25¢

For Jack

from Aunt Edna

June 22, 1933.

MINUTE BIOGRAPHIES

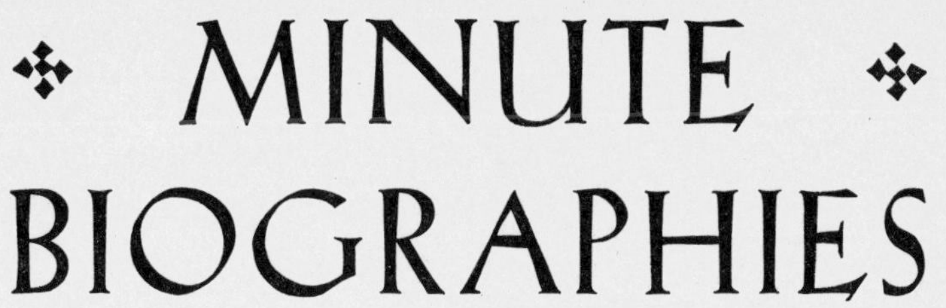

MINUTE BIOGRAPHIES

(Trademark Registration Applied For)

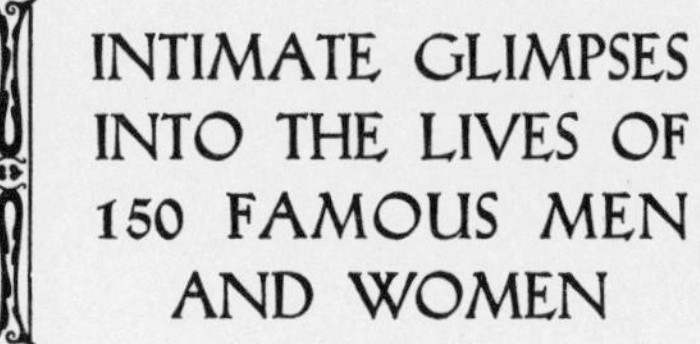

INTIMATE GLIMPSES INTO THE LIVES OF 150 FAMOUS MEN AND WOMEN

by

SAMUEL NISENSON

and

ALFRED PARKER

GROSSET & DUNLAP

Publishers

Printed in the United States of America

FOREWORD

Henry Ward Beecher once said: *Biography is the home aspect of history.*

Biography brings to each one of us, however humble and obscure, the things we should know about the great who have gone before. To remain ignorant of the high lights of those lives which have left such indelible impressions upon the history of the world, or to permit our children to remain in ignorance of them, is to deprive ourselves, and them, of that heritage these great men and women have left to us.

In the one or two hundred words of text which go to make up each "minute biography" the artist and editor naturally could not hope to do justice to the life of any one of the one hundred and fifty men and women who have been selected for this volume; but it is their hope and belief that the boy or girl, or the adult, will find from the brief glimpses this book affords into these lives that his interest has been aroused, and he will want to go on reading more about them, and learning more about them. A most fascinating world will open up before him!

If, however, the reader is not impelled to go deeper into the biographies of these great characters, he will at least have become intimately acquainted with the salient facts of their lives, not only through the medium of the text, but through the graphic power of the illustrations. Scrupulous care has been taken in securing only authentic portraits, from which the drawings have been made, and the textual facts have been most carefully investigated and corroborated as to their historical accuracy.

Samuel Nisenson
Alfred Parker

CONTENTS

THE MASTER DIPLOMAT
JOHN ADAMS
JOHN ADAMS, A HARVARD GRADUATE, AND A LAWYER, WAS ONE OF THE MIGHTY BRAINS BEHIND THE AMERICAN REVOLUTION . . . HE SUCCEEDED IN UNITING THE THIRTEEN COLONIES UNDER ONE LEADER, GENERAL WASHINGTON . . . AT THE END OF THE WAR IT WAS HE WHO SIGNED THE TREATY WITH ENGLAND THAT MADE AMERICA FREE! . . .
ADAMS WAS OUR FIRST AMBASSADOR TO ENGLAND . . THE ENGLISH KING TRIED TO TRICK HIM ON ONE OCCASION BY SAYING, "I HEAR YOU ARE NOT ATTACHED TO FRANCE" ADAMS IMMEDIATELY REPLIED, "I HAVE NO ATTACHMENT BUT TO MY OWN COUNTRY!" . . .
AFTER SERVING AS VICE-PRESIDENT UNDER GEORGE WASHINGTON, ADAMS WAS ELECTED THE SECOND PRESIDENT OF THE UNITED STATES . . HE LIVED TO SEE HIS SON, JOHN QUINCY ADAMS BECOME THE SIXTH PRESIDENT . . . . . .

· · BORN – 1735 – DIED – 1826 · ·

THE UGLY SLAVE WHO TOLD BEAUTIFUL FABLES!
AESOP
AESOP, IN THE DAYS OF CROESUS, KING OF LYDIA, WAS AN UGLY AND DEFORMED SLAVE·· AS A RE-WARD FOR HIS WISDOM, HIS MASTER FREED HIM AND HE MADE HIS WAY TO THE COURT OF CROESUS, WHERE HE BECAME FAMOUS AS A SAGE AND WIT · · · · · ·
THE PEOPLE OF DELPHI, AESOP'S NATIVE CITY, KILLED HIM BECAUSE OF HIS SAR-CASTIC CRITICISMS OF THEIR HABITS AND CUSTOMS·· AFTER HIS DEATH, PESTILENCE AND DISEASE FELL ON THE INHABITANTS OF THE CITY, AND TWO HUNDRED YEARS LATER, A STATUE OF HIM, BY LYSIPPUS, WAS ERECTED AT ATHENS AND PLACED IN FRONT OF THE STATUES OF THE SEVEN SAGES · · ·
AESOP USED TO SIT ON DOORSTEPS AND IN STREETS, RECOUNTING HIS BEAUTIFUL FABLES ABOUT FAMILIAR ANIMALS · · THESE STORIES HAD WISE MORALS ATTACHED TO THEM AND, AFTER 2500 YEARS, ARE STILL FAMOUS! ·

···BORN-620-B.C-DIED-560-B.C.·

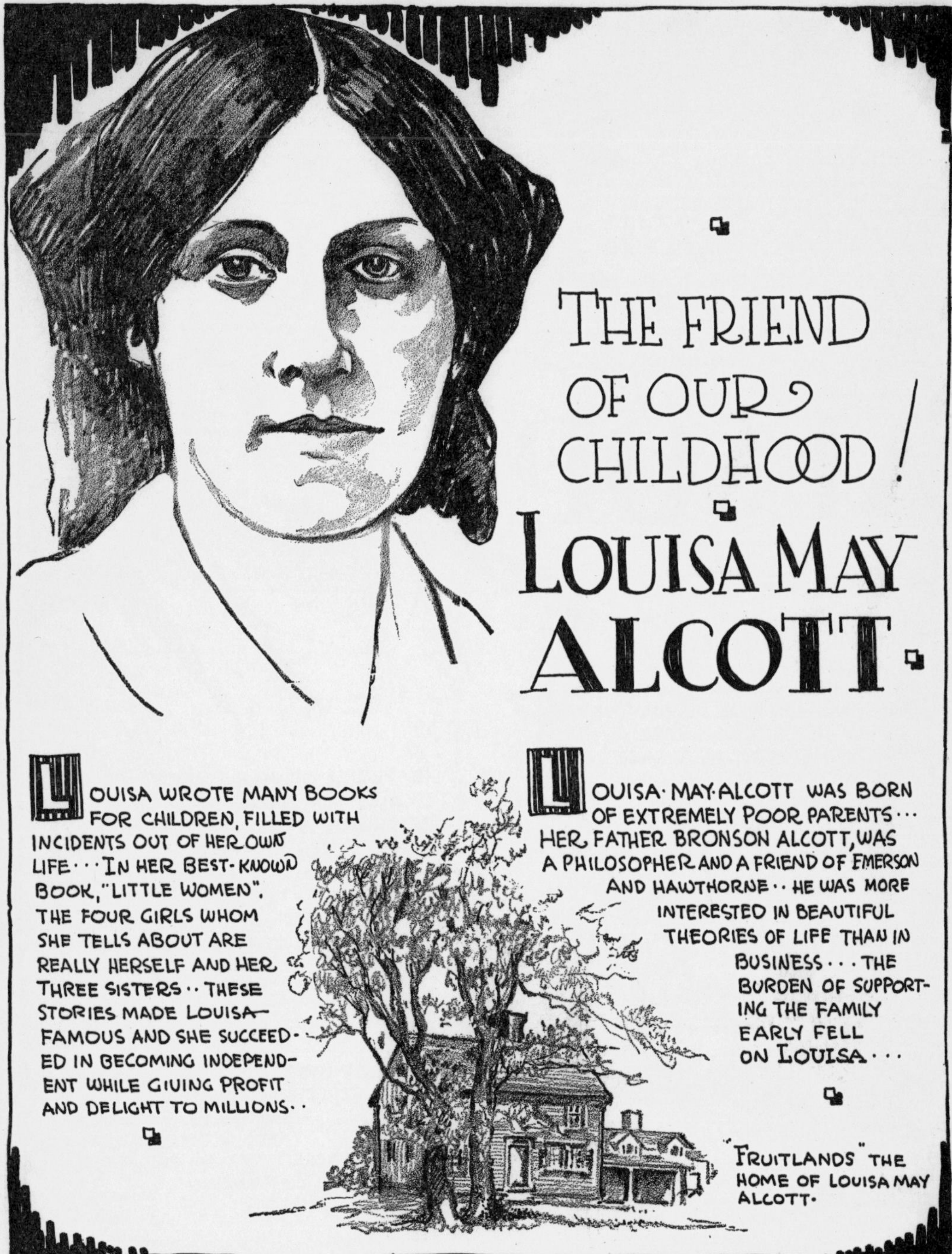
THE FRIEND OF OUR CHILDHOOD!
LOUISA MAY ALCOTT
LOUISA WROTE MANY BOOKS FOR CHILDREN, FILLED WITH INCIDENTS OUT OF HER OWN LIFE... IN HER BEST-KNOWN BOOK, "LITTLE WOMEN", THE FOUR GIRLS WHOM SHE TELLS ABOUT ARE REALLY HERSELF AND HER THREE SISTERS.. THESE STORIES MADE LOUISA FAMOUS AND SHE SUCCEEDED IN BECOMING INDEPENDENT WHILE GIVING PROFIT AND DELIGHT TO MILLIONS..
LOUISA MAY ALCOTT WAS BORN OF EXTREMELY POOR PARENTS... HER FATHER BRONSON ALCOTT, WAS A PHILOSOPHER AND A FRIEND OF EMERSON AND HAWTHORNE.. HE WAS MORE INTERESTED IN BEAUTIFUL THEORIES OF LIFE THAN IN BUSINESS... THE BURDEN OF SUPPORTING THE FAMILY EARLY FELL ON LOUISA...
"FRUITLANDS" THE HOME OF LOUISA MAY ALCOTT.

..BORN-1832-DIED-1888..

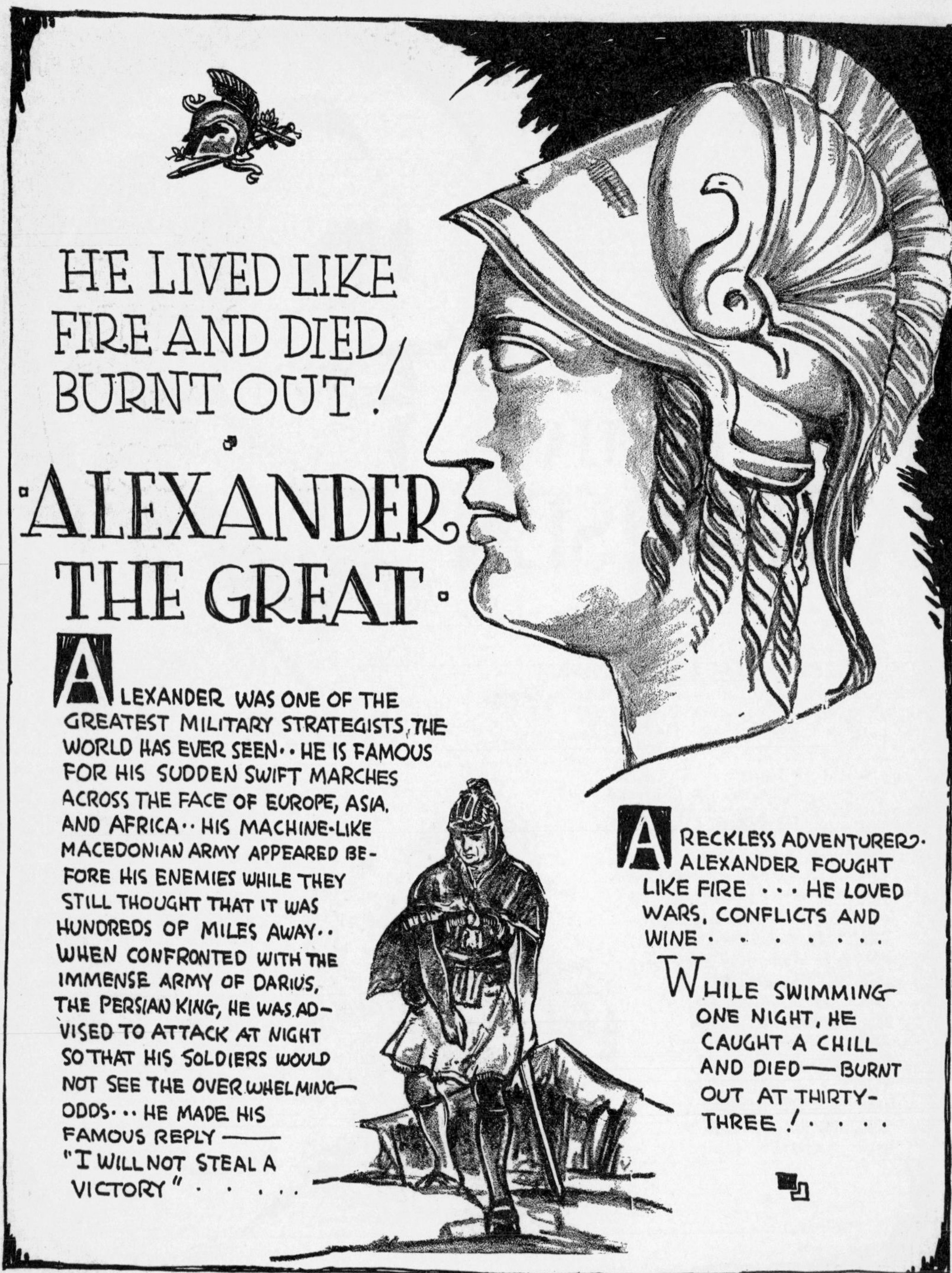
HE LIVED LIKE FIRE AND DIED BURNT OUT!
ALEXANDER THE GREAT
ALEXANDER WAS ONE OF THE GREATEST MILITARY STRATEGISTS THE WORLD HAS EVER SEEN.. HE IS FAMOUS FOR HIS SUDDEN SWIFT MARCHES ACROSS THE FACE OF EUROPE, ASIA, AND AFRICA.. HIS MACHINE-LIKE MACEDONIAN ARMY APPEARED BEFORE HIS ENEMIES WHILE THEY STILL THOUGHT THAT IT WAS HUNDREDS OF MILES AWAY.. WHEN CONFRONTED WITH THE IMMENSE ARMY OF DARIUS, THE PERSIAN KING, HE WAS ADVISED TO ATTACK AT NIGHT SO THAT HIS SOLDIERS WOULD NOT SEE THE OVERWHELMING ODDS... HE MADE HIS FAMOUS REPLY —— "I WILL NOT STEAL A VICTORY" . . . .
A RECKLESS ADVENTURER. ALEXANDER FOUGHT LIKE FIRE . . . HE LOVED WARS, CONFLICTS AND WINE . . . .
WHILE SWIMMING ONE NIGHT, HE CAUGHT A CHILL AND DIED —— BURNT OUT AT THIRTY-THREE! . . . .

... BORN. 356 BC — DIED 323 B.C. ...

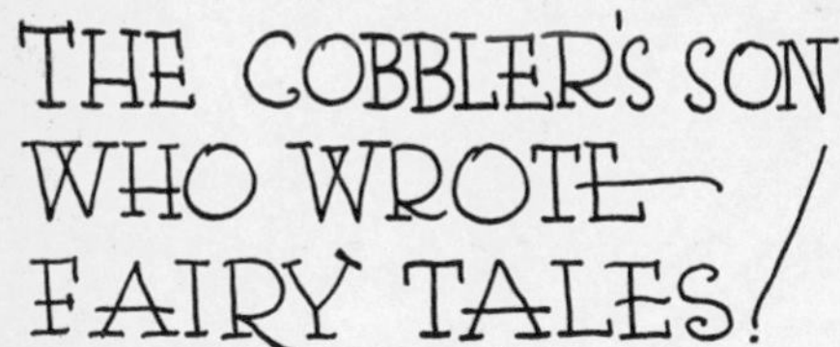
THE COBBLER'S SON
WHO WROTE
FAIRY TALES!

HANS CHRISTIAN ANDERSEN

ANDERSEN WAS BORN IN DENMARK, THE SON OF A POOR SHOEMAKER. A SENSITIVE, HIGHLY-STRUNG BOY, HE HAD A WONDERFUL IMAGINATION. INSTEAD OF GOING TO SCHOOL, HE STAYED AT HOME MOST OF THE TIME, DREAMING OF STRANGE CREATURES AND PLAYING WITH THE TOY THEATRE THAT HE BUILT FOR HIMSELF ... WHEN HE WAS ELEVEN, HIS FATHER DIED, AND, WITH ONLY NINE DOLLARS IN HIS POCKET AND A LITTLE BUNDLE OF CLOTHES ON HIS BACK, HE STARTED FOR COPENHAGEN TO SEEK FAME AND FORTUNE .. BUT HE WAS TO HAVE MANY A SAD AND HUNGRY DAY BEFORE HIS NAME WAS KNOWN THROUGHOUT EUROPE ....

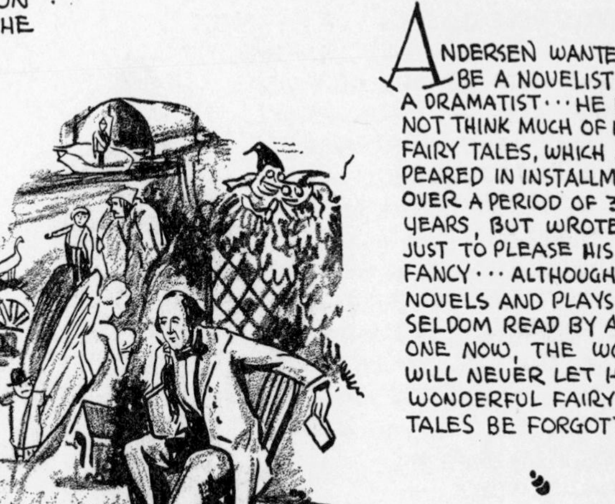

ANDERSEN WANTED TO BE A NOVELIST OR A DRAMATIST ... HE DID NOT THINK MUCH OF HIS FAIRY TALES, WHICH APPEARED IN INSTALLMENTS OVER A PERIOD OF 37 YEARS, BUT WROTE THEM JUST TO PLEASE HIS OWN FANCY ... ALTHOUGH HIS NOVELS AND PLAYS ARE SELDOM READ BY ANYONE NOW, THE WORLD WILL NEVER LET HIS WONDERFUL FAIRY TALES BE FORGOTTEN

... BORN-1805- DIED-1875 ...

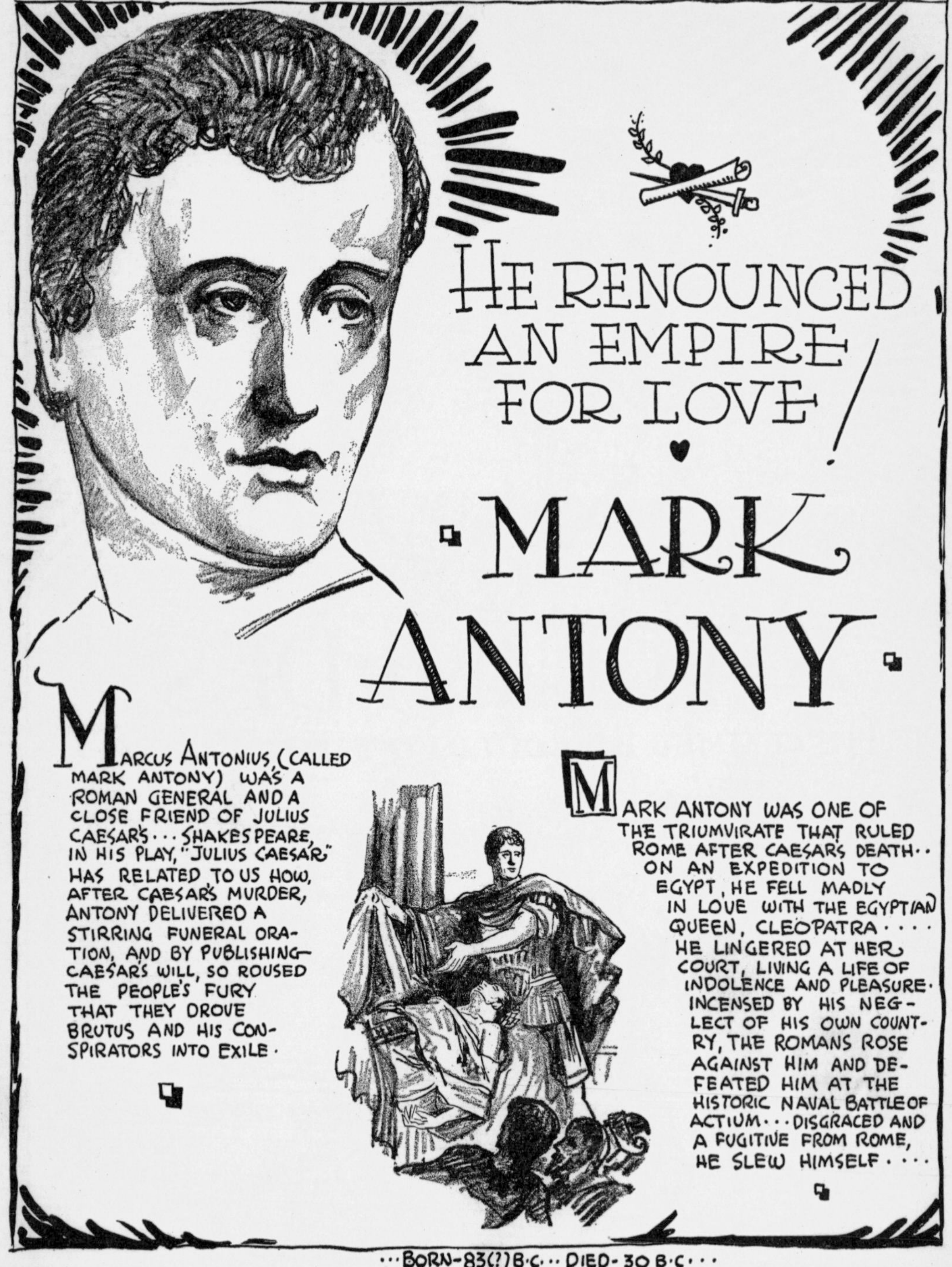
HE RENOUNCED AN EMPIRE FOR LOVE!
MARK ANTONY
MARCUS ANTONIUS (CALLED MARK ANTONY) WAS A ROMAN GENERAL AND A CLOSE FRIEND OF JULIUS CAESAR'S . . . SHAKESPEARE, IN HIS PLAY, "JULIUS CAESAR" HAS RELATED TO US HOW, AFTER CAESAR'S MURDER, ANTONY DELIVERED A STIRRING FUNERAL ORATION, AND BY PUBLISHING CAESAR'S WILL, SO ROUSED THE PEOPLE'S FURY THAT THEY DROVE BRUTUS AND HIS CONSPIRATORS INTO EXILE.
MARK ANTONY WAS ONE OF THE TRIUMVIRATE THAT RULED ROME AFTER CAESAR'S DEATH . . ON AN EXPEDITION TO EGYPT, HE FELL MADLY IN LOVE WITH THE EGYPTIAN QUEEN, CLEOPATRA . . . . HE LINGERED AT HER COURT, LIVING A LIFE OF INDOLENCE AND PLEASURE. INCENSED BY HIS NEGLECT OF HIS OWN COUNTRY, THE ROMANS ROSE AGAINST HIM AND DEFEATED HIM AT THE HISTORIC NAVAL BATTLE OF ACTIUM . . . DISGRACED AND A FUGITIVE FROM ROME, HE SLEW HIMSELF . . . .

... BORN - 83(?) B.C. ... DIED - 30 B.C. ...

ARCHIMEDES

HE CLAIMED HE COULD LIFT THE EARTH!

ARCHIMEDES WAS ASKED BY THE KING TO DISCOVER IF THE ROYAL CROWN WAS MADE OF PURE GOLD. IT WAS A PUZZLING PROBLEM . . . ONE DAY WHILE STEPPING INTO HIS BATH-TUB ARCHIMEDES NOTICED HOW THE WATER RAN OVER. THIS GAVE HIM AN IDEA AS TO HOW TO TEST THE CROWN . . HE WAS SO OVERJOYED THAT HE RAN HOME WITHOUT ANY CLOTHES ON, SHOUTING, "EUREKA, EUREKA"— "I HAVE FOUND IT, I HAVE FOUND IT!" . . . .

ARCHIMEDES WROTE BOOKS ON GEOMETRY AND MECHANICS . . HE CLAIMED THAT A SMALL FORCE COULD MOVE A GREAT WEIGHT, AND SAID: "GIVE ME A PLACE TO STAND AND I WILL MOVE THE EARTH!"

WHEN HIS NATIVE CITY, SYRACUSE, WAS CAPTURED, ARCHIMEDES WAS KILLED BY A ROMAN SOLDIER, AS HE WAS DRAWING A DIAGRAM IN THE SAND.

BORN - 287 B.C. - DIED - 212 B.C. . . .

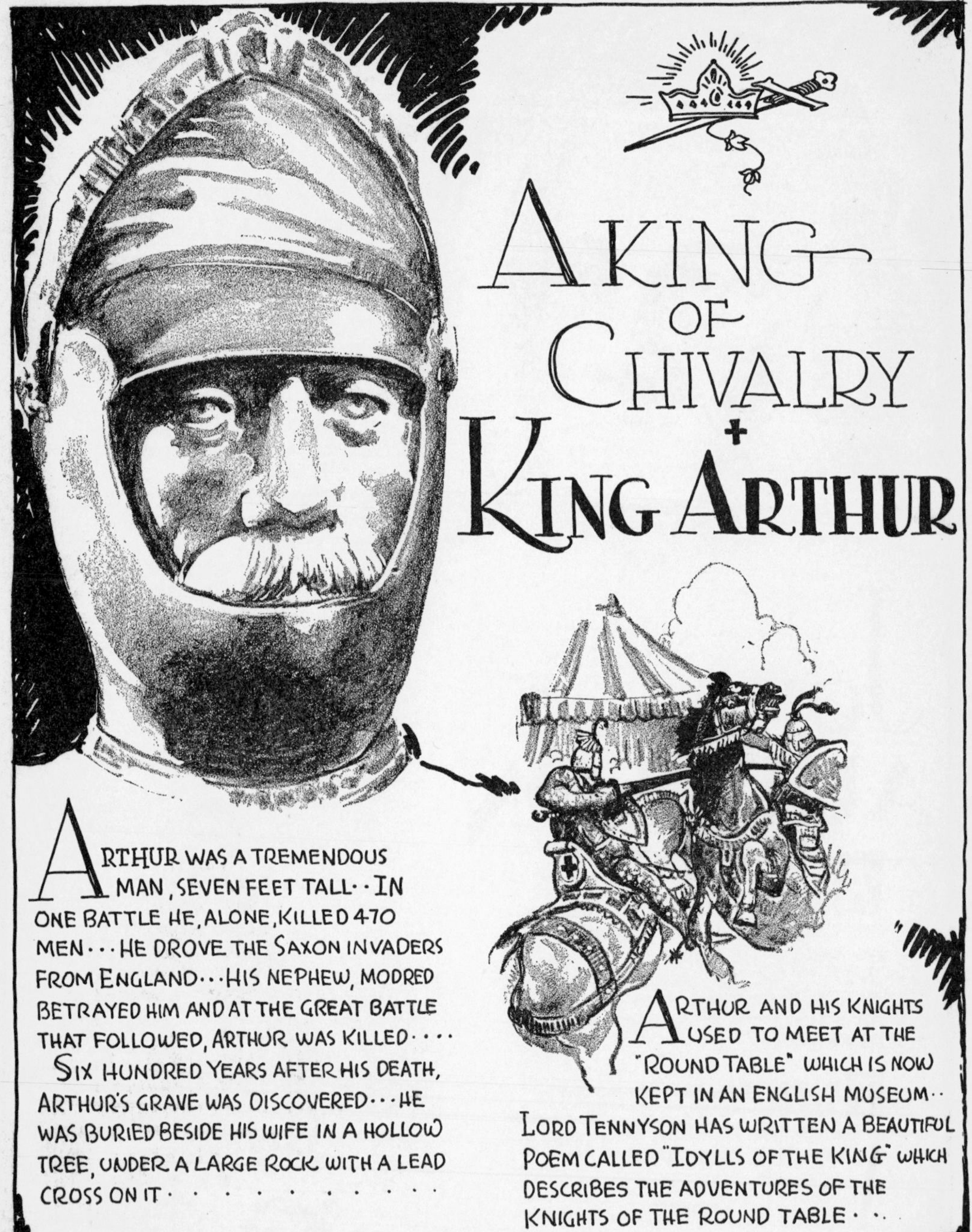

A KING OF CHIVALRY
✠ KING ARTHUR

ARTHUR WAS A TREMENDOUS MAN, SEVEN FEET TALL · · IN ONE BATTLE HE, ALONE, KILLED 470 MEN · · · HE DROVE THE SAXON INVADERS FROM ENGLAND · · · HIS NEPHEW, MODRED BETRAYED HIM AND AT THE GREAT BATTLE THAT FOLLOWED, ARTHUR WAS KILLED · · · ·

SIX HUNDRED YEARS AFTER HIS DEATH, ARTHUR'S GRAVE WAS DISCOVERED · · · HE WAS BURIED BESIDE HIS WIFE IN A HOLLOW TREE, UNDER A LARGE ROCK WITH A LEAD CROSS ON IT · · · · · · · · ·

ARTHUR AND HIS KNIGHTS USED TO MEET AT THE "ROUND TABLE" WHICH IS NOW KEPT IN AN ENGLISH MUSEUM · · LORD TENNYSON HAS WRITTEN A BEAUTIFUL POEM CALLED "IDYLLS OF THE KING" WHICH DESCRIBES THE ADVENTURES OF THE KNIGHTS OF THE ROUND TABLE · · ·

· · BORN. 480? — DIED 542 · · ·

HE TAUGHT US ABOUT BIRDS!
JOHN AUDUBON WAS BORN IN LOUISIANA, THE SON OF A FRENCH ADMIRAL AND A SPANISH LADY·· HE WAS SENT TO FRANCE TO STUDY PAINTING, BUT RETURNED TO THE UNITED STATES AND OPENED A STORE IN KENTUCKY·· HE LIKED TO WANDER IN THE WOODS, STUDYING BIRDS, AND PAID NO ATTENTION TO HIS BUSINESS·· THE STORE FAILED AND HE EARNED A LIVING BY GIVING LESSONS IN DRAWING, FENCING AND DANCING— ....
JOHN AUDUBON
AUDUBON TRAVELLED ALL THROUGH THE UNITED STATES AND CANADA, SKETCHING BIRDS··· HE PUBLISHED A BOOK— "BIRDS OF AMERICA" WHICH CONTAINS PAINTINGS OF MORE THAN 1000 BIRDS·· HE IS THE FATHER OF NATURE STUDY IN AMERICA ·········
TOWARD THE END OF HIS LIFE, AUDUBON SETTLED ON THE HUDSON RIVER AT AUDUBON PARK, WHICH IS NOW PART OF NEW YORK CITY···

—BORN 1780?— DIED·1851—

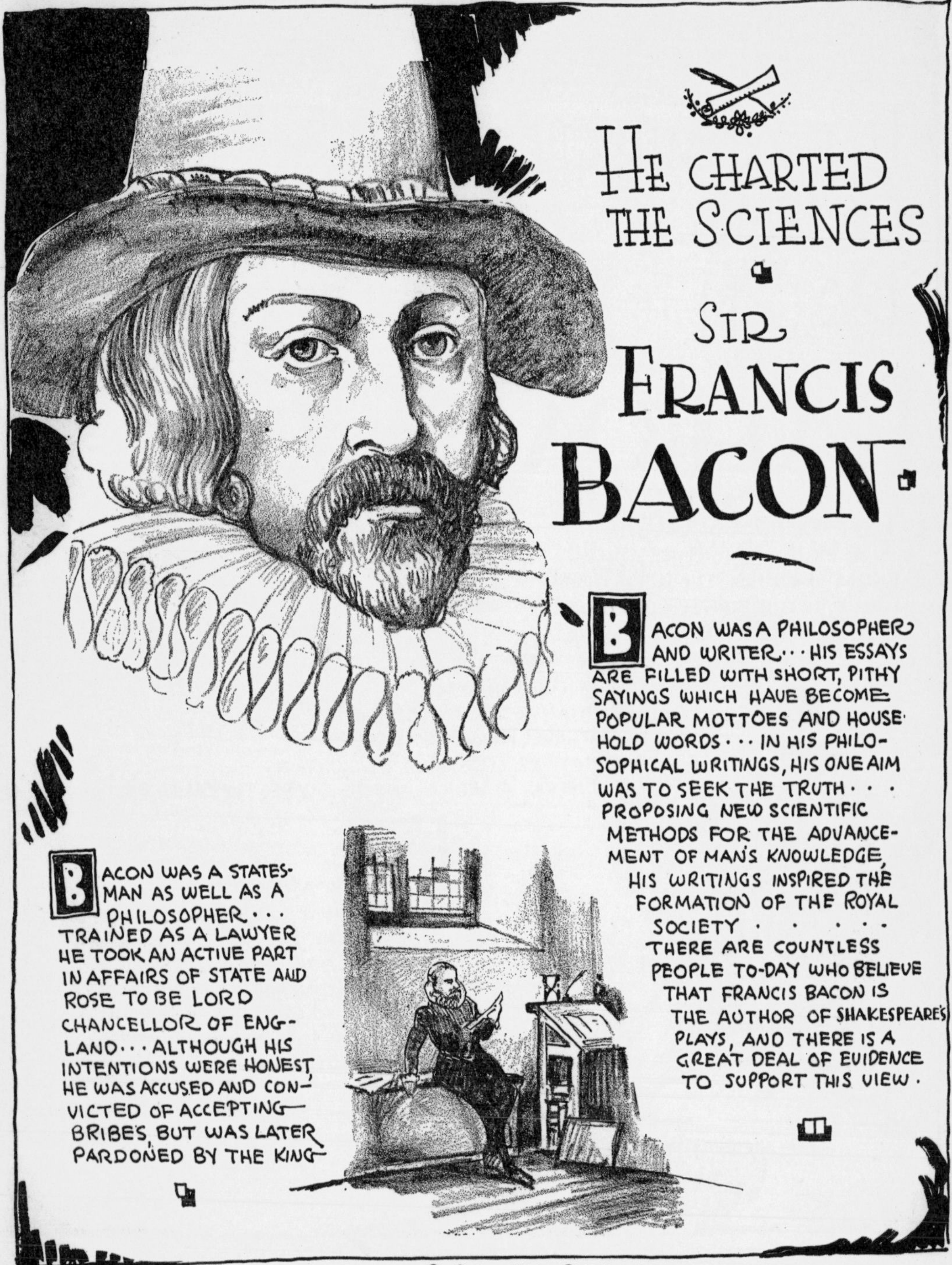
HE CHARTED THE SCIENCES
SIR FRANCIS BACON
BACON WAS A PHILOSOPHER AND WRITER... HIS ESSAYS ARE FILLED WITH SHORT, PITHY SAYINGS WHICH HAVE BECOME POPULAR MOTTOES AND HOUSEHOLD WORDS... IN HIS PHILOSOPHICAL WRITINGS, HIS ONE AIM WAS TO SEEK THE TRUTH... PROPOSING NEW SCIENTIFIC METHODS FOR THE ADVANCEMENT OF MAN'S KNOWLEDGE, HIS WRITINGS INSPIRED THE FORMATION OF THE ROYAL SOCIETY.... THERE ARE COUNTLESS PEOPLE TO-DAY WHO BELIEVE THAT FRANCIS BACON IS THE AUTHOR OF SHAKESPEARE'S PLAYS, AND THERE IS A GREAT DEAL OF EVIDENCE TO SUPPORT THIS VIEW.
BACON WAS A STATESMAN AS WELL AS A PHILOSOPHER... TRAINED AS A LAWYER HE TOOK AN ACTIVE PART IN AFFAIRS OF STATE AND ROSE TO BE LORD CHANCELLOR OF ENGLAND... ALTHOUGH HIS INTENTIONS WERE HONEST, HE WAS ACCUSED AND CONVICTED OF ACCEPTING BRIBES, BUT WAS LATER PARDONED BY THE KING

...BORN-1561- DIED-1626...

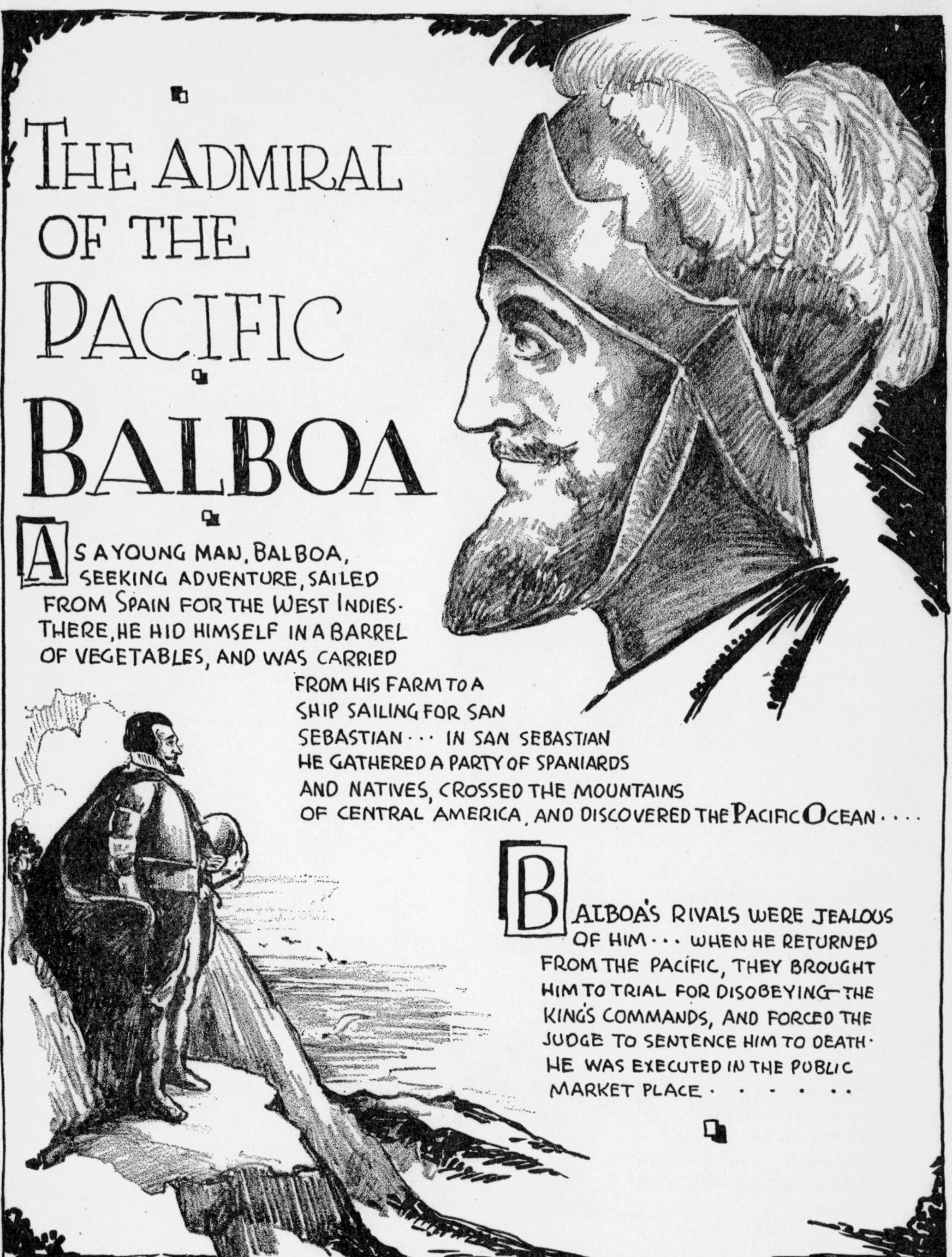
THE ADMIRAL
OF THE
PACIFIC
BALBOA
AS A YOUNG MAN, BALBOA,
SEEKING ADVENTURE, SAILED
FROM SPAIN FOR THE WEST INDIES.
THERE, HE HID HIMSELF IN A BARREL
OF VEGETABLES, AND WAS CARRIED
FROM HIS FARM TO A
SHIP SAILING FOR SAN
SEBASTIAN ... IN SAN SEBASTIAN
HE GATHERED A PARTY OF SPANIARDS
AND NATIVES, CROSSED THE MOUNTAINS
OF CENTRAL AMERICA, AND DISCOVERED THE PACIFIC OCEAN ....
BALBOA'S RIVALS WERE JEALOUS
OF HIM ... WHEN HE RETURNED
FROM THE PACIFIC, THEY BROUGHT
HIM TO TRIAL FOR DISOBEYING THE
KING'S COMMANDS, AND FORCED THE
JUDGE TO SENTENCE HIM TO DEATH.
HE WAS EXECUTED IN THE PUBLIC
MARKET PLACE . . . . . .

... BORN - 1475 - DIED - 1517 ...

THE GREATEST SHOWMAN ON EARTH!
PHINEAS T. BARNUM
BARNUM WAS BORN IN CONNECTICUT... HE LOVED PUBLICITY AND BALLYHOO AND WAS A SHOWMAN BY NATURE... SCRUPULOUSLY HONEST THOUGH HE WAS, HE LIKED TO HUMBUG PEOPLE, AND HIS WAS THE SAYING, "THERE'S A FOOL BORN EVERY MINUTE!"... HIS "AMERICAN MUSEUM" IN N.Y. WHERE HE EXHIBITED THE FEEJEE MERMAID, TOM THUMB, THE MIDGET AND THE QUEER ASSORTMENT OF ANIMALS THAT HE BROUGHT TO THIS COUNTRY, PROVED HIS STATEMENT BY EARNING A FORTUNE FOR HIM.....
BARNUM LOST FORTUNES AS EASILY AS HE MADE THEM.. HIS MUSEUM AND HIS CIRCUS WERE BOTH DESTROYED BY FIRE BUT HE ALWAYS CAME BACK WITH A GREATER AND MORE SUCCESSFUL SHOW.. HIS EIGHTY-ONE YEARS WERE FILLED WITH RICH EXPERIENCES AND NOT MANY PEOPLE HAVE ENJOYED LIFE AS THOROUGHLY AS HE DID...
IT WAS BARNUM WHO BROUGHT THE SWEDISH OPERA SINGER, JENNY LIND, TO AMERICA UNDER A FABULOUS CONTRACT FOR THE FAMOUS CONCERTS AT CASTLE GARDEN....

... BORN-1810-DIED-1891 ...

THAT LONELY GIANT of MUSIC! BEETHOVEN

IMAGINE A MUSICIAN BEING DEAF! . . . . .
BEETHOVEN WAS DEAF MOST OF HIS LIFE . . . HE NEVER HEARD A SINGLE NOTE OF HIS GREATEST WORK THE NINTH SYMPHONY! . . . .

HE WAS VERY SENSITIVE ABOUT HIS UGLINESS, AND SO, DESPITE HIS MANY LOVES, HE NEVER MARRIED . . HE WAS HOT-TEMPERED . . . AWKWARD . . . AND LONELY . . . AND HAD VERY FEW REAL FRIENDS HE HAD TO STRUGGLE FOR MONEY ALL HIS LIFE . .

BEETHOVEN'S DEATH MASK . .

IN SPITE OF THESE GREAT HANDICAPS, BEETHOVEN WROTE SOME OF THE MOST NOBLE MUSIC THAT THE WORLD HAS EVER HEARD! . . . . . .

. . BORN · 1770 — DIED · 1827 ·

SARAH BERNHARDT
(ROSINE BERNARD) WAS BORN IN PARIS, WAS BROUGHT UP IN A CONVENT, AND AS A YOUNG GIRL ENTERED THE FRENCH CONSERVATORY TO STUDY ACTING ... ALTHOUGH SHE SUFFERED BADLY FROM STAGE FRIGHT, HER WONDERFUL INTERPRETATIONS, HER MARVELOUS MEMORY AND ESPECIALLY HER UNFORGETTABLE, GOLDEN VOICE MADE HER THE GREATEST ACTRESS OF HER DAY . . . .
"THE DIVINE SARAH!"
BERNHARDT WAS A TIRELESS WORKER · DESPITE THE LOSS AT 70 OF ONE OF HER LEGS, SHE CONTINUED HER PERFORMANCES FOR THE BENEFIT OF THE SOLDIERS AT THE FRONT, AND ON THE EVE OF HER DEATH, WHEN SHE WAS ALMOST 80, SHE ACTED FOR THE MOVIES! . . . .
BERNHARDT LIVED HER OWN LIFE, DOING JUST WHAT HER FANCY DICTATED · · SHE WAS THE IDOL OF THE ENTIRE WORLD, AND IN ORDER TO PERPETUATE HER MEMORY, ONLY ONE WORD WAS NECESSARY ON HER TOMBSTONE -BERNHARDT!

BORN-1845-DIED-1923 ···

THE IRON
CHANCELLOR

PRINCE OTTO EDUARD LEOPOLD VON

BISMARCK

AS A YOUNG MILITARY STUDENT, BISMARCK WAS A SPLENDID DUELLIST AND A GREAT DRINKER.. AS HE GREW OLDER, HE MADE HIS WAY INTO PARLIAMENT, BECAME AN AMBASSADOR AND FINALLY PRIME MINISTER... BY A SERIES OF WARS, HE ADDED MANY NEW LANDS TO GERMANY'S DOMAIN, UNITED HER UNDER ONE EMPEROR, WILLIAM I, AND MADE HER A WORLD POWER.. ......

IT WAS LARGELY THROUGH BISMARCK'S GENIUS THAT GERMANY BECAME A GREAT NATION... HE PASSED LAWS TO HELP THE WORKING CLASSES AND HIS POLICY WAS ONE OF PEACE.. HE WAS A VERY STRONG-WILLED MAN. WHEN THE GERMAN CHAMBERS ONCE OPPOSED HIM ON A BUDGET, HE SIMPLY DISMISSED THEM, AND TOLD THEM HE WOULD HAVE TO DO WITHOUT THEM. . . .

BISMARCK SERVED THREE EMPERORS. HIS EPITAPH READS.. "A FAITHFUL GERMAN SERVANT OF WILLIAM I" . . . . .

... BORN. 1815 — DIED 1898 ...

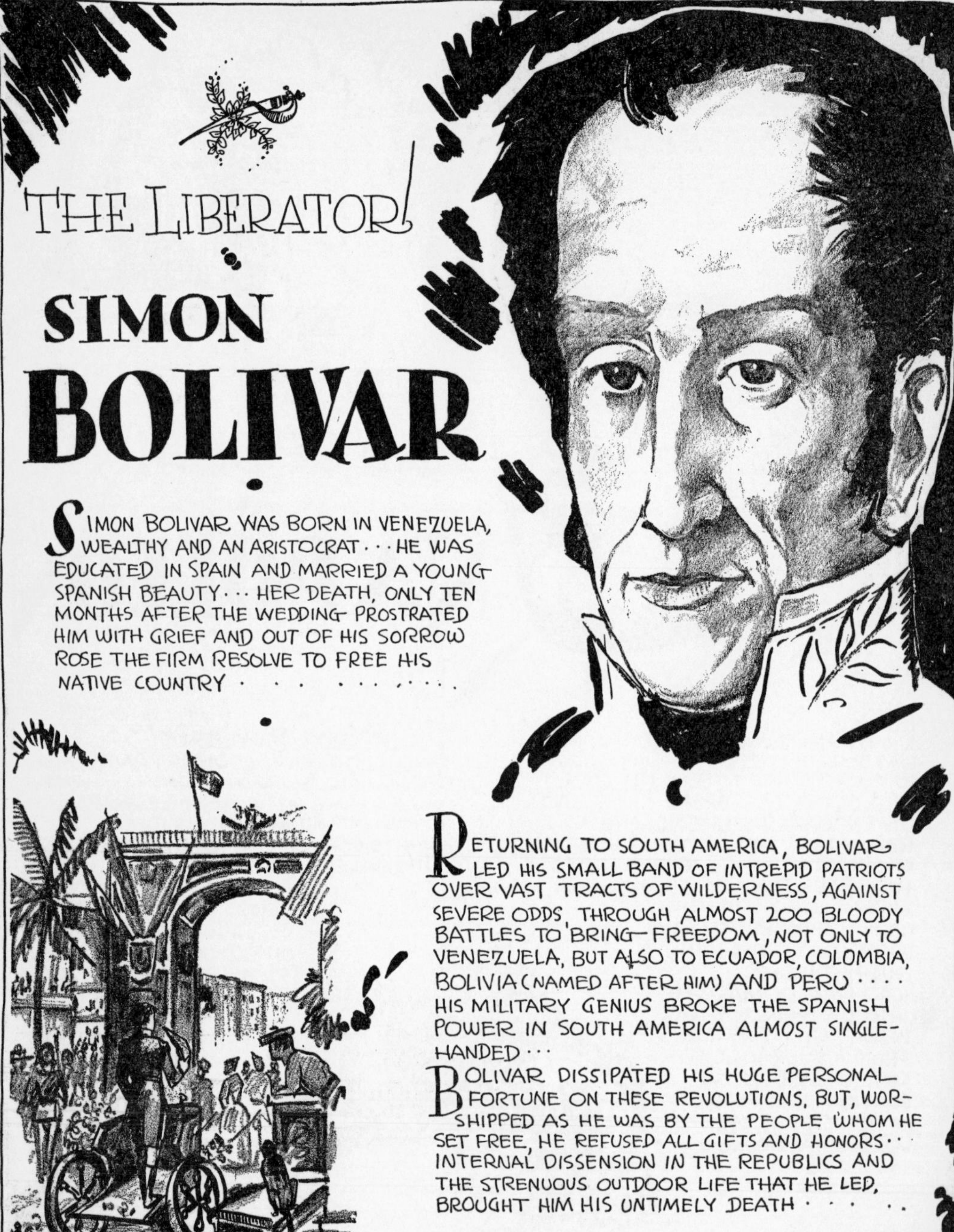

THE LIBERATOR!

SIMON BOLIVAR

SIMON BOLIVAR WAS BORN IN VENEZUELA, WEALTHY AND AN ARISTOCRAT . . . HE WAS EDUCATED IN SPAIN AND MARRIED A YOUNG SPANISH BEAUTY . . . HER DEATH, ONLY TEN MONTHS AFTER THE WEDDING PROSTRATED HIM WITH GRIEF AND OUT OF HIS SORROW ROSE THE FIRM RESOLVE TO FREE HIS NATIVE COUNTRY . . . .

RETURNING TO SOUTH AMERICA, BOLIVAR LED HIS SMALL BAND OF INTREPID PATRIOTS OVER VAST TRACTS OF WILDERNESS, AGAINST SEVERE ODDS, THROUGH ALMOST 200 BLOODY BATTLES TO BRING FREEDOM, NOT ONLY TO VENEZUELA, BUT ALSO TO ECUADOR, COLOMBIA, BOLIVIA (NAMED AFTER HIM) AND PERU . . . . HIS MILITARY GENIUS BROKE THE SPANISH POWER IN SOUTH AMERICA ALMOST SINGLE-HANDED . . .

BOLIVAR DISSIPATED HIS HUGE PERSONAL FORTUNE ON THESE REVOLUTIONS, BUT, WORSHIPPED AS HE WAS BY THE PEOPLE WHOM HE SET FREE, HE REFUSED ALL GIFTS AND HONORS . . . INTERNAL DISSENSION IN THE REPUBLICS AND THE STRENUOUS OUTDOOR LIFE THAT HE LED, BROUGHT HIM HIS UNTIMELY DEATH . . . . .

. . . BORN-1783-DIED-1830 . . .

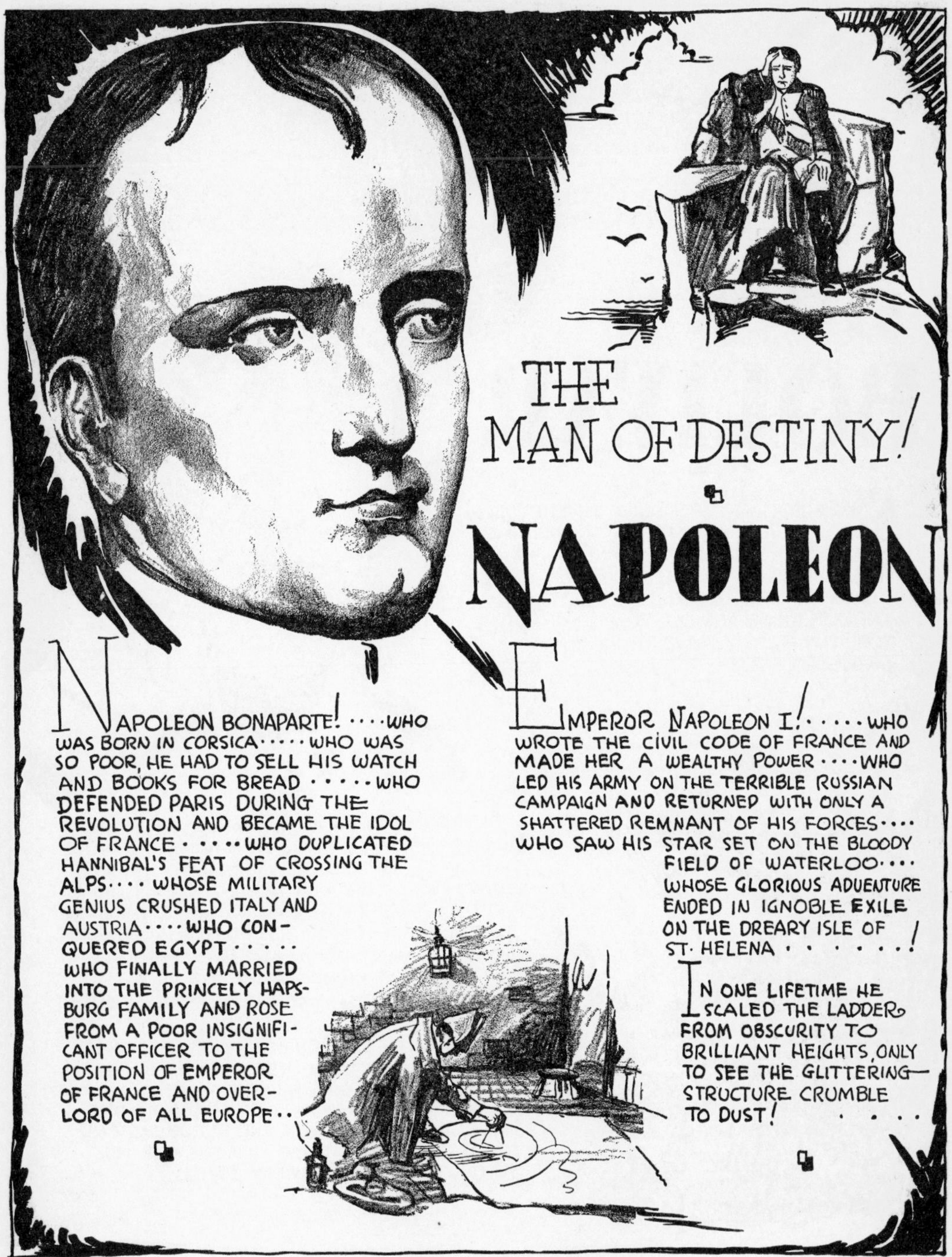
THE MAN OF DESTINY!
NAPOLEON
NAPOLEON BONAPARTE! .... WHO WAS BORN IN CORSICA .... WHO WAS SO POOR, HE HAD TO SELL HIS WATCH AND BOOKS FOR BREAD ..... WHO DEFENDED PARIS DURING THE REVOLUTION AND BECAME THE IDOL OF FRANCE ..... WHO DUPLICATED HANNIBAL'S FEAT OF CROSSING THE ALPS .... WHOSE MILITARY GENIUS CRUSHED ITALY AND AUSTRIA .... WHO CONQUERED EGYPT ..... WHO FINALLY MARRIED INTO THE PRINCELY HAPSBURG FAMILY AND ROSE FROM A POOR INSIGNIFICANT OFFICER TO THE POSITION OF EMPEROR OF FRANCE AND OVERLORD OF ALL EUROPE ..
EMPEROR NAPOLEON I! ..... WHO WROTE THE CIVIL CODE OF FRANCE AND MADE HER A WEALTHY POWER .... WHO LED HIS ARMY ON THE TERRIBLE RUSSIAN CAMPAIGN AND RETURNED WITH ONLY A SHATTERED REMNANT OF HIS FORCES .... WHO SAW HIS STAR SET ON THE BLOODY FIELD OF WATERLOO .... WHOSE GLORIOUS ADVENTURE ENDED IN IGNOBLE EXILE ON THE DREARY ISLE OF ST. HELENA .... !
IN ONE LIFETIME HE SCALED THE LADDER FROM OBSCURITY TO BRILLIANT HEIGHTS, ONLY TO SEE THE GLITTERING STRUCTURE CRUMBLE TO DUST! ...

... BORN-1769- DIED-1821 ...

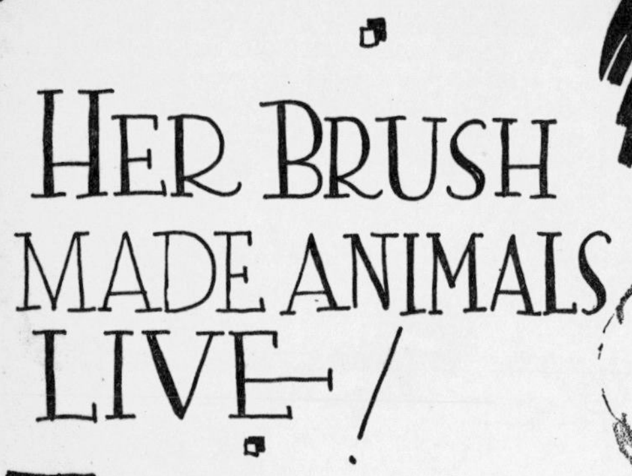
HER BRUSH
MADE ANIMALS
LIVE!

WHEN ROSA WAS A LITTLE GIRL, SHE LIKED TO PLAY BOYS' GAMES.. SHE WAS SENT TO A GIRLS' FINISHING SCHOOL.. ONE DAY SHE ORGANIZED A GAME OF SOLDIERS AND CHARGED A ROSE BUSH, COMPLETELY DESTROYING IT... THE ROSES WERE THE PRIDE OF THE SCHOOL AND SO SHE WAS DISMISSED.........

ROSA WAS TAUGHT TO DRAW BY HER FATHER, WHO WAS AN ARTIST.. SHE USED TO WANDER AROUND THE MARKET-PLACES, IN MENS CLOTHES, DRAWING PICTURES OF ANIMALS... SHE LOVED ANIMALS AND KEPT DOZENS OF PETS, AMONG THEM A LION...

ROSA BONHEUR

ROSA BECAME WORLD FAMOUS AS A PAINTER OF ANIMALS AND THE EMPRESS EUGÉNIE OF FRANCE MADE HER A MEMBER OF THE LEGION OF HONOR...

THE FAMOUS "HORSE FAIR" PAINTED BY ROSA BONHEUR, NOW HANGING IN THE METROPOLITAN MUSEUM OF ART, IN NEW YORK.....

BORN-1822-DIED 1899...

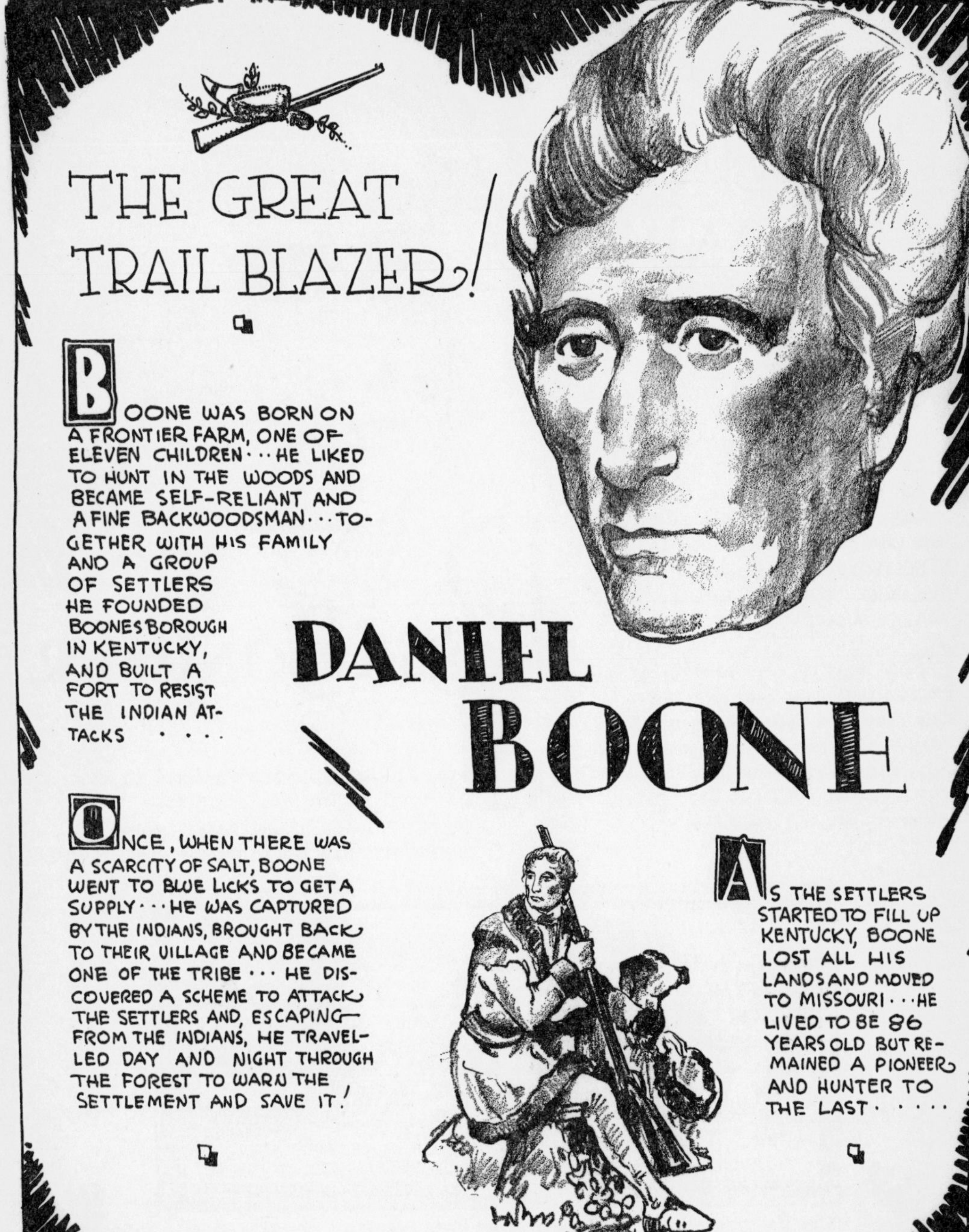
THE GREAT TRAIL BLAZER!
BOONE WAS BORN ON A FRONTIER FARM, ONE OF ELEVEN CHILDREN . . . HE LIKED TO HUNT IN THE WOODS AND BECAME SELF-RELIANT AND A FINE BACKWOODSMAN . . . TOGETHER WITH HIS FAMILY AND A GROUP OF SETTLERS HE FOUNDED BOONESBOROUGH IN KENTUCKY, AND BUILT A FORT TO RESIST THE INDIAN ATTACKS . . . .
DANIEL BOONE
ONCE, WHEN THERE WAS A SCARCITY OF SALT, BOONE WENT TO BLUE LICKS TO GET A SUPPLY . . . HE WAS CAPTURED BY THE INDIANS, BROUGHT BACK TO THEIR VILLAGE AND BECAME ONE OF THE TRIBE . . . HE DISCOVERED A SCHEME TO ATTACK THE SETTLERS AND, ESCAPING FROM THE INDIANS, HE TRAVELLED DAY AND NIGHT THROUGH THE FOREST TO WARN THE SETTLEMENT AND SAVE IT!
AS THE SETTLERS STARTED TO FILL UP KENTUCKY, BOONE LOST ALL HIS LANDS AND MOVED TO MISSOURI . . . HE LIVED TO BE 86 YEARS OLD BUT REMAINED A PIONEER AND HUNTER TO THE LAST . . . .

. . . BORN · 1735 — DIED · 1820 . .

LUCREZIA BORGIA

·The SIREN OF THE RENAISSANCE·

LUCREZIA WAS A FAMOUS BEAUTY·· SHE WAS A GAY YOUNG GIRL; BY NATURE, CHARMING, PATIENT, GENEROUS AND DISCREET·· HOWEVER, SHE WAS BROUGHT UP AMIDST DISSIPATION AND INTRIGUE·· HER AMBITIOUS FATHER RULED HER LIFE TO SUIT HIS OWN ENDS·· AS A RESULT, GOSSIP HAS GIVEN HER A BAD NAME·

AT SEVENTEEN LUCREZIA FELL IN LOVE WITH THE DUKE OF BISCEGLI, AND MARRIED HIM·· HE WAS MURDERED BY HER BROTHER CESARE BORGIA, WHO WAS ANOTHER BAD INFLUENCE IN HER LIFE.. SHE WAS THEN MARRIED OFF TO THE DUKE OF FERRARA AND MOVED AWAY FROM THE EVIL SURROUNDINGS OF HER FATHER'S COURT·· ONCE AWAY FROM ROME, LUCREZIA'S TENDER AND AFFECTIONATE NATURE ASSERTED ITSELF·· SHE GATHERED FAMOUS MEN AND ARTISTS AT HER COURT, AND DEVOTED THE REST OF HER LIFE TO THE UPBRINGING OF HER CHILDREN AND TO CHARITY· . . . .

··BORN-1480··DIED·1519

THE MAN WHO GAVE US SAMUEL JOHNSON!
BOSWELL CAME TO LONDON AT 19, A YOUNG SCOTCH LAWYER WHO ADMITTEDLY SOUGHT PLEASURE AND DID NOT CARE WHETHER THE WORLD LAUGHED AT OR WITH HIM ... HE MET SAMUEL JOHNSON, THIRTY YEARS HIS SENIOR, IN A LITTLE BOOKSHOP, AND THERE BEGAN THE LIFE-LONG INTIMACY WHICH RESULTED IN BOSWELL'S FAMOUS BIOGRAPHY OF THE LEARNED DOCTOR . . . . .
JAMES BOSWELL
BUT THIS FRIENDSHIP WAS THE ONLY LIGHT IN BOSWELL'S LIFE ... HIS MEETING WITH VOLTAIRE AND ROUSSEAU, HIS MARRIAGE AT 29 TO A VERY BEAUTIFUL GIRL, AND HIS SCOTTISH TOUR WITH JOHNSON WERE OVERSHADOWED BY HIS UNLUCKY SPECULATIONS, HIS QUARRELS WITH HIS FATHER AND HIS TENDENCY TOWARD DRUNKENESS UNTIL, WORN OUT HE DIED AT 55, A PATHETIC FAILURE! . . . . . .
REGARDED FOR A LONG TIME AS AN INSPIRED IDIOT, BOSWELL IS NOW RECOGNIZED AS A SKILLFUL AND CONSCIENTIOUS ARTIST, WHO GAVE US IN HIS GREAT BIOGRAPHY AN ENCYCLOPEDIA OF 18th CENTURY SOCIAL LIFE . . . .

... BORN - 1740 - DIED - 1795

HIS SOUL GOES MARCHING ON!
JOHN BROWN WAS A NEW ENGLAND FARMER AND SHEEPRAISER .... INTENSELY RELIGIOUS BY NATURE, HE WAS OBSESSED WITH THE IDEA THAT IT WAS HIS MISSION ON EARTH TO DESTROY SLAVERY, AND PLAYED A PROMINENT PART IN THE BLOODY ANTI-SLAVERY RIOTS IN KANSAS, BEFORE THE CIVIL WAR . . . . . .
JOHN BROWN
MONTHS BEFORE WAR WAS DECLARED BETWEEN THE STATES, BROWN, WITH THE AID OF HIS SONS (HE HAD TWENTY CHILDREN) AND SOME NEGROES CAPTURED THE U.S. ARSENAL AT HARPER'S FERRY, WEST VIRGINIA .... THE ATTEMPT TO ROUSE THE SLAVES FAILED AND HE WAS HANGED FOR MURDER AND TREASON . . . .
ALTHOUGH HIS FANATICISM ACTUALLY ACCOMPLISHED NOTHING, HE WAS CONSIDERED A MARTYR AND HIS ILL-STARRED VENTURE WAS ONE OF THE CONTRIBUTING CAUSES OF THE CIVIL WAR . . . .
THE SONG, "JOHN BROWN'S BODY" HAS IMMORTALIZED THE MAN WHO DIED AS A TRAITOR FOR WHAT SHORTLY AFTERWARDS WAS TO BE A JUST CAUSE . . . .

..BORN-1800-DIED-1859...

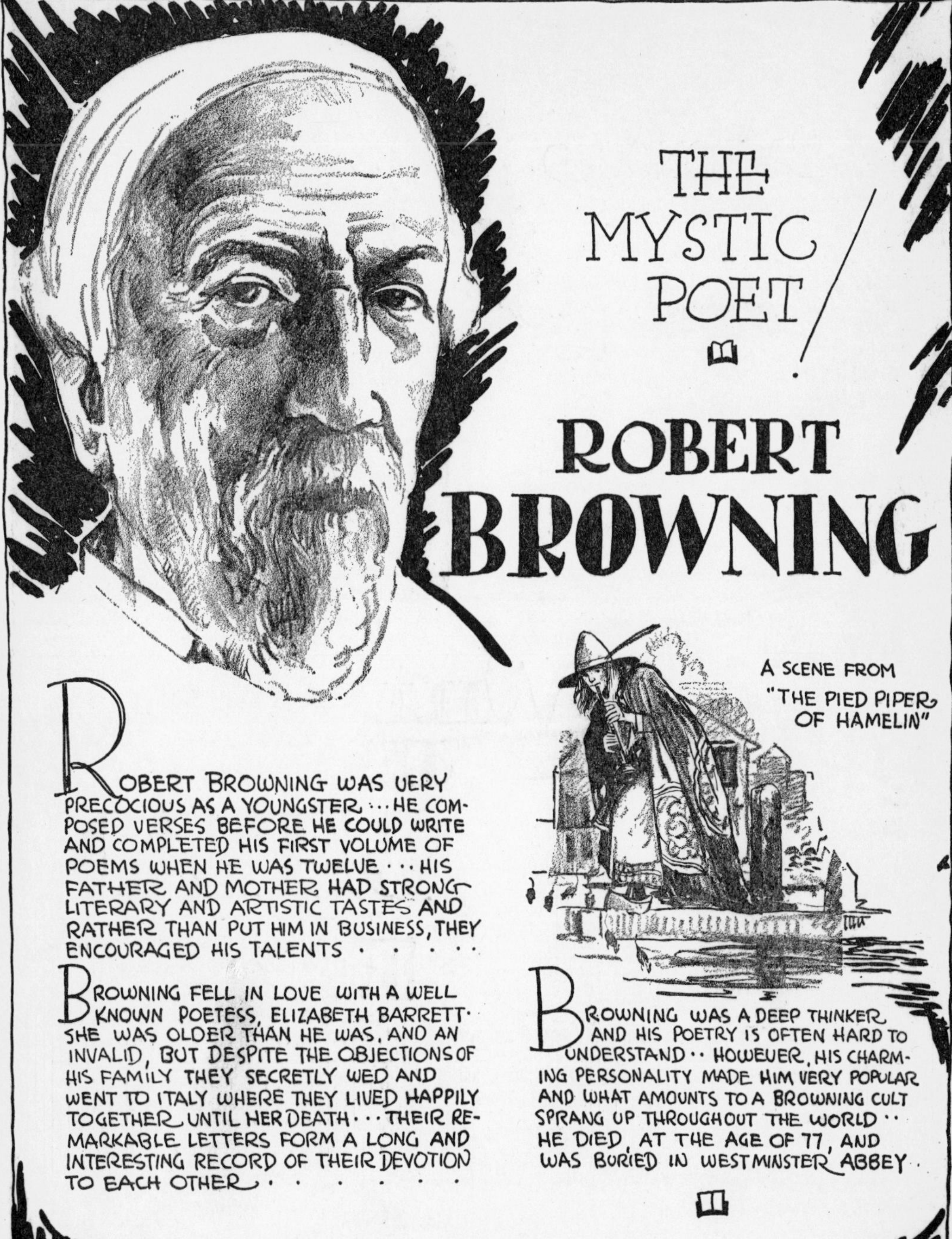

THE MYSTIC POET

ROBERT BROWNING

A SCENE FROM "THE PIED PIPER OF HAMELIN"

ROBERT BROWNING WAS VERY PRECOCIOUS AS A YOUNGSTER ... HE COMPOSED VERSES BEFORE HE COULD WRITE AND COMPLETED HIS FIRST VOLUME OF POEMS WHEN HE WAS TWELVE ... HIS FATHER AND MOTHER HAD STRONG LITERARY AND ARTISTIC TASTES AND RATHER THAN PUT HIM IN BUSINESS, THEY ENCOURAGED HIS TALENTS . . . . .

BROWNING FELL IN LOVE WITH A WELL KNOWN POETESS, ELIZABETH BARRETT · SHE WAS OLDER THAN HE WAS, AND AN INVALID, BUT DESPITE THE OBJECTIONS OF HIS FAMILY THEY SECRETLY WED AND WENT TO ITALY WHERE THEY LIVED HAPPILY TOGETHER UNTIL HER DEATH ... THEIR REMARKABLE LETTERS FORM A LONG AND INTERESTING RECORD OF THEIR DEVOTION TO EACH OTHER . . . . . .

BROWNING WAS A DEEP THINKER AND HIS POETRY IS OFTEN HARD TO UNDERSTAND ·· HOWEVER, HIS CHARMING PERSONALITY MADE HIM VERY POPULAR AND WHAT AMOUNTS TO A BROWNING CULT SPRANG UP THROUGHOUT THE WORLD ·· HE DIED, AT THE AGE OF 77, AND WAS BURIED IN WESTMINSTER ABBEY .

··· BORN · 1812 - DIED - 1889 ···

THE SILVER-TONGUED COMMONER

BRYAN WAS BORN IN ILLINOIS ... HE EARLY DISCOVERED HIS POWER TO SWAY AN AUDIENCE, AND HIS TALENT FOR DECLAIMING WAS ENCOURAGED BY HIS PARENTS ... ELECTED TO CONGRESS FROM NEBRASKA, HIS ADOPTED STATE, BRYAN'S ELOQUENT THREE HOUR SPEECH, IN DEFENSE OF SILVER COINAGE EARNED FOR HIM A REPUTATION AS AN ORATOR AND WAS ONE OF THE HIGH SPOTS IN THE CONTROVERSY ... IT WAS HIS FAMOUS "CROSS OF GOLD" ORATION AT THE DEMOCRATIC NATIONAL CONVENTION WHICH WON HIM THE NOMINATION OF HIS PARTY FOR PRESIDENT IN 1896 ....

WILLIAM JENNINGS BRYAN

BRYAN SOUGHT THE PRESIDENCY TWICE MORE, AND IN ONE CAMPAIGN OF SPEECH-MAKING COVERED 18,000 MILES! ... IN 1912, HE TOOK HIS SEAT IN WILSON'S CABINET AS SECRETARY OF STATE, BUT RESIGNED IN 1915 BECAUSE OF POLITICAL DIFFERENCES WITH THE PRESIDENT ..

BRYAN AGAIN ENTERED THE LIMELIGHT IN 1925, BY HIS DEFENSE OF THE BIBLE, IN THE EVOLUTION TEST CASE IN TENNESSEE, WHICH ATTRACTED THE ATTENTION OF THE ENTIRE WORLD .. A FEW DAYS AFTER THE CLOSE OF THE TRIAL, HIS FLUENT TONGUE WAS FOREVER STILLED BY HIS SUDDEN DEATH, BROUGHT ABOUT BY HIS EXERTIONS DURING THE TRIAL ...

... BORN - 1860 - DIED - 1925 ...

AMERICA'S
FIRST FAMOUS
POET . . .
WM· CULLEN
BRYANT
BRYANT, ONE OF AMERICA'S FIRST POETS, WAS A COUNTRY BOY · · THE SON OF A RURAL DOCTOR · · HE KNEW THE ALPHABET BEFORE HE WAS TWO AND AT FOURTEEN, HE HAD ALREADY HAD SEVERAL PATRIOTIC POEMS PRINTED IN NEWSPAPERS · · WHEN HE WAS TWENTY HE WROTE THE FAMOUS POEM "THANATOPSIS" ——
BRYANT BECAME EDITOR OF THE "NEW YORK EVENING POST" THE NEWSPAPER IS STILL PUBLISHED TO-DAY · · DURING THE FIFTY-TWO YEARS THAT HE HELD THAT POSITION, HE WROTE ABOUT THE AD— MINISTRATIONS OF TWELVE PRESIDENTS! · ·
BRYANT HAD A REMARKABLE MEMORY · · WHILE ON OCEAN TRIPS, HE WAS TOO SICK TO READ · · · HE WOULD SPEND HOURS RE- CITING— PAGE AFTER PAGE OF POETRY FROM MEMORY . . . . .

— BORN-1794-DIED-1878 —

"BONUS AGRICOLA"
LUTHER BURBANK
BURBANK WAS BORN IN MASSACHUSETTS, THE SON OF A FARMER · · · WHILE ATTENDING SCHOOL, HE FOUND, IN HIS VILLAGE LIBRARY, A SET OF DARWIN'S ESSAYS ON NATURE, AND READ THEM · · IT WAS THE TURNING POINT IN HIS LIFE · · INSPIRED BY THESE BOOKS TO CONDUCT HIS REVOLUTIONARY EXPERIMENTS, HE MOVED TO CALIFORNIA WHEN HE WAS 26, AND SET OUT, ON A FEW ACRES OF LAND, THE NURSERY GARDEN WHICH BECAME CELEBRATED THE WORLD OVER · HERE FOR 50 YEARS HE CARRIED ON HIS INVESTIGATIONS SOME OF HIS EXPERIMENTS TAKING 35 TO 40 YEARS TO COMPLETE! · ·
BURBANK HELPED MANKIND CONQUER NATURE AND MAKE HER SERVE HIS OWN ENDS, WHILE HE INCIDENTALLY REALIZED HIS PRIVATE AMBITION TO PRODUCE BETTER FRUITS AND FAIRER FLOWERS · · · ·

· · BORN - 1849 - DIED - 1926

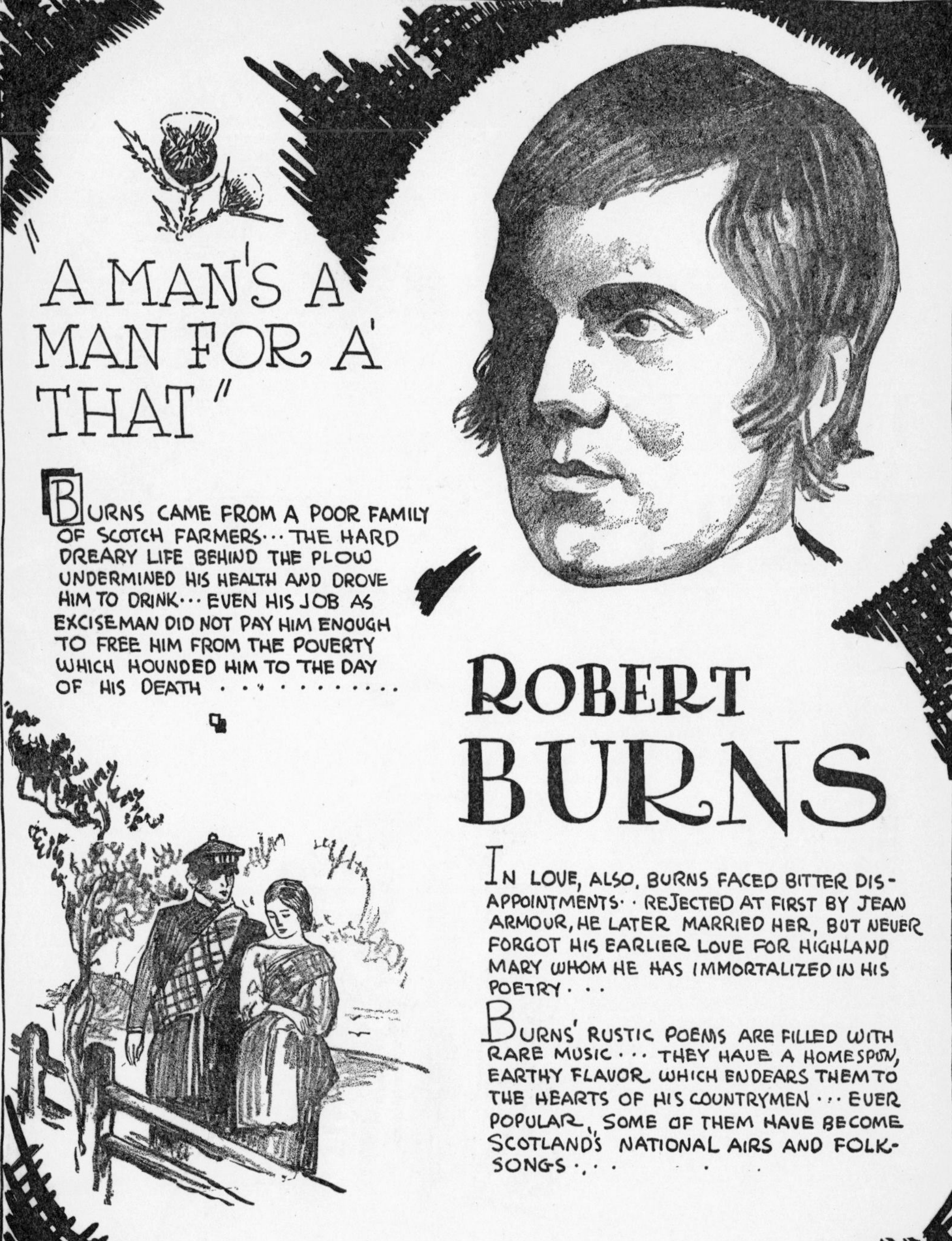
"A MAN'S A MAN FOR A' THAT"
BURNS CAME FROM A POOR FAMILY OF SCOTCH FARMERS... THE HARD DREARY LIFE BEHIND THE PLOW UNDERMINED HIS HEALTH AND DROVE HIM TO DRINK... EVEN HIS JOB AS EXCISEMAN DID NOT PAY HIM ENOUGH TO FREE HIM FROM THE POVERTY WHICH HOUNDED HIM TO THE DAY OF HIS DEATH ....
ROBERT BURNS
IN LOVE, ALSO, BURNS FACED BITTER DISAPPOINTMENTS.. REJECTED AT FIRST BY JEAN ARMOUR, HE LATER MARRIED HER, BUT NEVER FORGOT HIS EARLIER LOVE FOR HIGHLAND MARY WHOM HE HAS IMMORTALIZED IN HIS POETRY...
BURNS' RUSTIC POEMS ARE FILLED WITH RARE MUSIC... THEY HAVE A HOMESPUN, EARTHY FLAVOR WHICH ENDEARS THEM TO THE HEARTS OF HIS COUNTRYMEN... EVER POPULAR, SOME OF THEM HAVE BECOME SCOTLAND'S NATIONAL AIRS AND FOLK-SONGS.....

....BORN-1756-DIED-1796....

THE GREAT ADVENTURER
AARON BURR
AARON BURR WAS BORN IN NEWARK, N.J. BOTH HIS PARENTS DIED WHEN HE WAS THREE YEARS OLD AND HE WAS BROUGHT UP BY AN UNCLE.. HE DISTINGUISHED HIMSELF AS A BRAVE SOLDIER DURING THE REVOLUTIONARY WAR AND LATER BECAME ATTORNEY-GENERAL OF NEW YORK STATE . . . .
BURR WAS VICE-PRESIDENT UNDER JEFFERSON AND ORGANIZED TAMMANY, THE POLITICAL CLUB... HE WAS CONTINUALLY BEING OPPOSED AND ATTACKED BY ALEXANDER HAMILTON.. HE CHALLENGED HAMILTON TO A PISTOL DUEL, FOUGHT AT WEEHAWKEN, N.J., AND KILLED HIM! . .
AFTER THE DUEL, BURR BECAME AN OUTCAST, BUT CAME BACK TO THE UNITED STATES, PURCHASED SOME LAND IN LOUISIANA, AND TRIED TO FORM A NEW STATE.. HE WAS ARRESTED AND TRIED FOR TREASON.. ALTHOUGH FOUND NOT GUILTY, HE HAD TO FLEE TO EUROPE TO ESCAPE PUBLIC OPINION . . .
AT 77, BURR MARRIED A WEALTHY WIDOW, BUT SOON LEFT HER . . .
HE DIED THREE YEARS LATER ON STATEN ISLAND.N.Y.

... BORN-1756-DIED..1836..

HE LIVED WITH NATURE!

JOHN BURROUGHS

JOHN BURROUGH'S ANCESTORS WERE ALL FARMERS.. HE LOVED THE WOODS AND FIELDS, AND AS A BOY, WORKED ON HIS FATHER'S FARM WHILE ATTENDING SCHOOL. . AFTER READING AUDUBON'S BOOKS, HE BECAME INTERESTED IN BIRDS.. HE TRAVELLED ALL OVER NORTH AMERICA STUDYING NATURE, AND WROTE MANY INTERESTING BOOKS ABOUT BIRDS. . . . .

"JOHN O' BIRDS," AS HIS FRIENDS CALLED HIM, WORKED AS A HIRED FARM HAND AND AS A GOVERNMENT CLERK TO GET MONEY TO EDUCATE HIMSELF . . . HE LIVED IN A COTTAGE CALLED "SLABSIDES", WHICH BECAME THE CENTER FOR VISITORS FROM ALL OVER THE WORLD . . . . IN 1903, HE WAS PRESIDENT ROOSEVELT'S COMPANION ON A TRIP THROUGH YELLOW STONE PARK. . . . .

. . . BORN 1837 . . DIED 1921 . . .

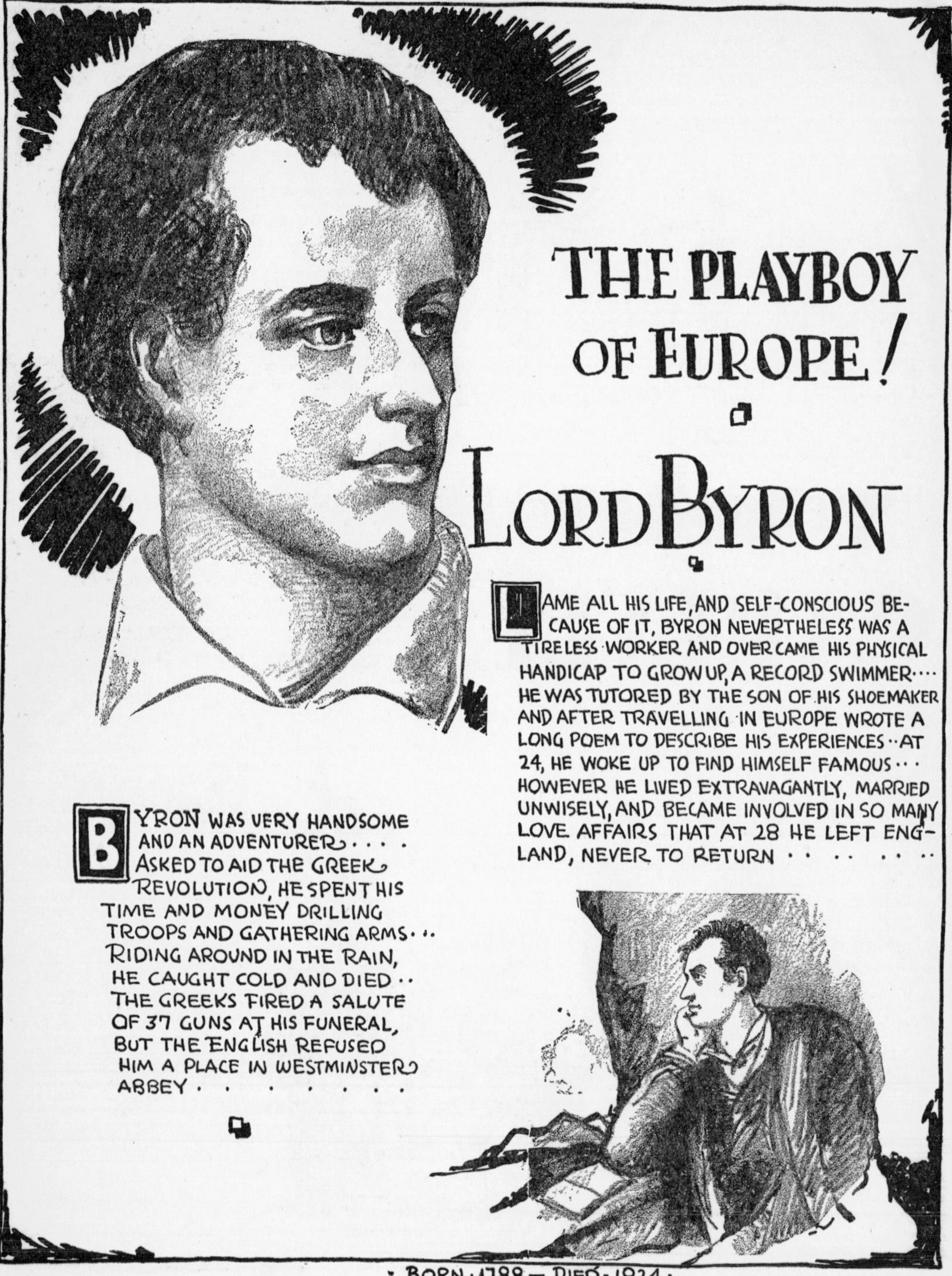
THE PLAYBOY OF EUROPE!
LORD BYRON
LAME ALL HIS LIFE, AND SELF-CONSCIOUS BECAUSE OF IT, BYRON NEVERTHELESS WAS A TIRELESS WORKER AND OVERCAME HIS PHYSICAL HANDICAP TO GROW UP A RECORD SWIMMER.... HE WAS TUTORED BY THE SON OF HIS SHOEMAKER AND AFTER TRAVELLING IN EUROPE WROTE A LONG POEM TO DESCRIBE HIS EXPERIENCES.. AT 24, HE WOKE UP TO FIND HIMSELF FAMOUS... HOWEVER HE LIVED EXTRAVAGANTLY, MARRIED UNWISELY, AND BECAME INVOLVED IN SO MANY LOVE AFFAIRS THAT AT 28 HE LEFT ENGLAND, NEVER TO RETURN . . . .
BYRON WAS VERY HANDSOME AND AN ADVENTURER.... ASKED TO AID THE GREEK REVOLUTION, HE SPENT HIS TIME AND MONEY DRILLING TROOPS AND GATHERING ARMS... RIDING AROUND IN THE RAIN, HE CAUGHT COLD AND DIED.. THE GREEKS FIRED A SALUTE OF 37 GUNS AT HIS FUNERAL, BUT THE ENGLISH REFUSED HIM A PLACE IN WESTMINSTER ABBEY . . . .

• BORN • 1788 — DIED • 1824 •

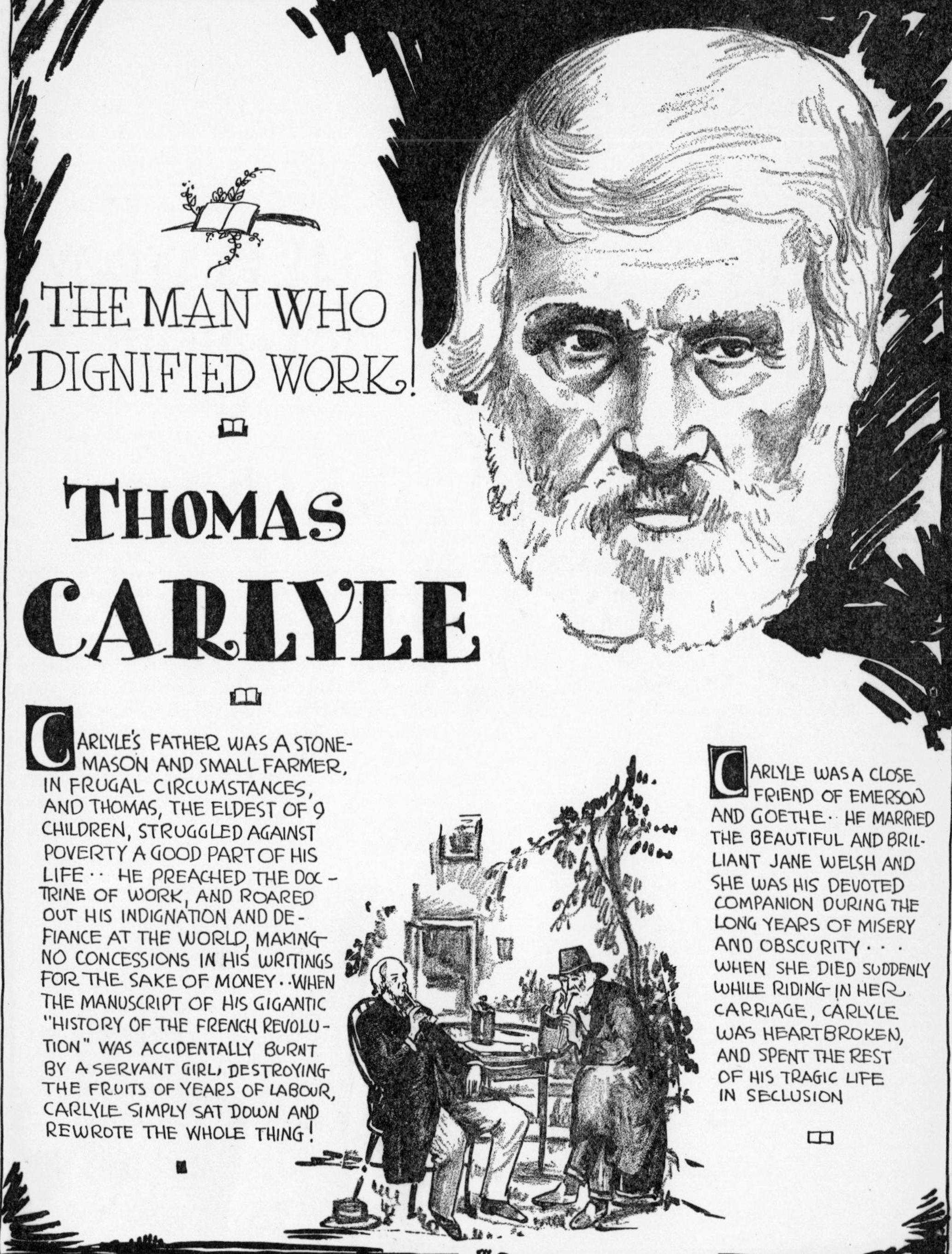
THE MAN WHO
DIGNIFIED WORK!
THOMAS
CARLYLE
CARLYLE'S FATHER WAS A STONE-MASON AND SMALL FARMER, IN FRUGAL CIRCUMSTANCES, AND THOMAS, THE ELDEST OF 9 CHILDREN, STRUGGLED AGAINST POVERTY A GOOD PART OF HIS LIFE.. HE PREACHED THE DOCTRINE OF WORK, AND ROARED OUT HIS INDIGNATION AND DEFIANCE AT THE WORLD, MAKING NO CONCESSIONS IN HIS WRITINGS FOR THE SAKE OF MONEY.. WHEN THE MANUSCRIPT OF HIS GIGANTIC "HISTORY OF THE FRENCH REVOLUTION" WAS ACCIDENTALLY BURNT BY A SERVANT GIRL, DESTROYING THE FRUITS OF YEARS OF LABOUR, CARLYLE SIMPLY SAT DOWN AND REWROTE THE WHOLE THING!
CARLYLE WAS A CLOSE FRIEND OF EMERSON AND GOETHE. HE MARRIED THE BEAUTIFUL AND BRILLIANT JANE WELSH AND SHE WAS HIS DEVOTED COMPANION DURING THE LONG YEARS OF MISERY AND OBSCURITY... WHEN SHE DIED SUDDENLY WHILE RIDING IN HER CARRIAGE, CARLYLE WAS HEARTBROKEN, AND SPENT THE REST OF HIS TRAGIC LIFE IN SECLUSION

·BORN-1795-DIED-1881

A STEEL BARON
WHO HELPED
EDUCATE THE WORLD
ANDREW
CARNEGIE
"CARNEGIE CAME FROM A FAMILY OF SCOTCH WEAVERS. . . WHEN THEY EMIGRATED TO AMERICA, YOUNG ANDREW WENT TO WORK IN A COTTON FACTORY. HE SOON FOUND TELEGRAPHY AND TRAIN DISPATCHING MORE TO HIS LIKING, AND DURING THE CIVIL WAR, HE WAS PUT IN CHARGE OF THE NORTHERN RAILROAD OPERATIONS . . . .
ALTHOUGH HE WROTE MORE THAN HALF A DOZEN BOOKS, IT IS AS A PHILANTHROPIST THAT CARNEGIE IS BEST KNOWN. . . . HIS PRINCELY GIFTS — HUNDREDS OF MILLIONS OF DOLLARS — STAGGER THE IMAGINATION. . HE DONATED FORTUNES FOR SCIENTIFIC RESEARCH, BUILT THE PEACE PALACE AT THE HAGUE AND ESTABLISHED TRUST FUNDS FOR NEEDY STUDENTS AND PROFESSORS. . . HIS GREATEST EFFORTS WERE IN BEHALF OF EDUCATION AND THE 2500 LIBRARIES THAT HE BUILT IN ENGLAND AND AMERICA ARE HIS MOST LASTING MONUMENT.
CARNEGIE FORESAW THE USE OF STEEL IN CONSTRUCTION, AND FROM A SMALL PLANT, HE EXPANDED HIS MANUFACTURING INTERESTS UNTIL HE HAD THE ENTIRE INDUSTRY IN HIS GRASP! .

. . . BORN - 1835 — DIED - 1919 . . .

· A GERMAN PRINCESS WHO BECAME A GREAT RUSSIAN EMPRESS · ·

CATHERINE THE GREAT

CATHERINE WAS A GERMAN PRINCESS BY BIRTH · · AT 16 SHE WAS MARRIED TO THE GRAND DUKE PETER, HEIR TO THE RUSSIAN THRONE · · HER HUSBAND WAS A WEAKLING AND DEMENTED, AND SHE DESPISED HIM · · SHE HAD MANY LOVERS— HER CHIEF MINISTERS AND TRUSTED AGENTS AMONG THEM, AND HER LIFE WAS THE SCANDAL OF ALL EUROPE · · · ·

CATHERINE BECAME EMPRESS AT 33 AND RULED RUSSIA FOR 34 YEARS · · SHE WAS DIPLOMATIC AND INTELLIGENT AND MADE THE RUSSIAN COURT AS CULTIVATED AS ANY IN EUROPE · · · · ·

SHE WROTE WITTY LETTERS AND A GREAT MANY BOOKS— AMONG THEM A HISTORY OF RUSSIA · · · · · ·

· · BORN-1729- DIED-1796 · · ·

BENVENUTO
CELLINI
CHILD OF ITALY ... PUPIL OF MICHELANGELO ... PET OF POPES AND KINGS ... BRAWLER ... GOLDSMITH ... SCULPTOR ... TROUBADOUR ... BOASTER ... ASSASSIN ... AND COLORFUL GENIUS .....
CELLINIS FIERY TEMPER MADE HIM HATED AND FEARED ... IF HE HAD NOT BEEN AS SKILLED WITH HIS DAGGER AS HE WAS WITH HIS TOOLS, IT IS DOUBTFUL IF HE WOULD HAVE LIVED TO THE AGE OF 71 ... HOWEVER, HIS BEAUTIFUL CRAFTSMANSHIP WON HIM THE FAVOR OF POWERFUL MEN . . . .
CELLINI NEVER MARRIED .... HE WROTE HIS OWN BIOGRAPHY, A RACY BOOK FULL OF HIS PASSIONS, HIS HATREDS AND HIS ADVENTURES ... IT IS ONE OF THE MOST FASCINATING, EXCITING BOOKS IN EXISTENCE . . . . .

... BORN · 1500 — DIED · 1571 ...

THE POET OF THE PIANO!
FRÉDÉRIC CHOPIN
CHOPIN WAS BORN IN POLAND, THE SON OF A FRENCH PROFESSOR·· EVEN AS A LAD, HIS GENIUS AS A PIANO PLAYER MADE HIM THE PET OF POLISH SOCIETY···· HIS DEBUT IN VIENNA WAS AN OVERWHELMING SUCCESS AND IN PARIS, WHERE HE FINALLY SETTLED, HE BECAME THE IDOL OF THE FASHIONABLE WORLD · · · · · · ·
CHOPINS LOVE AFFAIR WITH MME. DUDEVANT (THE WRITER, GEORGE SAND) IS ONE OF THE FAMOUS ONES IN HISTORY· WHEN HIS FRAIL BODY BROKE UNDER THE STRAIN OF HIS CONSTANT ACTIVITY, GEORGE SAND TOOK HIM TO THE ISLAND OF MAJORCA·· HERE, HER CAREFUL NURSING GAVE HIM A FRESH LEASE ON LIFE — BUT ONLY A TEMPORARY ONE·· ·HE DIED BEFORE HE REACHED HIS FORTIETH YEAR ·
CHOPIN LABOURED LONG AND HARD TO MAKE HIS MUSIC PERFECT AND HIS MELANCHOLY COMPOSITIONS ARE FILLED WITH GENUINE POETRY

BORN-1810- DIED-1849·

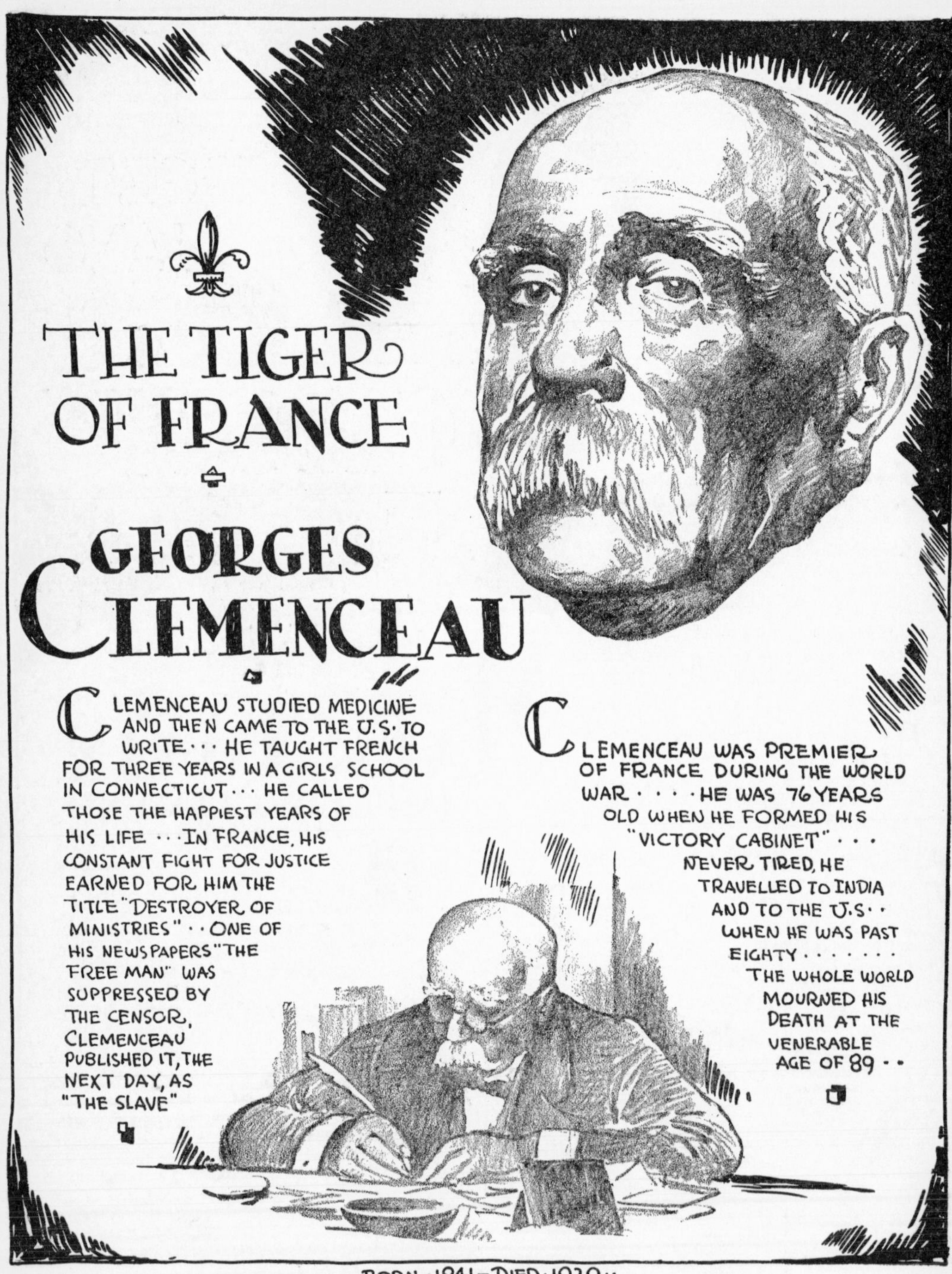
THE TIGER
OF FRANCE
GEORGES
CLEMENCEAU
CLEMENCEAU STUDIED MEDICINE AND THEN CAME TO THE U.S. TO WRITE . . . HE TAUGHT FRENCH FOR THREE YEARS IN A GIRLS SCHOOL IN CONNECTICUT . . . HE CALLED THOSE THE HAPPIEST YEARS OF HIS LIFE . . . IN FRANCE, HIS CONSTANT FIGHT FOR JUSTICE EARNED FOR HIM THE TITLE "DESTROYER OF MINISTRIES" . . ONE OF HIS NEWSPAPERS "THE FREE MAN" WAS SUPPRESSED BY THE CENSOR, CLEMENCEAU PUBLISHED IT, THE NEXT DAY, AS "THE SLAVE"
CLEMENCEAU WAS PREMIER OF FRANCE DURING THE WORLD WAR . . . . HE WAS 76 YEARS OLD WHEN HE FORMED HIS "VICTORY CABINET" . . . NEVER TIRED, HE TRAVELLED TO INDIA AND TO THE U.S. . WHEN HE WAS PAST EIGHTY . . . . THE WHOLE WORLD MOURNED HIS DEATH AT THE VENERABLE AGE OF 89 . .

· · BORN - 1841 - DIED · 1929 · ·

HE LAUGHED AT LIFE!
HE WAS BORN IN A LITTLE MISSOURI TOWN, HANNIBAL, LIVED IN THE FARWEST, IN NEW YORK AND IN EUROPE AND WORKED AS A RIVER PILOT ON THE MISSISSIPPI · · IN TAKING SOUNDINGS OF THE RIVER BOTTOM THE PILOTS CALLED OUT "MARK THREE, MARK HALF, MARK TWAIN," ETC. THE WORDS "MARK TWAIN" BECAME HIS PEN NAME · · · · · · · · ·
HE LOVED TO SPECULATE AND WAS CONSTANTLY INVESTING IN HAIR-BRAINED SCHEMES — GOLD MINES, OLD FARMS, PRINTING MACHINES AND SO ON ·
HIS FAMOUS BOYS' STORIES "TOM SAWYER" AND "HUCKLEBERRY FINN" ARE ENJOYED BY YOUNG AND OLD ALIKE · · ·
MARK TWAIN
(SAMUEL L · CLEMENS)
FAMOUS AS A HUMORIST AND ALWAYS LAUGHING, YET THERE IS A BITTER STRAIN IN HIS HUMOR AND HE DID NOT ENJOY LIFE · · A LADY ONCE KISSED HIS HAND AND SAID, "GOD MUST LOVE YOU!" — "I HOPE SO!" HE ANSWERED AND ADDED LATER, "I GUESS SHE HASN'T HEARD OF OUR STRAINED RELATIONSHIP!" —

· · BORN – 1835 – DIED – 1910 · ·

The ENCHANTRESS OF THE EAST
CLEOPATRA
LOVELY BEYOND COMPARISON, PROFICIENT IN EIGHT LANGUAGES, WITTY, GRACEFUL AND LEARNED, CLEOPATRA, THE LAST QUEEN OF EGYPT, CAME TO THE THRONE AT THE AGE OF SEVENTEEN ... SHE SHARED THE ROYAL SEAT WITH HER BROTHER, PTOLEMY, WHO WAS TWELVE YEARS OLD ... UNDER THIS JOINT RULERSHIP, CIVIL WAR SOON DISRUPTED THE STATE AND CLEOPATRA FLED TO SYRIA ... SHE DETERMINED TO OBTAIN CAESAR'S HELP AND, AS THE STORY GOES, HAD HERSELF BROUGHT TO HIM, ROLLED IN A CARPET .. CAPTIVATED BY HER BEAUTY, HE OVERTHREW PTOLEMY AND BECAME CLEOPATRA'S LOVER . HE TOOK HER TO ROME, WHERE SHE LIVED UNTIL HE WAS MURDERED . . . . .
BROUGHT TO ACCOUNT BY MARK ANTONY, CLEOPATRA BEWITCHED HIM ALSO AND THEY LIVED TOGETHER IN LUXURY AND DISSIPATION UNTIL HIS DEFEAT AT ACTIUM .. FEARING ROMAN VENGEANCE, SHE COMMITTED SUICIDE BY ALLOWING A POISONOUS SNAKE TO BITE HER, AND WAS BURIED IN THE SAME TOMB WITH ANTONY . . . . .

... BORN - 69 B.C. — DIED - 30 B.C. ...

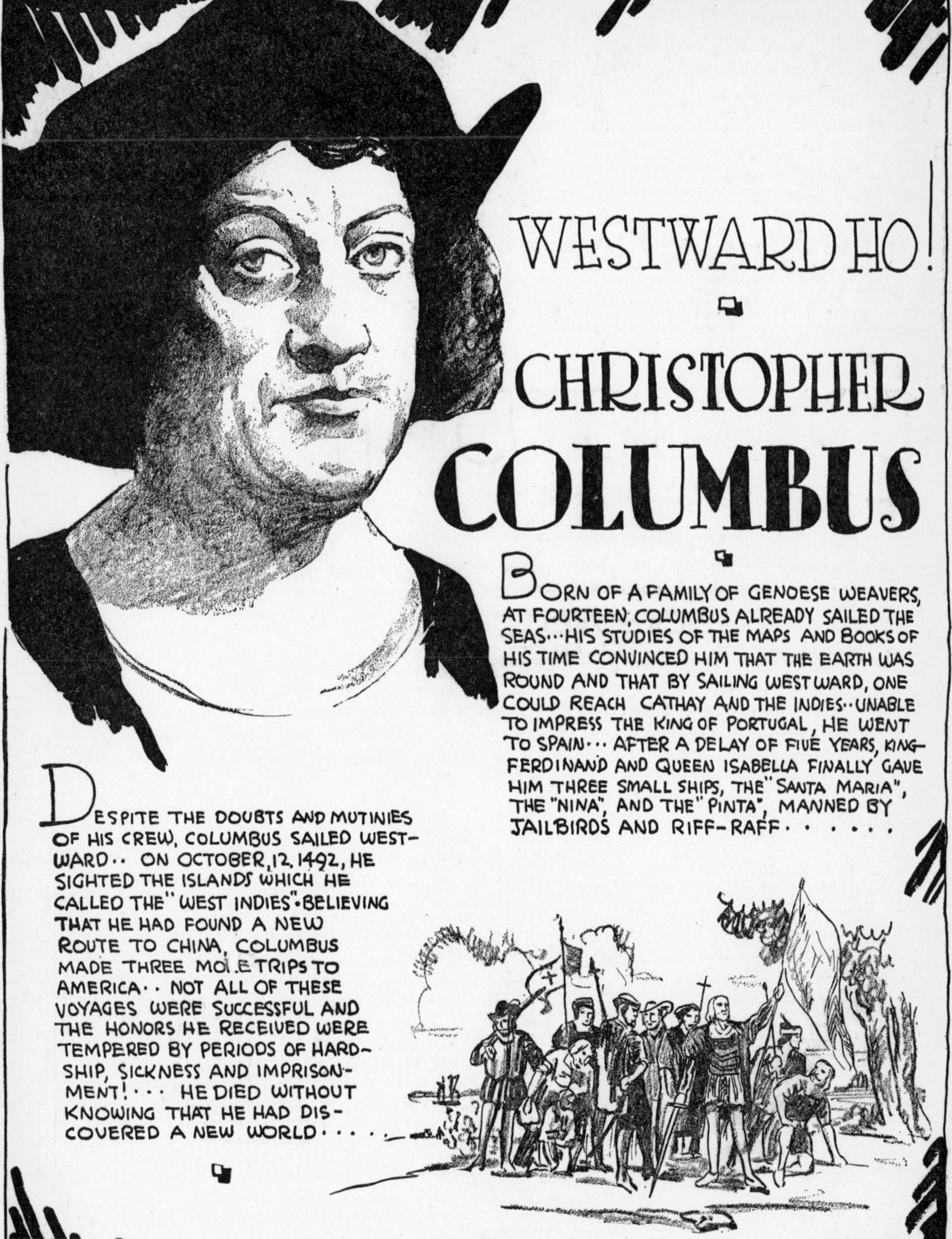
WESTWARD HO!
CHRISTOPHER
COLUMBUS
BORN OF A FAMILY OF GENOESE WEAVERS, AT FOURTEEN, COLUMBUS ALREADY SAILED THE SEAS··· HIS STUDIES OF THE MAPS AND BOOKS OF HIS TIME CONVINCED HIM THAT THE EARTH WAS ROUND AND THAT BY SAILING WESTWARD, ONE COULD REACH CATHAY AND THE INDIES·· UNABLE TO IMPRESS THE KING OF PORTUGAL, HE WENT TO SPAIN··· AFTER A DELAY OF FIVE YEARS, KING FERDINAND AND QUEEN ISABELLA FINALLY GAVE HIM THREE SMALL SHIPS, THE "SANTA MARIA", THE "NINA", AND THE "PINTA", MANNED BY JAILBIRDS AND RIFF-RAFF · · · · ·
DESPITE THE DOUBTS AND MUTINIES OF HIS CREW, COLUMBUS SAILED WESTWARD·· ON OCTOBER, 12, 1492, HE SIGHTED THE ISLANDS WHICH HE CALLED THE "WEST INDIES"· BELIEVING THAT HE HAD FOUND A NEW ROUTE TO CHINA, COLUMBUS MADE THREE MORE TRIPS TO AMERICA·· NOT ALL OF THESE VOYAGES WERE SUCCESSFUL AND THE HONORS HE RECEIVED WERE TEMPERED BY PERIODS OF HARDSHIP, SICKNESS AND IMPRISONMENT!··· HE DIED WITHOUT KNOWING THAT HE HAD DISCOVERED A NEW WORLD · · · · ·

··BORN-1446 OR 1451- DIED-1506···

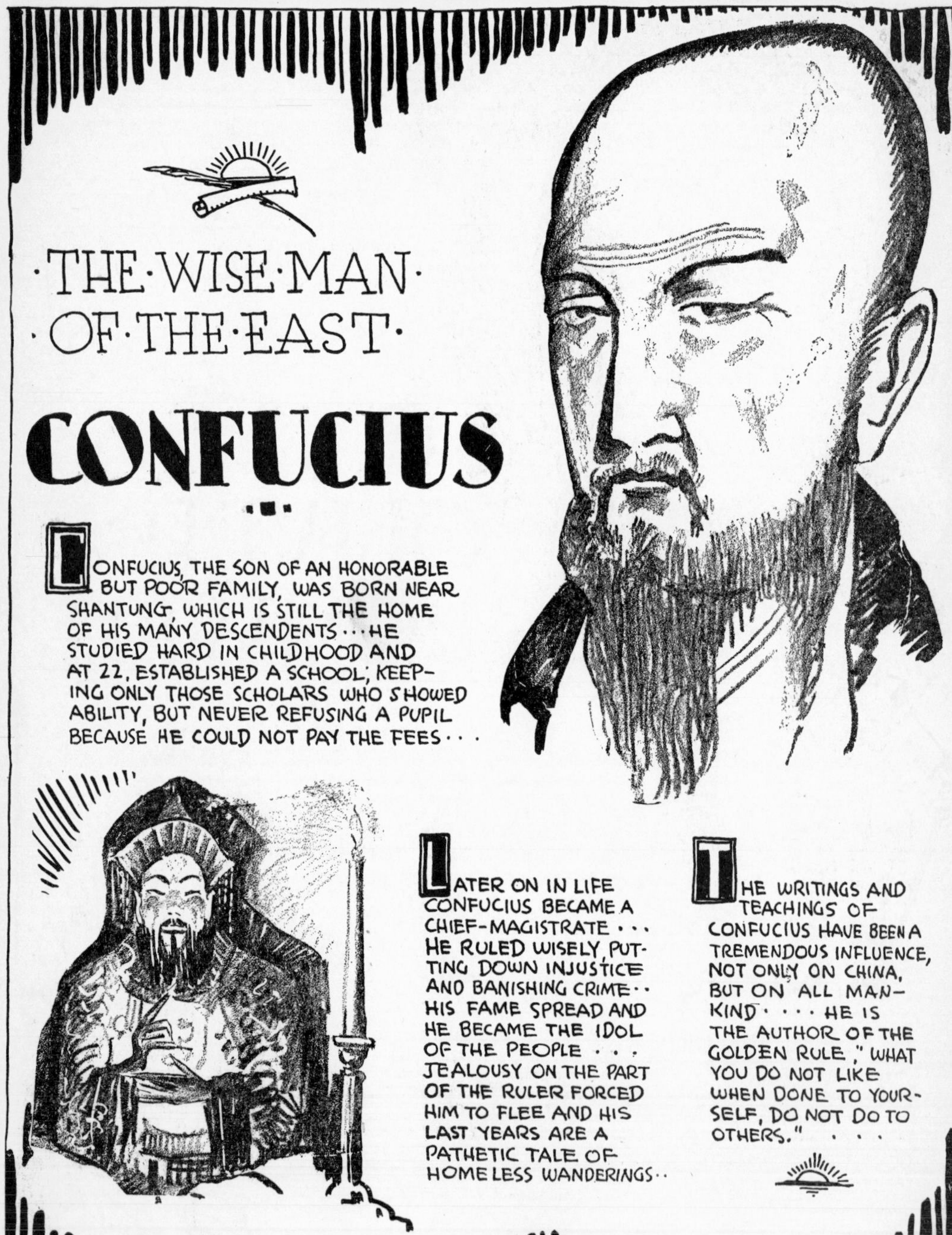
·THE·WISE·MAN·
·OF·THE·EAST·
CONFUCIUS
CONFUCIUS, THE SON OF AN HONORABLE BUT POOR FAMILY, WAS BORN NEAR SHANTUNG, WHICH IS STILL THE HOME OF HIS MANY DESCENDENTS ··· HE STUDIED HARD IN CHILDHOOD AND AT 22, ESTABLISHED A SCHOOL; KEEPING ONLY THOSE SCHOLARS WHO SHOWED ABILITY, BUT NEVER REFUSING A PUPIL BECAUSE HE COULD NOT PAY THE FEES ···
LATER ON IN LIFE CONFUCIUS BECAME A CHIEF-MAGISTRATE ··· HE RULED WISELY, PUTTING DOWN INJUSTICE AND BANISHING CRIME ·· HIS FAME SPREAD AND HE BECAME THE IDOL OF THE PEOPLE ··· JEALOUSY ON THE PART OF THE RULER FORCED HIM TO FLEE AND HIS LAST YEARS ARE A PATHETIC TALE OF HOMELESS WANDERINGS ··
THE WRITINGS AND TEACHINGS OF CONFUCIUS HAVE BEEN A TREMENDOUS INFLUENCE, NOT ONLY ON CHINA, BUT ON ALL MANKIND ···· HE IS THE AUTHOR OF THE GOLDEN RULE, " WHAT YOU DO NOT LIKE WHEN DONE TO YOURSELF, DO NOT DO TO OTHERS." ···
··· BORN - 550 - B.C. - DIED - 478 B.C. ···

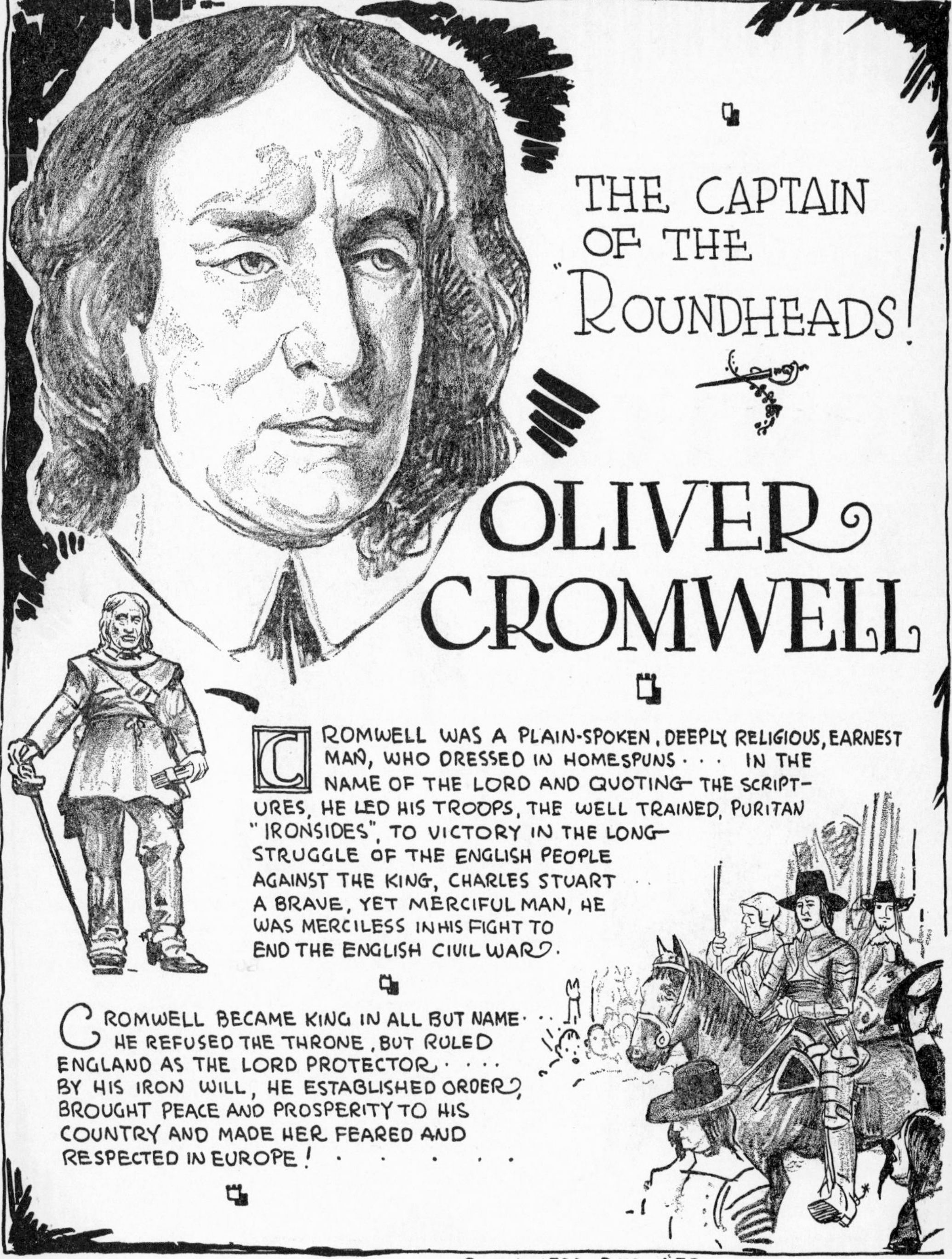
THE CAPTAIN OF THE "ROUNDHEADS"!
OLIVER CROMWELL
CROMWELL WAS A PLAIN-SPOKEN, DEEPLY RELIGIOUS, EARNEST MAN, WHO DRESSED IN HOMESPUNS . . . IN THE NAME OF THE LORD AND QUOTING THE SCRIPTURES, HE LED HIS TROOPS, THE WELL TRAINED, PURITAN "IRONSIDES", TO VICTORY IN THE LONG STRUGGLE OF THE ENGLISH PEOPLE AGAINST THE KING, CHARLES STUART . . A BRAVE, YET MERCIFUL MAN, HE WAS MERCILESS IN HIS FIGHT TO END THE ENGLISH CIVIL WAR.
CROMWELL BECAME KING IN ALL BUT NAME . . HE REFUSED THE THRONE, BUT RULED ENGLAND AS THE LORD PROTECTOR . . . . BY HIS IRON WILL, HE ESTABLISHED ORDER, BROUGHT PEACE AND PROSPERITY TO HIS COUNTRY AND MADE HER FEARED AND RESPECTED IN EUROPE! . . . . . .

· · · BORN - 1599 - DIED - 1658 · · ·

HE GLORIFIED HELL!
DANTE
DANTE WAS INTERESTED IN POLITICS AND HELPED GOVERN HIS NATIVE CITY FLORENCE.
BECAUSE OF A QUARREL HE WAS CONDEMNED TO BE BURNT ALIVE
HE HAD TO SPEND THE REST OF HIS LIFE WANDERING, TO ESCAPE THE PENALTY.
WHEN HE WAS NINE YEARS OLD, DANTE FELL IN LOVE WITH A BEAUTIFUL GIRL, BEATRICE . . . SHE DIED WHILE STILL YOUNG.
HE WROTE A LONG MAJESTIC POEM ABOUT HEAVEN AND HELL, INSPIRED BY HIS LOVE FOR HER . . . IT IS FULL OF MARVELOUS LEARNING AND IS NOW ONE OF THE WORLD'S GRANDEST TREASURES, AND IS CALLED THE "DIVINE COMEDY."

· · BORN · 1265 — DIED · 1321 · ·

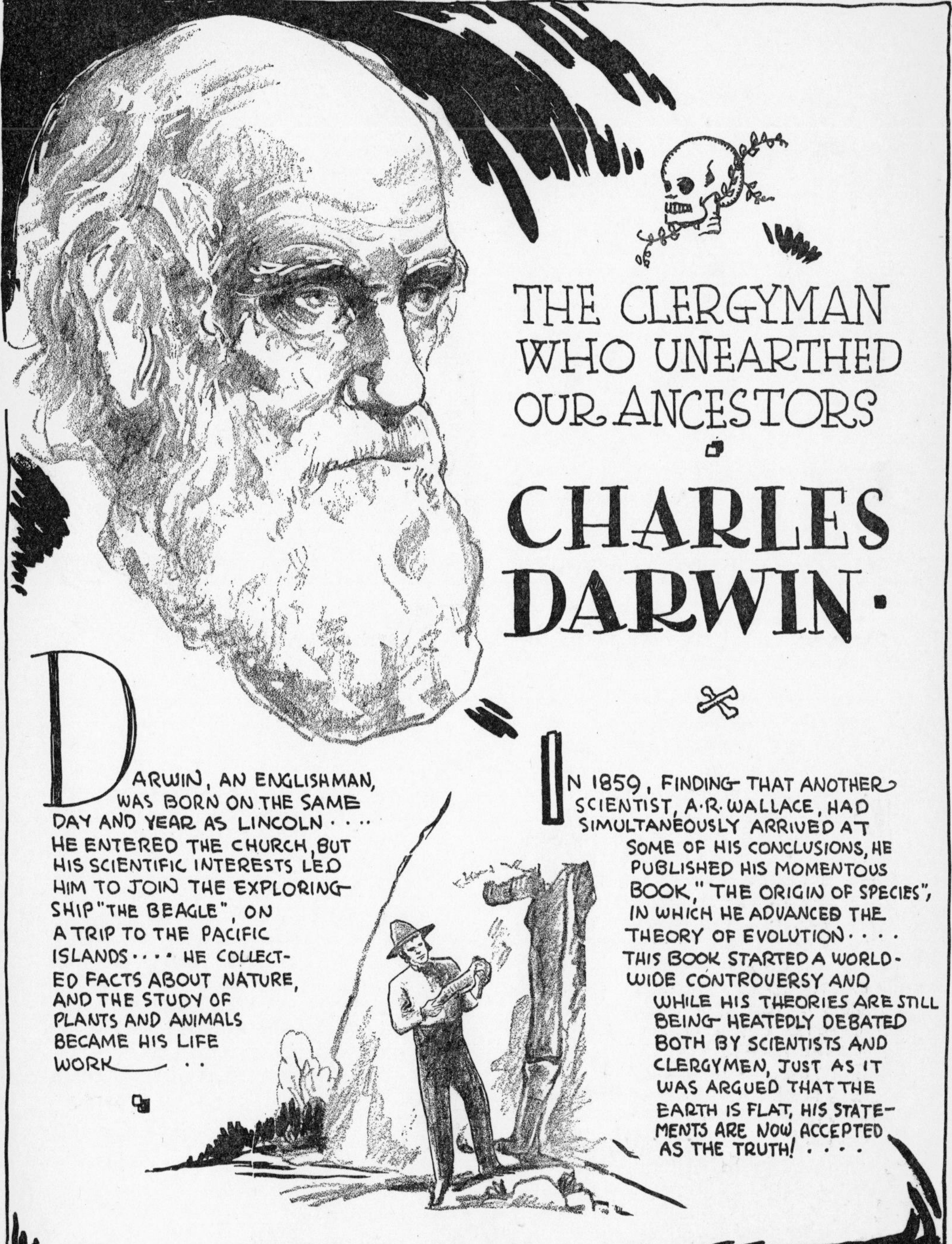
THE CLERGYMAN
WHO UNEARTHED
OUR ANCESTORS
CHARLES
DARWIN
DARWIN, AN ENGLISHMAN, WAS BORN ON THE SAME DAY AND YEAR AS LINCOLN .... HE ENTERED THE CHURCH, BUT HIS SCIENTIFIC INTERESTS LED HIM TO JOIN THE EXPLORING SHIP "THE BEAGLE", ON A TRIP TO THE PACIFIC ISLANDS .... HE COLLECTED FACTS ABOUT NATURE, AND THE STUDY OF PLANTS AND ANIMALS BECAME HIS LIFE WORK ..
IN 1859, FINDING THAT ANOTHER SCIENTIST, A.R. WALLACE, HAD SIMULTANEOUSLY ARRIVED AT SOME OF HIS CONCLUSIONS, HE PUBLISHED HIS MOMENTOUS BOOK, "THE ORIGIN OF SPECIES", IN WHICH HE ADVANCED THE THEORY OF EVOLUTION .... THIS BOOK STARTED A WORLD-WIDE CONTROVERSY AND WHILE HIS THEORIES ARE STILL BEING HEATEDLY DEBATED BOTH BY SCIENTISTS AND CLERGYMEN, JUST AS IT WAS ARGUED THAT THE EARTH IS FLAT, HIS STATEMENTS ARE NOW ACCEPTED AS THE TRUTH! ....
... BORN-1809-DIED-1882 ...

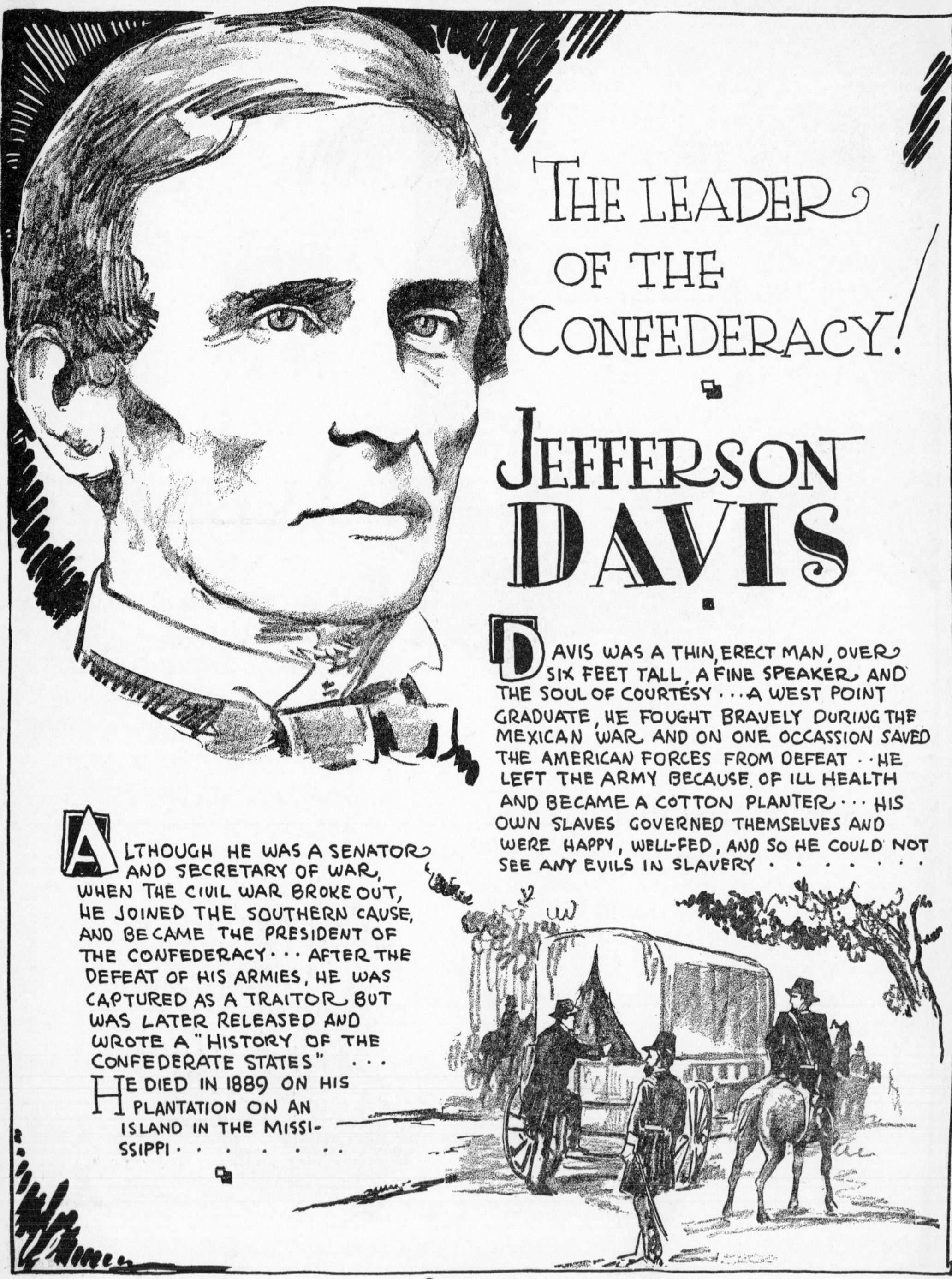
THE LEADER OF THE CONFEDERACY!
JEFFERSON DAVIS
DAVIS WAS A THIN, ERECT MAN, OVER SIX FEET TALL, A FINE SPEAKER AND THE SOUL OF COURTESY . . . A WEST POINT GRADUATE, HE FOUGHT BRAVELY DURING THE MEXICAN WAR AND ON ONE OCCASSION SAVED THE AMERICAN FORCES FROM DEFEAT . . HE LEFT THE ARMY BECAUSE OF ILL HEALTH AND BECAME A COTTON PLANTER . . . HIS OWN SLAVES GOVERNED THEMSELVES AND WERE HAPPY, WELL-FED, AND SO HE COULD NOT SEE ANY EVILS IN SLAVERY . . . .
ALTHOUGH HE WAS A SENATOR AND SECRETARY OF WAR, WHEN THE CIVIL WAR BROKE OUT, HE JOINED THE SOUTHERN CAUSE, AND BECAME THE PRESIDENT OF THE CONFEDERACY . . . AFTER THE DEFEAT OF HIS ARMIES, HE WAS CAPTURED AS A TRAITOR BUT WAS LATER RELEASED AND WROTE A "HISTORY OF THE CONFEDERATE STATES" . . .
HE DIED IN 1889 ON HIS PLANTATION ON AN ISLAND IN THE MISSISSIPPI . . . .

. . . BORN-1808 — DIED · 1889 . . .

AN ARTIST WHO POKED FUN AT PEOPLE!

HONORÉ DAUMIER

IMPRISONED FOR BEING CLEVER! DAUMIER WAS A HARD WORKER AND DID ABOUT 5000 DRAWINGS DURING HIS LIFE. . HE DREW A CLEVER CARTOON OF THE KING. FOR THIS HE WAS PUT IN JAIL...

WHILE **DAUMIER** LIVED HE HAD TO STRUGGLE AGAINST POVERTY AND LACK OF APPRECIATION. . . . IN 1870, HE WAS OFFERED THE CROSS OF **LEGION OF HONOR**. HE REFUSED IT!

TO ADD TO HIS TROUBLES, HE BECAME BLIND!

DAUMIER IS NOW RECOGNIZED AS THE MOST IMPORTANT FRENCH PAINTER AND CARICATURIST OF THE **NINETEENTH CENTURY** . . .

· · BORN 1808 — DIED 1879 · ·

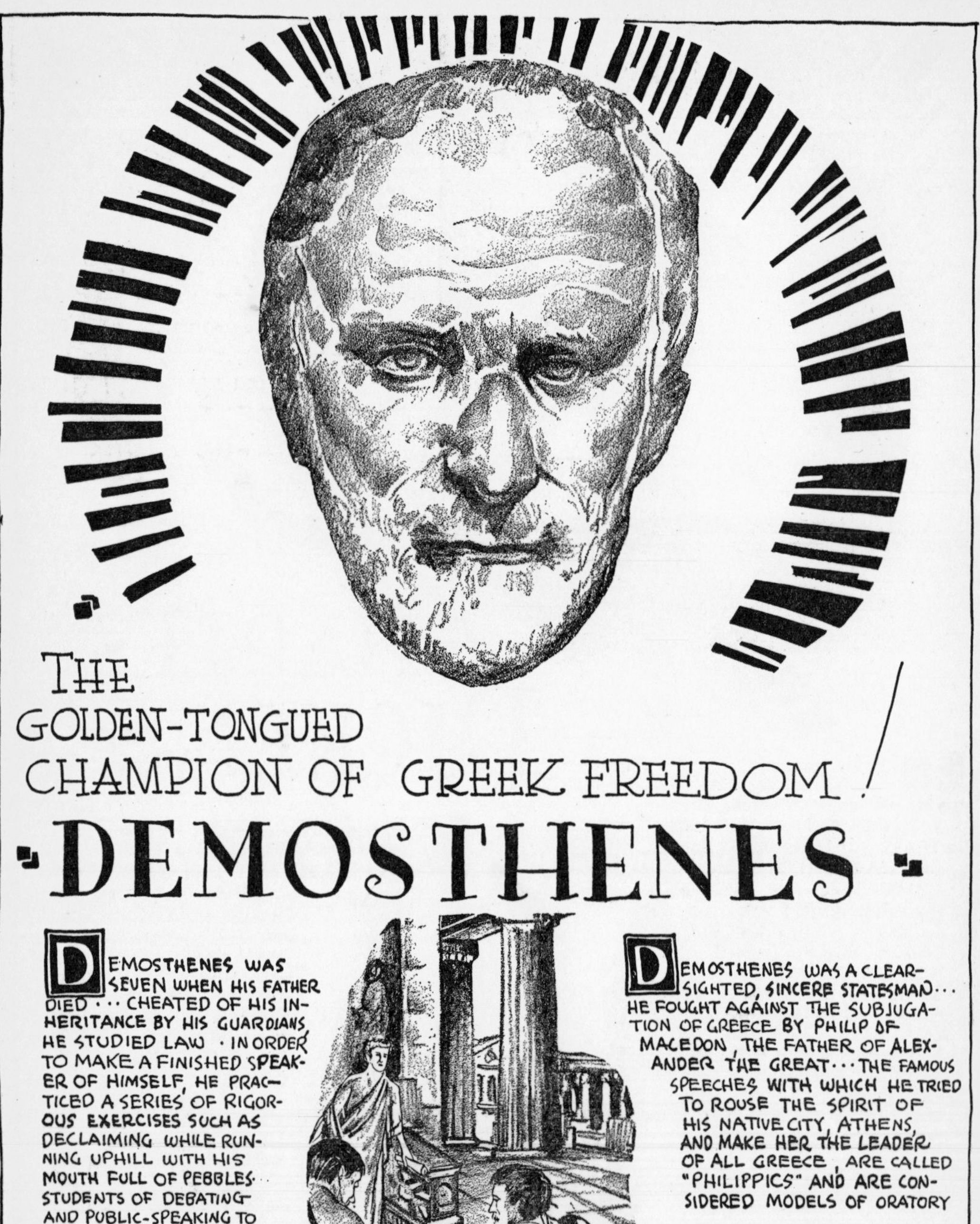
THE
GOLDEN-TONGUED
CHAMPION OF GREEK FREEDOM!
DEMOSTHENES
DEMOSTHENES WAS SEVEN WHEN HIS FATHER DIED ... CHEATED OF HIS INHERITANCE BY HIS GUARDIANS, HE STUDIED LAW · IN ORDER TO MAKE A FINISHED SPEAKER OF HIMSELF, HE PRACTICED A SERIES OF RIGOROUS EXERCISES SUCH AS DECLAIMING WHILE RUNNING UPHILL WITH HIS MOUTH FULL OF PEBBLES .. STUDENTS OF DEBATING AND PUBLIC-SPEAKING TO THIS DAY STUDY THE METHODS OF DEMOSTHENES ...
DEMOSTHENES WAS A CLEAR-SIGHTED, SINCERE STATESMAN ... HE FOUGHT AGAINST THE SUBJUGATION OF GREECE BY PHILIP OF MACEDON, THE FATHER OF ALEXANDER THE GREAT ... THE FAMOUS SPEECHES WITH WHICH HE TRIED TO ROUSE THE SPIRIT OF HIS NATIVE CITY, ATHENS, AND MAKE HER THE LEADER OF ALL GREECE, ARE CALLED "PHILIPPICS" AND ARE CONSIDERED MODELS OF ORATORY

... BORN-384 B.C.· DIED··322 B.C.

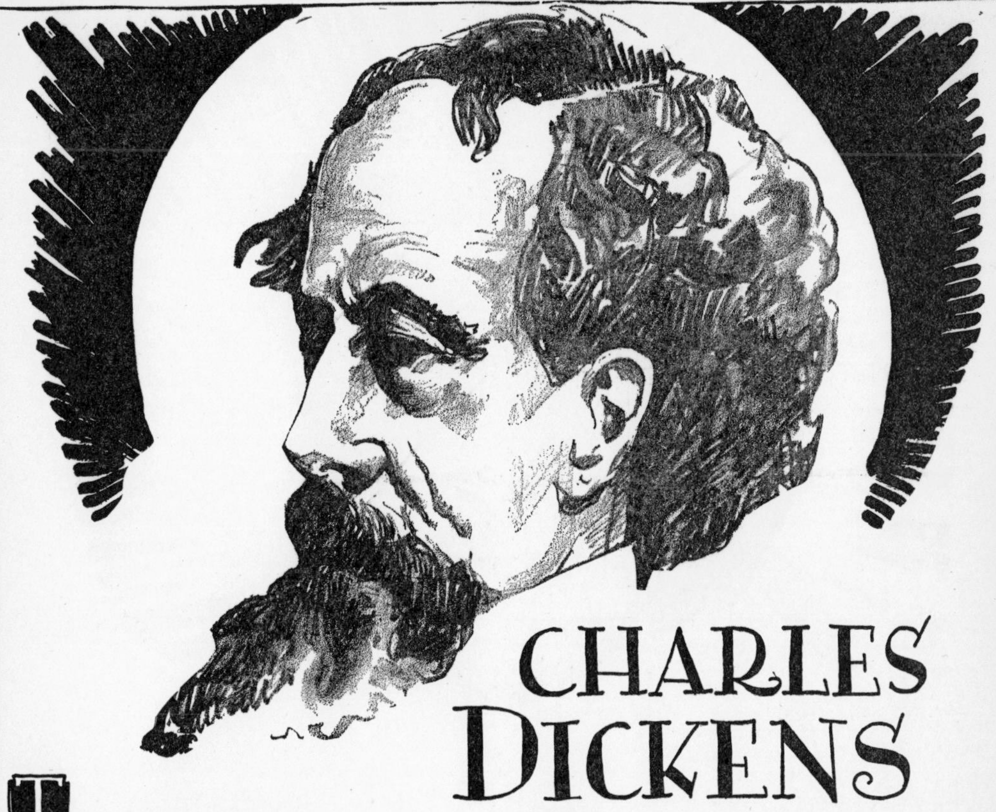

CHARLES DICKENS

THROWN ON HIS OWN RESOURCES WHEN HE WAS TEN YEARS OLD, DICKENS' WATCHFUL, CRITICAL EYE NOTED AND REMEMBERED THE HARDSHIPS AND PLEASURES OF THE POOR . . . THIS KNOWLEDGE FORMED THE FOUNDATION FOR HIS SERIES OF GREAT NOVELS ABOUT THE MIDDLE AND LOWER CLASSES . . . HE WORKED AS A NEWSPAPER REPORTER AND WITH THE APPEARANCE OF THE "PICKWICK PAPERS" HE ENTERED THE LIMELIGHT AS A HUMOROUS WRITER.

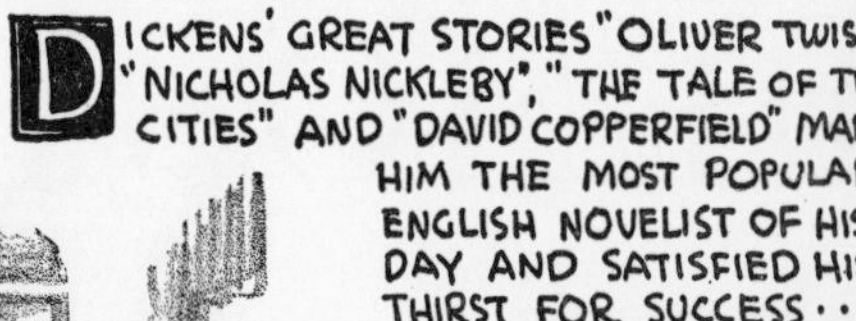

DICKENS' GREAT STORIES "OLIVER TWIST", "NICHOLAS NICKLEBY", "THE TALE OF TWO CITIES" AND "DAVID COPPERFIELD" MADE HIM THE MOST POPULAR ENGLISH NOVELIST OF HIS DAY AND SATISFIED HIS THIRST FOR SUCCESS . . . . . HIS CHARACTERS, CARICATURES OF HIS FAMILY AND FRIENDS ARE HUMAN AND REAL, AND UNDER HIS SUBTLE TOUCH BECOME UNFORGETABLE . . . . . .

DICKENS JOURNEYED TO AMERICA TWICE AND RECEIVED A ROYAL WELCOME BOTH TIMES.

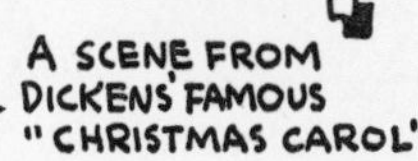

A SCENE FROM DICKENS' FAMOUS "CHRISTMAS CAROL"

. . . BORN-1812-DIED-1870 . . .

THE NOVELIST-POLITICIAN!
BENJAMIN DISRAELI
WEALTHY AND AN ARISTOCRAT, DISRAELI EARLY RESOLVED TO ENTER POLITICS. AFTER MANY DEFEATS, HE GAINED A SEAT IN THE ENGLISH HOUSE OF COMMONS. ROMANTIC BY NATURE, HIS DANDYISH DRESS AND FLOWERY, DRAMATIC SPEECH, CAUSED THE HOUSE TO LAUGH HIM DOWN, BUT NOT UNTIL HE HAD PROMISED HIS HEARERS THAT SOME DAY THEY WOULD HAVE TO LISTEN TO HIM...
HIS PROPHESY CAME TRUE. AS PRIME MINISTER OF ENGLAND, HE WON THE AFFECTION OF QUEEN VICTORIA BY HIS LOYAL PATRIOTISM, HIS COURTLY DEFERENCE AND SUBTLE FLATTERY... HIS GREATEST SERVICE TO ENGLAND WAS THE PURCHASE, ON HIS OWN AUTHORITY OF THE SUEZ CANAL... FINALLY, THE TITLE EARL OF BEACONSFIELD WAS BESTOWED ON HIM AND HE ENTERED THE HOUSE OF LORDS!
DISRAELI WAS A NOVELIST AS WELL AS A STATESMAN, AND HIS SPICY SOCIETY STORIES ARE FILLED WITH KEEN WIT AND CLEVER SITUATIONS...

... BORN - 1804 - DIED - 1881 ...

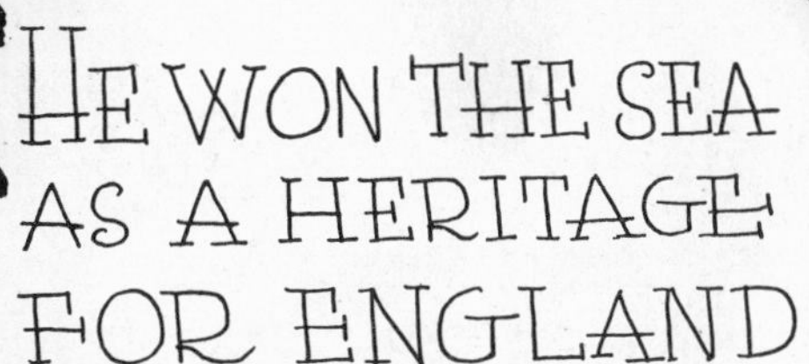
HE WON THE SEA
AS A HERITAGE
FOR ENGLAND

Sir Francis DRAKE

DRAKE, THE SON OF A CLERGYMAN, SPENT HIS YOUTH AS AN APPRENTICE ON SLAVE TRADE VESSELS TO THE NEW WORLD AS HE GREW OLDER, HE TURNED TO PRIVATEERING (A POLITE TERM FOR PIRACY) AND ENRICHED ENGLISH COFFERS AT THE EXPENSE OF SPANISH SHIPPING HIS LIGHTNING SWIFT RAIDS BEWILDERED HIS ENEMIES AND MADE HIM THE MOST FEARED AND RESPECTED ANTAGONIST OF THE SPANISH CROWN . . . . . .

DRAKE WAS THE FIRST ENGLISHMAN TO SAIL AROUND THE WORLD HE CAPTURED MANY PRIZES ON THE WAY AND RETURNED LADEN WITH TREASURE. AS A REWARD QUEEN ELIZABETH KNIGHTED HIM

DRAKE'S GREATEST TRIUMPH WAS YET TO COME IN 1588, THE SPANISH ARMADA, THE MOST POWERFUL FLOTILLA EVER ASSEMBLED IN ALL HISTORY, SET SAIL TO INVADE ENGLAND.. DRAKE LED THE COUNTER-ATTACK AND DISPLAYING SUPERB SEAMANSHIP, SCATTERED AND BURNT THE SPANISH FLEET.. THIS SWEEPING VICTORY BROKE THE POWER OF SPAIN AND MADE ENGLAND MISTRESS OF THE SEAS FOR THREE CENTURIES! . . .

... BORN-1539? - DIED-1595

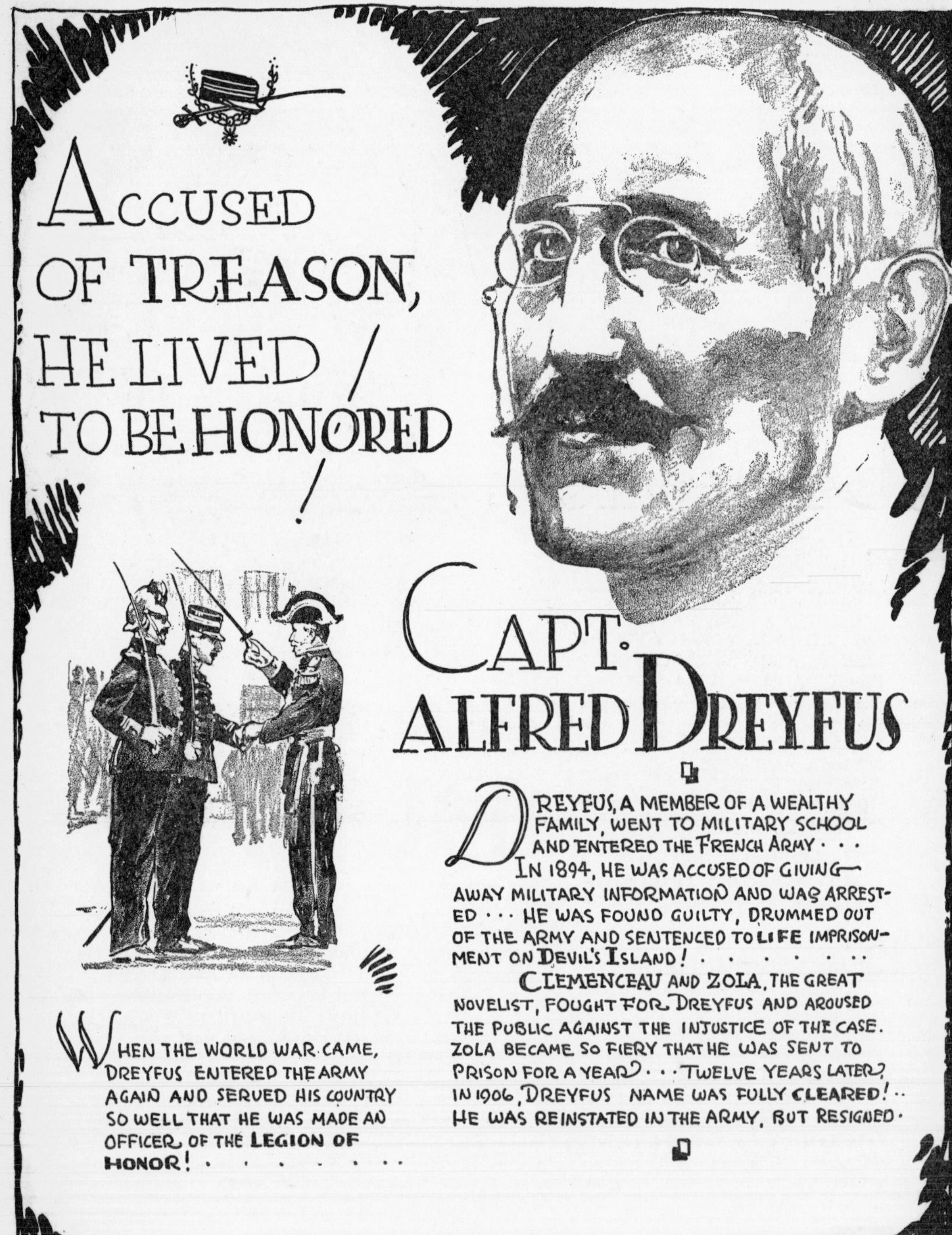
ACCUSED OF TREASON, HE LIVED TO BE HONORED!
CAPT. ALFRED DREYFUS
DREYFUS, A MEMBER OF A WEALTHY FAMILY, WENT TO MILITARY SCHOOL AND ENTERED THE FRENCH ARMY . . . IN 1894, HE WAS ACCUSED OF GIVING AWAY MILITARY INFORMATION AND WAS ARRESTED . . . HE WAS FOUND GUILTY, DRUMMED OUT OF THE ARMY AND SENTENCED TO LIFE IMPRISONMENT ON DEVIL'S ISLAND! . . . .
CLEMENCEAU AND ZOLA, THE GREAT NOVELIST, FOUGHT FOR DREYFUS AND AROUSED THE PUBLIC AGAINST THE INJUSTICE OF THE CASE. ZOLA BECAME SO FIERY THAT HE WAS SENT TO PRISON FOR A YEAR . . . TWELVE YEARS LATER, IN 1906, DREYFUS NAME WAS FULLY CLEARED! . . HE WAS REINSTATED IN THE ARMY, BUT RESIGNED.
WHEN THE WORLD WAR CAME, DREYFUS ENTERED THE ARMY AGAIN AND SERVED HIS COUNTRY SO WELL THAT HE WAS MADE AN OFFICER OF THE LEGION OF HONOR! . . . .

• • BORN-1859 — • •

THE FOURTH MUSKETEER!
ALEXANDRE DUMAS
· PÈRE ·
DUMAS LOST ALL HIS MONEY THROUGH HIS GENEROSITY AND HAD TO WRITE MORE THAN 1200 VOLUMES TO PAY BACK HIS CREDITORS · · · · ·
HIS SON, ALEXANDRE DUMAS, ALSO BECAME A FAMOUS WRITER · · · ·
"THE THREE MUSKETEERS"— "TWENTY YEARS AFTER"— AND "THE COUNT OF MONTE CRISTO"— ARE SOME OF DUMAS' BEST KNOWN STORIES · · · · · · ·
DUMAS' GRANDFATHER WAS A MARQUIS, HIS GRANDMOTHER A NEGRESS AND HIS FATHER, A GREAT GENERAL UNDER NAPOLEON · · · · ·
DUMAS HIMSELF LOVED ADVENTURE · · · HE TOOK A PROMINENT PART IN THE REVOLUTIONS OF 1830 AND 1848 AND WAS FORCED TO FLEE FROM FRANCE TO SWITZERLAND AND RUSSIA · · · · EVEN AT THE AGE OF 58, HE JOINED GARIBALDI ON ONE OF HIS REVOLUTIONARY EXPEDITIONS ·

· · · BORN - 1802 - DIED - 1870 · · ·

THE WIZARD of MENLO PARK
THOMAS ALVA EDISON
EDISON WAS BORN IN A LITTLE OHIO TOWN AND HAD VERY LITTLE SCHOOLING ... AT SEVEN HE WAS A "NEWS BUTCHER" ON A RAILROAD TRAIN ... LATER ON, HE PRINTED A WEEKLY NEWS SHEET, BY HAND, IN A SMOKING CAR WHICH HE FITTED UP AS A CHEMICAL LABORATORY ... ON ONE OCCASION, HIS CHEMICALS SET FIRE TO THE TRAIN, AND THE SEVERE BOX ON THE EAR THAT HE RECEIVED FROM THE CONDUCTOR AS A PARTING SHOT, LED TO A DEAFNESS WHICH HAS PERSISTED ALL HIS LIFE ....
AS A RESULT OF SAVING THE LIFE OF THE STATION MASTER'S LITTLE CHILD, EDISON GOT A NEW START AS A TELEGRAPH OPERATOR, BUT HIS GENIUS FOR TAKING THINGS APART AND IMPROVING THEM SOON LOST HIM THIS JOB.
HOWEVER, THE SAME GENIUS FINALLY BORE FRUIT... IT IS TO EDISON, THAT WE ARE INDEBTED FOR SUCH THINGS AS THE ELECTRIC LIGHT, MOVING PICTURES, THE PHONOGRAPH, THE RECORDS FOR WHICH HE MADE FROM HARD SOAP, THE ELECTRIC TRAIN, AND COUNTLESS OTHER INGENIOUS DEVICES ...

—BORN-1847—

THE VIRGIN QUEEN!
ELIZABETH WAS THE DAUGHTER OF HENRY VIII AND ANNE BOLEYN... HER FATHER BROUGHT HER UP LIKE A BOY, AND THE GOOD EDUCATION, THE COMMAND OF LANGUAGES, AND EVEN THE ABILITY TO SWEAR LIKE A MAN, ON OCCASION, WHICH SHE ACQUIRED, ALL STOOD HER IN GOOD STEAD WHEN AT 25, SHE BECAME QUEEN OF ENGLAND... AMIABLE AND WITTY ON THE SURFACE, HER RED HAIR PROCLAIMED THE TEMPER SHE WAS CAPABLE OF, AND HER IRON WILL BROOKED NO INTERFERENCE WITH THE POLICY WHICH SHE DICTATED FOR ENGLAND....
ELIZABETH
SINCE NO ENGLISH SUITOR WAS OF HER RANK, AND SINCE, BEING THOROUGHLY ENGLISH SHE COULD NOT STAND MOST OF THE ELIGIBLE FOREIGNERS, ELIZABETH NEVER MARRIED........
THE ILLUSTRIOUS COURT WHICH ELIZABETH GATHERED AROUND HER BOASTED SUCH NAMES AS BEN JONSON, SHAKESPEARE, FRANCIS BACON, WALTER RALEIGH, ESSEX AND DRAKE, AND MADE THE REIGN OF "GOOD QUEEN BESS" ONE OF THE MOST GLORIOUS IN ENGLISH HISTORY!

...BORN-1533-DIED-1603...

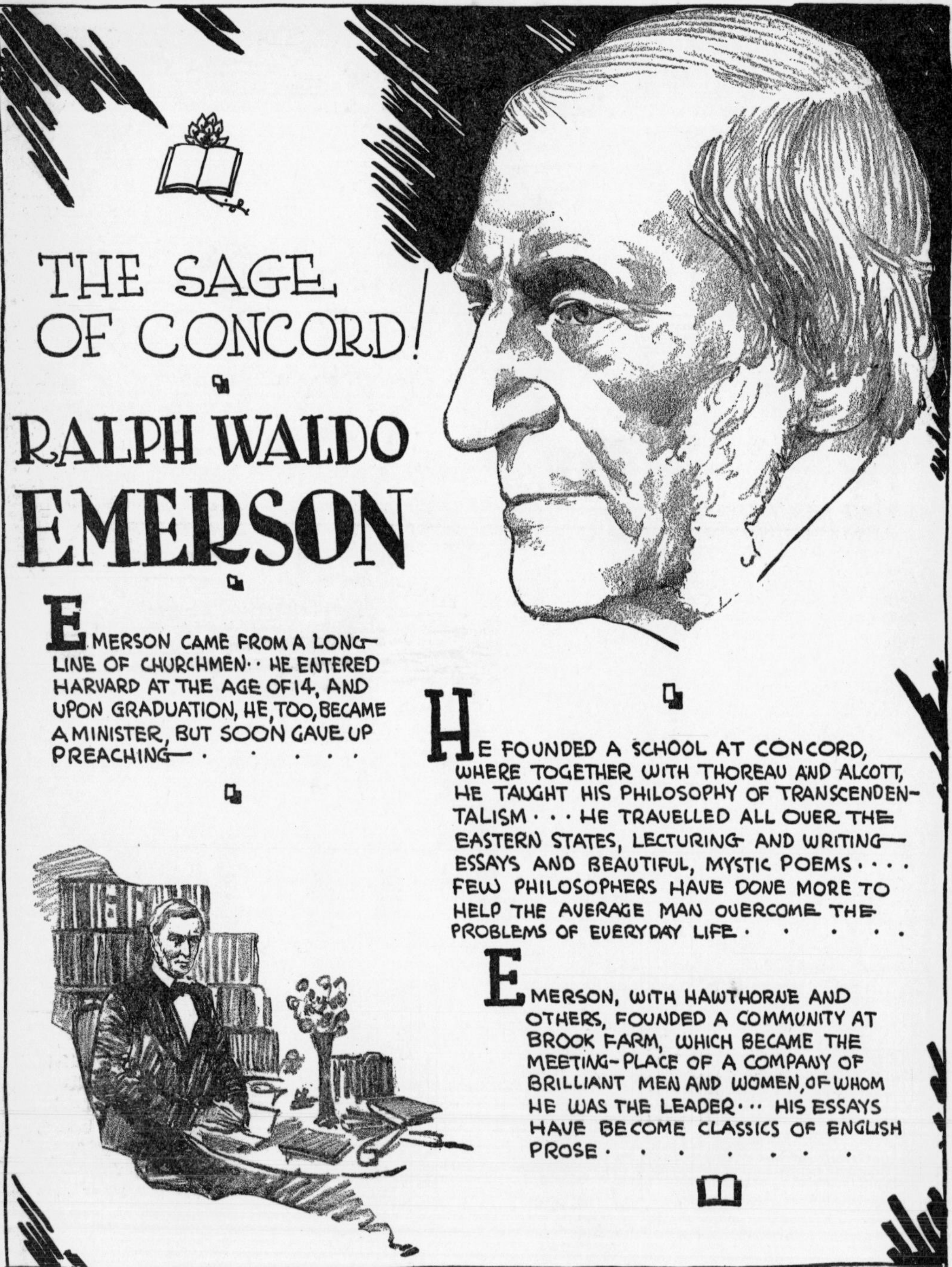
THE SAGE OF CONCORD!
RALPH WALDO EMERSON
EMERSON CAME FROM A LONG LINE OF CHURCHMEN · · HE ENTERED HARVARD AT THE AGE OF 14, AND UPON GRADUATION, HE, TOO, BECAME A MINISTER, BUT SOON GAVE UP PREACHING— · · · ·
HE FOUNDED A SCHOOL AT CONCORD, WHERE TOGETHER WITH THOREAU AND ALCOTT, HE TAUGHT HIS PHILOSOPHY OF TRANSCENDENTALISM · · · HE TRAVELLED ALL OVER THE EASTERN STATES, LECTURING AND WRITING— ESSAYS AND BEAUTIFUL, MYSTIC POEMS · · · · FEW PHILOSOPHERS HAVE DONE MORE TO HELP THE AVERAGE MAN OVERCOME THE PROBLEMS OF EVERYDAY LIFE · · · · ·
EMERSON, WITH HAWTHORNE AND OTHERS, FOUNDED A COMMUNITY AT BROOK FARM, WHICH BECAME THE MEETING-PLACE OF A COMPANY OF BRILLIANT MEN AND WOMEN, OF WHOM HE WAS THE LEADER · · · HIS ESSAYS HAVE BECOME CLASSICS OF ENGLISH PROSE · · · · · · ·

· · · BORN-1803-DIED-1882 · · ·

THE CHILDREN'S LAUREATE
FIELD WAS BORN IN MISSOURI, AND WAS BROUGHT UP IN NEW ENGLAND AFTER GAINING A HAPHAZARD COLLEGE EDUCATION, HE ENTERED UPON A NEWSPAPER CAREER AND WAS EMPLOYED ON ST LOUIS, DENVER, AND CHICAGO PAPERS. ALTHOUGH HE TURNED OUT HUNDREDS OF FANTASTIC SKETCHES AND HUMOROUS VERSES, HIS MOST BEAUTIFUL HANDIWORKS ARE HIS CHILDHOOD POEMS, AND "LITTLE BOY BLUE" AND SEEIN' THINGS AT NIGHT" WILL LONG REMAIN DEAR TO THE HEARTS OF CHILDREN . . . .
EUGENE FIELD
FIELD WAS A KEEN WIT AND AN INCURABLE PRACTICAL JOKER, AND MANY DELIGHTFUL STORIES ARE TOLD OF THE DISCOMFITING SITUATIONS THAT HE CREATED WHILE HE WAS IN THE MIDST OF HIS WORK AND AT THE HEIGHT OF HIS POWERS, FIELD, ONLY 45, PASSED AWAY QUIETLY IN HIS SLEEP, HIS DEATH COMING AS A SHOCK TO THE WORLD THAT HAD LEARNED TO LOVE THIS GENTLE, WHIMSICAL POET . . . .
A SCENE FROM FIELD'S POEM — "WYNKEN, BLYNKEN AND NOD"

· · · BORN - 1850 - DIED - 1895 · · ·

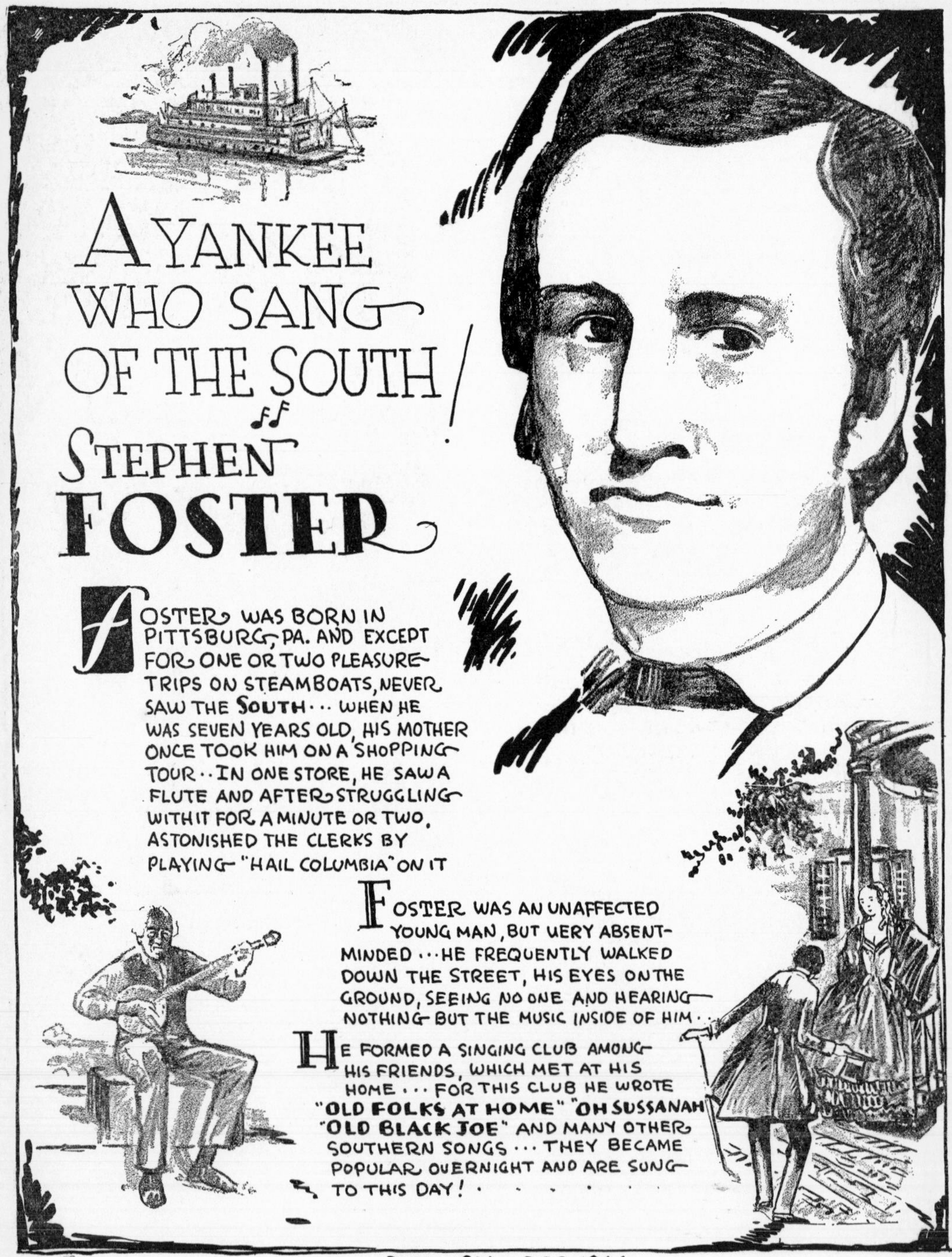
A YANKEE WHO SANG OF THE SOUTH!
STEPHEN FOSTER
FOSTER WAS BORN IN PITTSBURG, PA. AND EXCEPT FOR ONE OR TWO PLEASURE TRIPS ON STEAMBOATS, NEVER SAW THE SOUTH ... WHEN HE WAS SEVEN YEARS OLD, HIS MOTHER ONCE TOOK HIM ON A SHOPPING TOUR .. IN ONE STORE, HE SAW A FLUTE AND AFTER STRUGGLING WITH IT FOR A MINUTE OR TWO, ASTONISHED THE CLERKS BY PLAYING "HAIL COLUMBIA" ON IT
FOSTER WAS AN UNAFFECTED YOUNG MAN, BUT VERY ABSENT-MINDED ... HE FREQUENTLY WALKED DOWN THE STREET, HIS EYES ON THE GROUND, SEEING NO ONE AND HEARING NOTHING BUT THE MUSIC INSIDE OF HIM.
HE FORMED A SINGING CLUB AMONG HIS FRIENDS, WHICH MET AT HIS HOME ... FOR THIS CLUB HE WROTE "OLD FOLKS AT HOME" "OH SUSSANAH" "OLD BLACK JOE" AND MANY OTHER SOUTHERN SONGS ... THEY BECAME POPULAR OVERNIGHT AND ARE SUNG TO THIS DAY! . . . . .

.. BORN-1826 - DIED-1864 ..

"HE CAME TO SCOFF—"

ANATOLE FRANCE

FRANCE WAS A VERY WITTY AND WISE WRITER AND A STUDENT OF HUMAN NATURE . . . IN THE DISGUISE OF FANTASTIC STORIES, HIS BOOKS DESCRIBE WHAT IS COMIC AND EVIL IN PEOPLE, OFTEN IN A SARCASTIC MANNER . . .

ANATOLE FRANCE WAS THE SON OF A BOOK-SELLER . . . MME. DE CAILLAVET, A LOVER OF LITERATURE, URGED HIM TO WRITE AND BUILD UP HIS REPUTATION . . . HE STUDIED GREEK AND LATIN, AND READ FAR AND WIDE UNTIL HE REACHED HIS PLACE AT THE TOP OF FRENCH LITERATURE. WE CAN PICTURE HIM SITTING IN HIS LIBRARY, WHICH RESEMBLED A CHAPEL, WEARING A LONG BRIGHT-COLORED ROBE AND A VELVET SKULL CAP, PORING OVER HIS BOOKS . . .

ANATOLE FRANCE WAS THE PEN NAME OF JACQUES ANATOLE THIBAULT

. . . BORN - 1844 — DIED · 1924 . . .

THE MAN WHO CAPTURED LIGHTNING!

BENJAMIN FRANKLIN

A STATESMAN . . . WHO WAS ALSO FIRE-CHIEF . . . WRITER . . . INVENTOR . . . PRINTER . . AMBASSADOR . . . NEWSPAPER PUBLISHER . . . .

B·FRANKLIN
PRINTER
OOKS BOUGHT & SOLD

BY FLYING A KITE DURING A THUNDERSTORM HE DISCOVERED THAT ELECTRICITY AND LIGHTNING WERE THE SAME . . THIS LED TO HIS INVENTION OF THE LIGHTNING ROD, WHICH PROTECTS BUILDINGS FROM LIGHTNING — .

FRANKLIN HELPED WRITE THE DECLARATION OF INDEPENDENCE . . HE ALSO WROTE A BOOK FULL OF WISE AND WITTY SAYINGS, THE FAMOUS "POOR RICHARD'S ALMANAC" . . TWO HUNDRED YEARS AGO HE PRINTED A MAGAZINE, STILL BEING PUBLISHED TO-DAY — THE SATURDAY EVENING POST . . . .

HE WAS THE YOUNGEST OF FIFTEEN CHILDREN AND LIVED TO THE RIPE OLD AGE OF EIGHTY-FOUR. FRANKLIN WAS ONE OF THE GRANDEST MEN OF ALL TIME, EQUALLY LOVED IN EUROPE AND AMERICA . . . . . .

· · BORN · 1706 - DIED · 1790 · ·

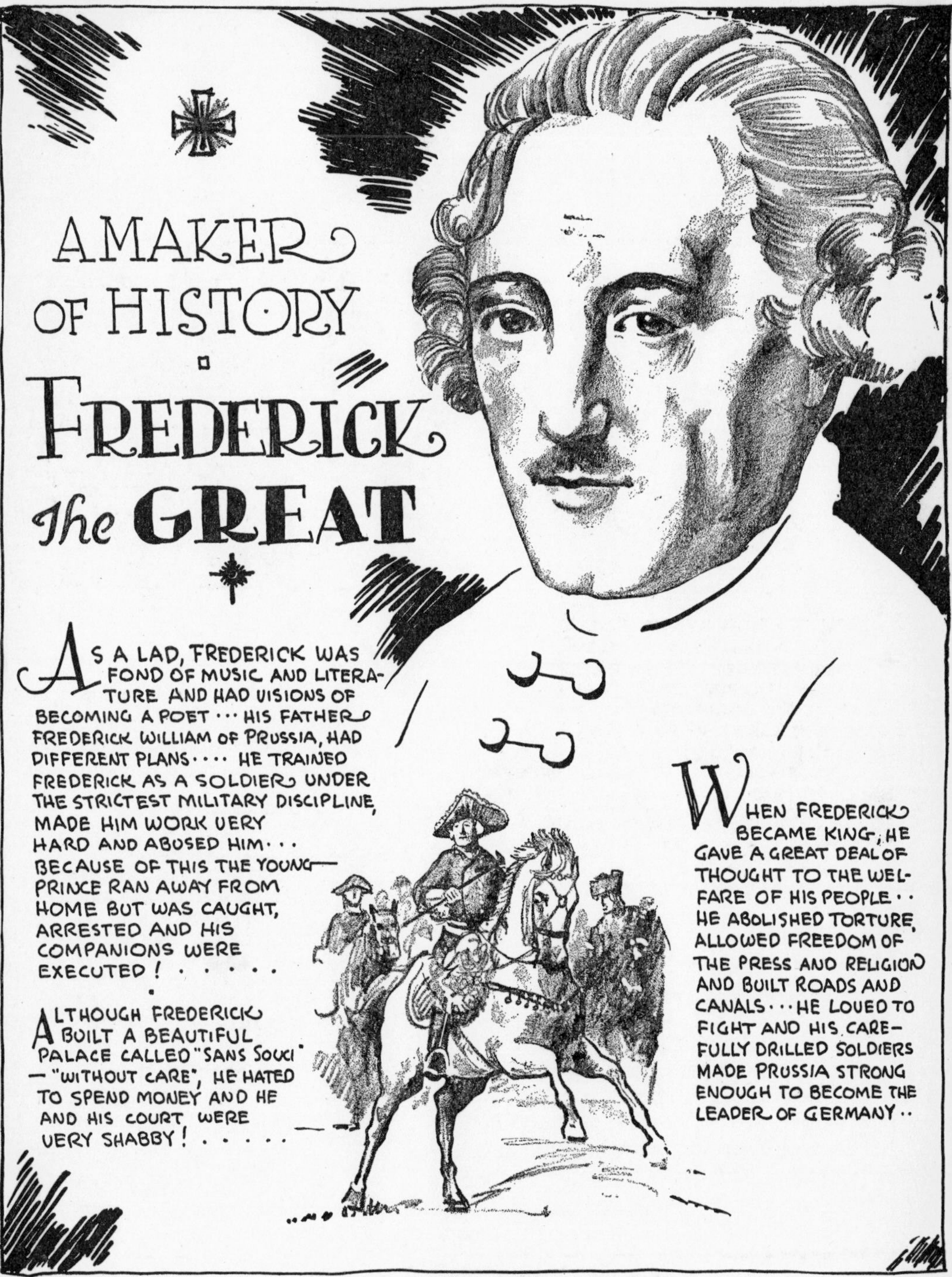
A MAKER OF HISTORY
FREDERICK the GREAT
AS A LAD, FREDERICK WAS FOND OF MUSIC AND LITERATURE AND HAD VISIONS OF BECOMING A POET ··· HIS FATHER FREDERICK WILLIAM OF PRUSSIA, HAD DIFFERENT PLANS···· HE TRAINED FREDERICK AS A SOLDIER UNDER THE STRICTEST MILITARY DISCIPLINE, MADE HIM WORK VERY HARD AND ABUSED HIM··· BECAUSE OF THIS THE YOUNG PRINCE RAN AWAY FROM HOME BUT WAS CAUGHT, ARRESTED AND HIS COMPANIONS WERE EXECUTED! .....
ALTHOUGH FREDERICK BUILT A BEAUTIFUL PALACE CALLED "SANS SOUCI" — "WITHOUT CARE", HE HATED TO SPEND MONEY AND HE AND HIS COURT WERE VERY SHABBY! .....
WHEN FREDERICK BECAME KING, HE GAVE A GREAT DEAL OF THOUGHT TO THE WELFARE OF HIS PEOPLE·· HE ABOLISHED TORTURE, ALLOWED FREEDOM OF THE PRESS AND RELIGION AND BUILT ROADS AND CANALS··· HE LOVED TO FIGHT AND HIS CAREFULLY DRILLED SOLDIERS MADE PRUSSIA STRONG ENOUGH TO BECOME THE LEADER OF GERMANY··

··· BORN-1712-DIED··1786-

THE PAINTER
WHO BUILT
THE FIRST STEAMBOAT
ROBERT
FULTON
BORN IN PENNSYLVANIA, ROBERT FULTON WAS APPRENTICED TO A JEWELER BUT TOOK UP PORTRAIT PAINTING AS A PROFESSION..... HE WENT TO ENGLAND TO STUDY PAINTING. THERE HE MET JAMES WATT, THE INVENTOR OF THE STEAM ENGINE, WHO INFLUENCED HIM TO BECOME AN INVENTOR...
IN PARIS HE BUILT A SUBMARINE, THE "NAUTILUS" AND OFFERED IT TO NAPOLEON, WHO REFUSED IT.. HE THEN BUILT THE FIRST STEAMBOAT, THE "CLERMONT".. PEOPLE SCOFFED AT IT AND CALLED IT "FULTON'S FOLLY"— BUT IT WAS A SUCCESS AND MADE TRIPS FROM NEW YORK TO ALBANY... FULTON ALSO INVENTED DEVICES FOR MAKING ROPE, FOR CUTTING AND POLISHING MARBLE AND FOR IMPROVING CANALS.

··BORN-1765··DIED-1815·

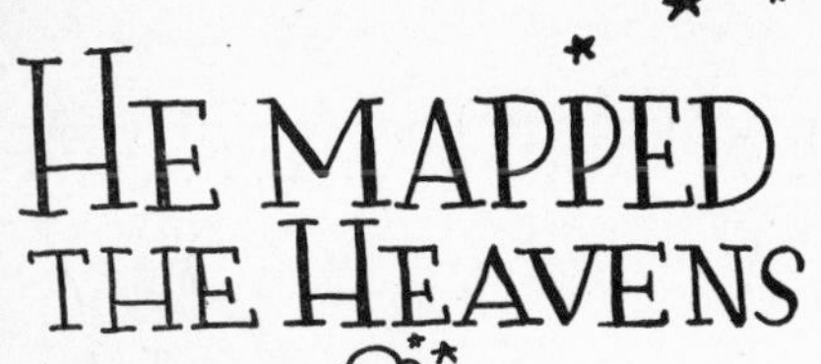

HE MAPPED THE HEAVENS

GALILEO WAS THE SON OF A MATHEMATICIAN AND SPENT HIS YOUTH IN A MONASTERY . . . . ALTHOUGH HE LIKED MUSIC AND PAINTING HE CONSTANTLY EXPERIMENTED WITH SCIENCE . . . HE INVENTED THE THERMOMETER AND USED A SWINGING PENDULUM TO MEASURE THE HUMAN PULSE . . . HE CONDUCTED THE FAMOUS EXPERIMENT OF DROPPING TWO DIFFERENT WEIGHTS FROM THE LEANING TOWER OF PISA TO SHOW THAT THEY FELL WITH THE SAME SPEED . . . .

GALILEO

GALILEO BUILT A POWERFUL TELESCOPE AND WITH IT DISCOVERED MANY NEW STARS AND PLANETS . . . HE BELIEVED, WITH COPERNICUS, THAT THE EARTH MOVED AROUND THE SUN, WHICH WAS CONTRARY TO THE DOCTRINES OF THE CHURCH . . . HE WAS EXAMINED BY THE INQUISITION, FORCED TO TAKE BACK HIS STATEMENTS, AND FORBIDDEN TO PUBLISH HIS LEARNED BOOKS . . . ALTHOUGH HE WAS CAREFULLY WATCHED, HE CONTINUED TO WORK UNTIL HE BECAME BLIND . . . .

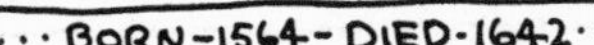

. . . BORN-1564-DIED-1642 . . .

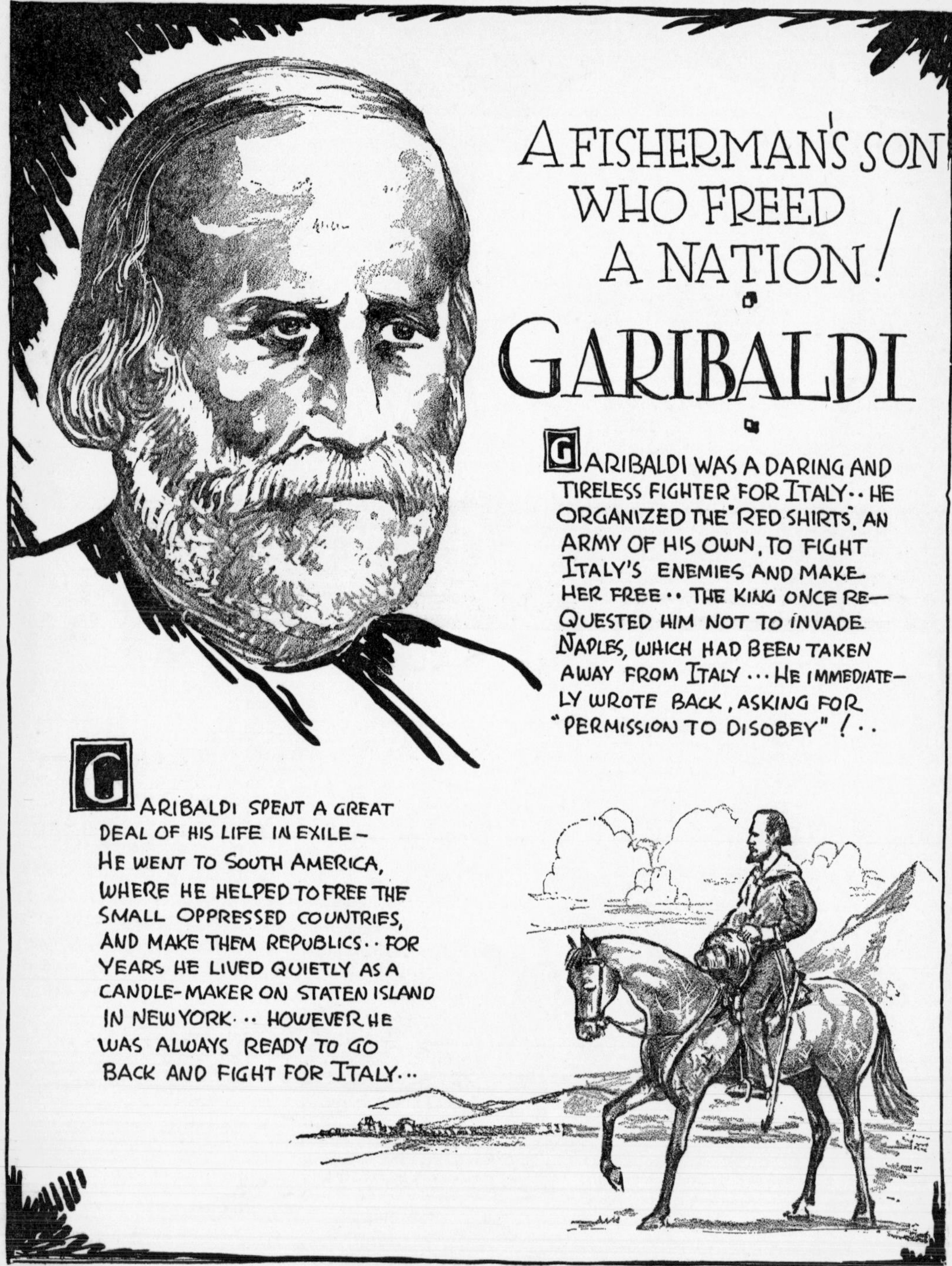
A FISHERMAN'S SON WHO FREED A NATION!
GARIBALDI
GARIBALDI WAS A DARING AND TIRELESS FIGHTER FOR ITALY.. HE ORGANIZED THE "RED SHIRTS", AN ARMY OF HIS OWN, TO FIGHT ITALY'S ENEMIES AND MAKE HER FREE.. THE KING ONCE REQUESTED HIM NOT TO INVADE NAPLES, WHICH HAD BEEN TAKEN AWAY FROM ITALY... HE IMMEDIATELY WROTE BACK, ASKING FOR "PERMISSION TO DISOBEY"!..
GARIBALDI SPENT A GREAT DEAL OF HIS LIFE IN EXILE - HE WENT TO SOUTH AMERICA, WHERE HE HELPED TO FREE THE SMALL OPPRESSED COUNTRIES, AND MAKE THEM REPUBLICS.. FOR YEARS HE LIVED QUIETLY AS A CANDLE-MAKER ON STATEN ISLAND IN NEW YORK.. HOWEVER HE WAS ALWAYS READY TO GO BACK AND FIGHT FOR ITALY...

...BORN·1807— DIED·1882..

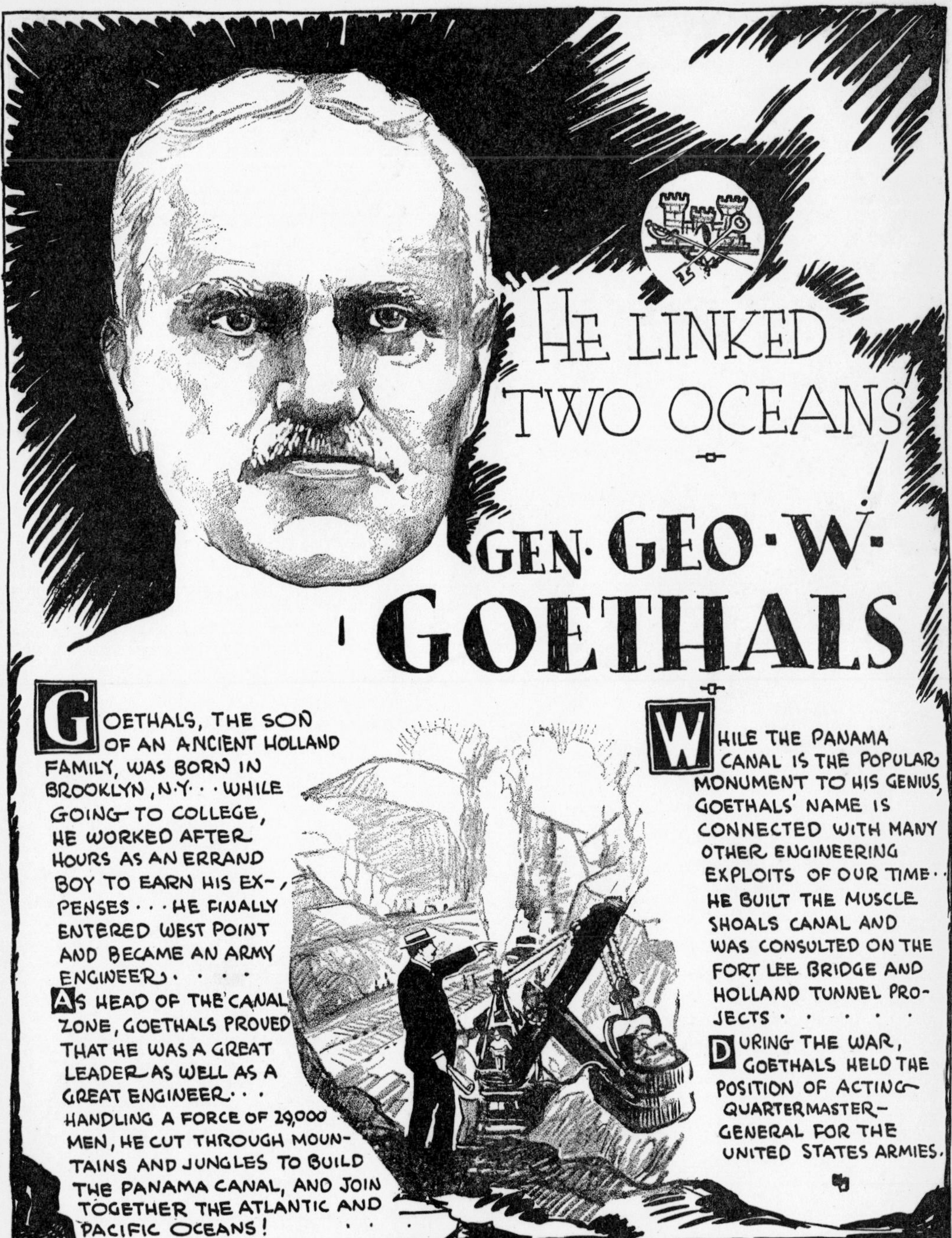
HE LINKED TWO OCEANS!
GEN. GEO. W. GOETHALS
GOETHALS, THE SON OF AN ANCIENT HOLLAND FAMILY, WAS BORN IN BROOKLYN, N.Y. . . WHILE GOING TO COLLEGE, HE WORKED AFTER HOURS AS AN ERRAND BOY TO EARN HIS EXPENSES . . . HE FINALLY ENTERED WEST POINT AND BECAME AN ARMY ENGINEER . . . .
AS HEAD OF THE CANAL ZONE, GOETHALS PROVED THAT HE WAS A GREAT LEADER AS WELL AS A GREAT ENGINEER . . . HANDLING A FORCE OF 29,000 MEN, HE CUT THROUGH MOUNTAINS AND JUNGLES TO BUILD THE PANAMA CANAL, AND JOIN TOGETHER THE ATLANTIC AND PACIFIC OCEANS! . . .
WHILE THE PANAMA CANAL IS THE POPULAR MONUMENT TO HIS GENIUS, GOETHALS' NAME IS CONNECTED WITH MANY OTHER ENGINEERING EXPLOITS OF OUR TIME . . HE BUILT THE MUSCLE SHOALS CANAL AND WAS CONSULTED ON THE FORT LEE BRIDGE AND HOLLAND TUNNEL PROJECTS . . . . .
DURING THE WAR, GOETHALS HELD THE POSITION OF ACTING QUARTERMASTER-GENERAL FOR THE UNITED STATES ARMIES.

. . . BORN-1858-DIED-1928 . .

THE MANY-SIDED MASTER!
ALTHOUGH HE WAS A LAWYER, SCIENTIST, PHILOSOPHER, POLITICAL WRITER, ART CRITIC, AND STATESMAN, IT IS AS GERMANY'S GREATEST POET THAT GOETHE IS ACCLAIMED TO-DAY... THE CROWNING GLORY OF HIS LIFE IS THE DRAMATIC POEM, "FAUST", BUILT AROUND AN ANCIENT LEGEND... IT TOOK HIM YEARS TO WRITE THIS TRAGIC TALE, WHICH HAS STIRRED THE HEARTS OF GENERATIONS IN SONG AND STORY . . . .
JOHANN WOLFGANG VON GOETHE
GOETHE LIVED HIS LIFE IN AN ATMOSPHERE OF CULTURE... THE POET SCHILLER WAS HIS CLOSE FRIEND, AS WAS BEETHOVEN, UNTIL HE AND GOETHE BOTH FELL IN LOVE WITH THE SAME WOMAN . . .
GOETHE TRAVELLED A GREAT DEAL IN ITALY BUT FINALLY MADE HIS HOME IN WEIMAR, IN SAXONY... THIS CITY HAS BECOME A SHRINE TO WHICH LOVERS OF LITERATURE COME FROM ALL OVER THE WORLD TO PAY REVERENCE TO HIS MEMORY . . . . .

....BORN-1749-DIED-1832....

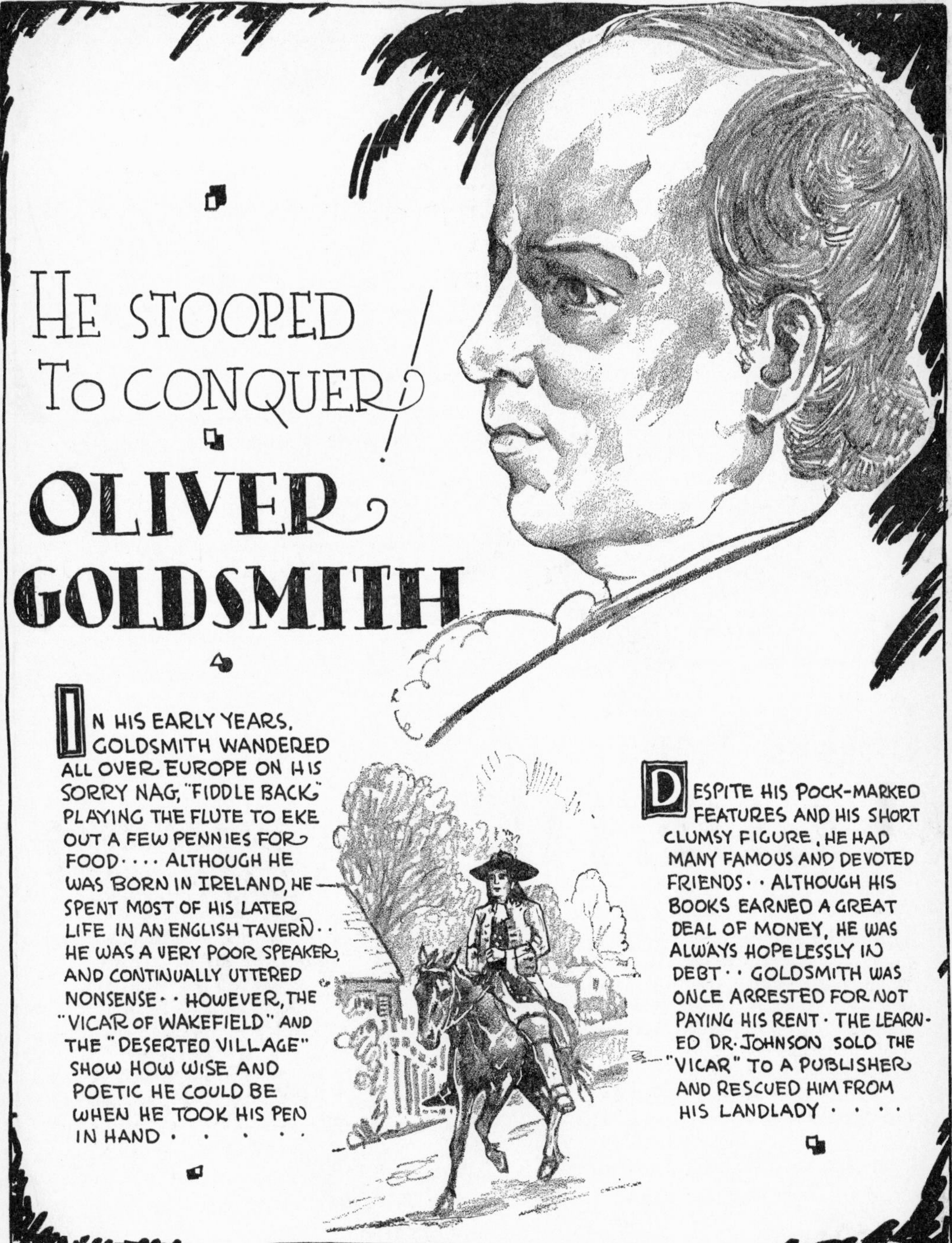
HE STOOPED TO CONQUER!
OLIVER GOLDSMITH
IN HIS EARLY YEARS, GOLDSMITH WANDERED ALL OVER EUROPE ON HIS SORRY NAG, "FIDDLE BACK," PLAYING THE FLUTE TO EKE OUT A FEW PENNIES FOR FOOD.... ALTHOUGH HE WAS BORN IN IRELAND, HE SPENT MOST OF HIS LATER LIFE IN AN ENGLISH TAVERN.. HE WAS A VERY POOR SPEAKER, AND CONTINUALLY UTTERED NONSENSE.. HOWEVER, THE "VICAR OF WAKEFIELD" AND THE "DESERTED VILLAGE" SHOW HOW WISE AND POETIC HE COULD BE WHEN HE TOOK HIS PEN IN HAND .....
DESPITE HIS POCK-MARKED FEATURES AND HIS SHORT CLUMSY FIGURE, HE HAD MANY FAMOUS AND DEVOTED FRIENDS.. ALTHOUGH HIS BOOKS EARNED A GREAT DEAL OF MONEY, HE WAS ALWAYS HOPELESSLY IN DEBT.. GOLDSMITH WAS ONCE ARRESTED FOR NOT PAYING HIS RENT. THE LEARNED DR. JOHNSON SOLD THE "VICAR" TO A PUBLISHER AND RESCUED HIM FROM HIS LANDLADY ....

·· BORN·1728–DIED·1774 ··

FROM PLOWBOY TO PRESIDENT!

ULYSSES S. GRANT

AT 39—A TANNER'S CLERK—A FAILURE!
AT 40—A MAJOR-GENERAL!
AT 47—PRESIDENT OF THE U.S.!

GRANT WAS A PLOWBOY ON HIS FATHER'S FARM... AGAINST HIS WILL, HE WAS SENT TO WEST POINT.... IN 1854, HIS DRINKING HABITS FORCED HIM TO RESIGN FROM THE ARMY... HE TRIED FARMING AND REAL ESTATE, FAILED AT BOTH AND WENT BACK TO HIS FATHER'S TANNING-SHOP... WHEN THE CIVIL WAR BROKE OUT IN 1861, HE COULD NOT EVEN GET BACK INTO THE ARMY.. FINALLY, HE RECEIVED A COMMISSION AND HIS SENSATIONAL VICTORIES RAPIDLY PROMOTED HIM TO THE POSITION OF COMMANDER-IN-CHIEF OF THE ARMIES..

GRANT WAS A SPLENDID HORSEMAN—THE BEST AT WEST POINT.. DURING THE MEXICAN WAR, IN 1848, HE FOUGHT SIDE BY SIDE WITH ROBERT E. LEE, WHO LATER OPPOSED HIM AS COMMANDER OF THE CONFEDERATE FORCES...

AFTER THE TERRIBLE BATTLE OF THE WILDERNESS, HE SAID—"I PROPOSE TO FIGHT IT OUT ON THIS LINE IF IT TAKES ALL SUMMER"!

..BORN·1822—DIED·1885..

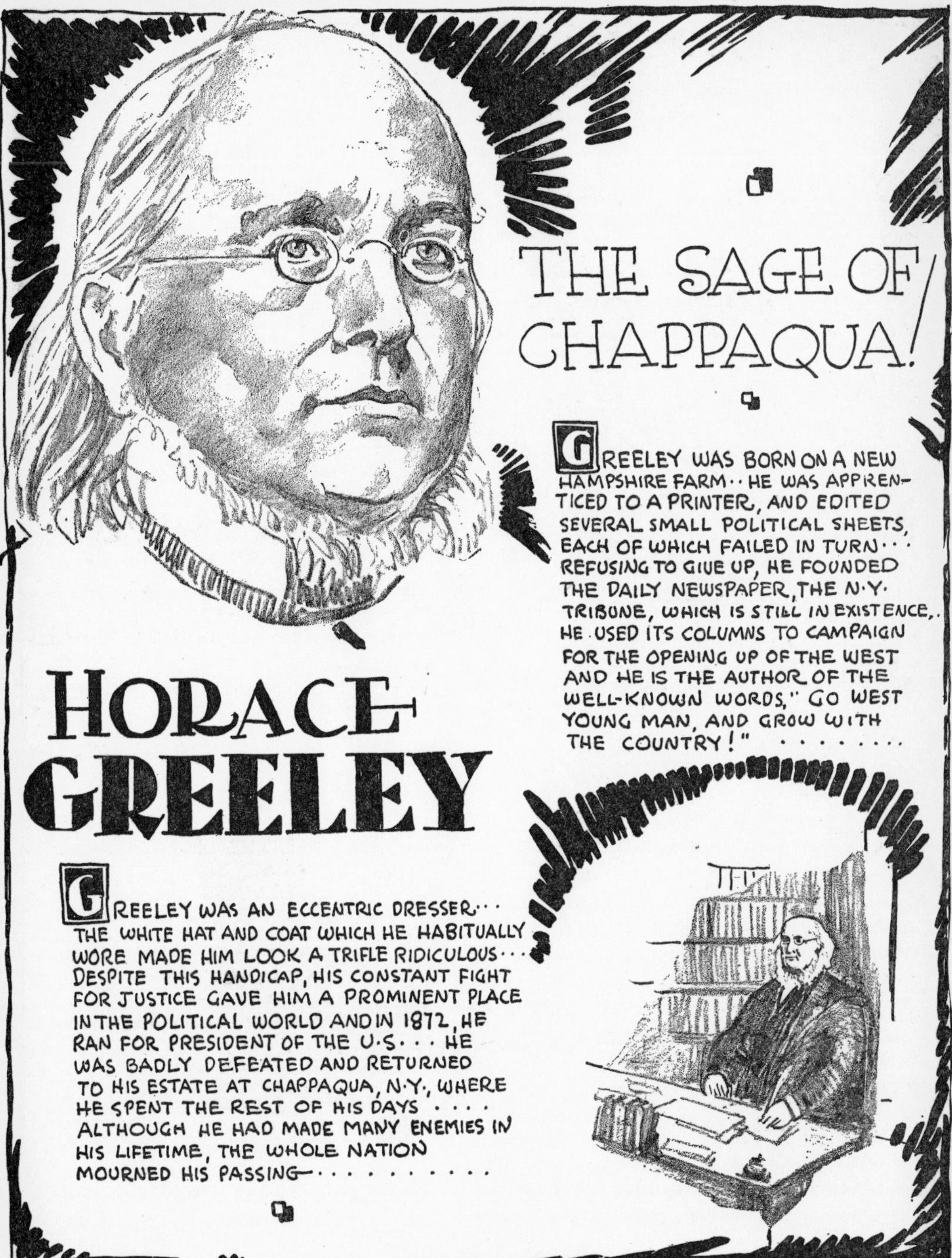
THE SAGE OF CHAPPAQUA!
GREELEY WAS BORN ON A NEW HAMPSHIRE FARM·· HE WAS APPRENTICED TO A PRINTER, AND EDITED SEVERAL SMALL POLITICAL SHEETS, EACH OF WHICH FAILED IN TURN··· REFUSING TO GIVE UP, HE FOUNDED THE DAILY NEWSPAPER, THE N·Y· TRIBUNE, WHICH IS STILL IN EXISTENCE. HE USED ITS COLUMNS TO CAMPAIGN FOR THE OPENING UP OF THE WEST AND HE IS THE AUTHOR OF THE WELL-KNOWN WORDS, "GO WEST YOUNG MAN, AND GROW WITH THE COUNTRY!" ....
HORACE GREELEY
GREELEY WAS AN ECCENTRIC DRESSER··· THE WHITE HAT AND COAT WHICH HE HABITUALLY WORE MADE HIM LOOK A TRIFLE RIDICULOUS··· DESPITE THIS HANDICAP, HIS CONSTANT FIGHT FOR JUSTICE GAVE HIM A PROMINENT PLACE IN THE POLITICAL WORLD AND IN 1872, HE RAN FOR PRESIDENT OF THE U·S··· HE WAS BADLY DEFEATED AND RETURNED TO HIS ESTATE AT CHAPPAQUA, N·Y·, WHERE HE SPENT THE REST OF HIS DAYS .... ALTHOUGH HE HAD MADE MANY ENEMIES IN HIS LIFETIME, THE WHOLE NATION MOURNED HIS PASSING ....

···BORN-1811-DIED-1872···

THE
SCHOOL-TEACHER
WHO DIED FOR
HIS COUNTRY!
NATHAN
HALE
NATHAN HALE, A CONNECTICUT BOY, WAS GRADUATED FROM YALE UNIVERSITY AND MADE TEACHING HIS VOCATION··· WHEN THE COLONIES REVOLTED AGAINST ENGLAND, HE JOINED THE ARMY AND SERVED BRAVELY DURING THE FIGHTING AROUND BOSTON ··· HE TOOK PART IN MANY DARING EXPLOITS, AMONG THEM, THE CAPTURE OF A BRITISH PROVISION SLOOP ····
WHEN HE WAS ONLY TWENTY YEARS OLD, HALE EMBARKED ON A DANGEROUS MISSION,··· DISGUISED AS A DUTCH SCHOOLMASTER, HE PENETRATED THE ENEMY LINES IN NEW YORK TO DISCOVER THEIR PLANS··· HE WAS CAUGHT, SENTENCED AS A SPY, AND HANGED THE NEXT DAY ··· A MARTYR TO THE CAUSE OF LIBERTY, HIS LAST WORDS WERE -- "MY ONLY REGRET IS THAT I HAVE BUT ONE LIFE TO LOSE FOR MY COUNTRY!"
··BORN-1756-DIED-1776···

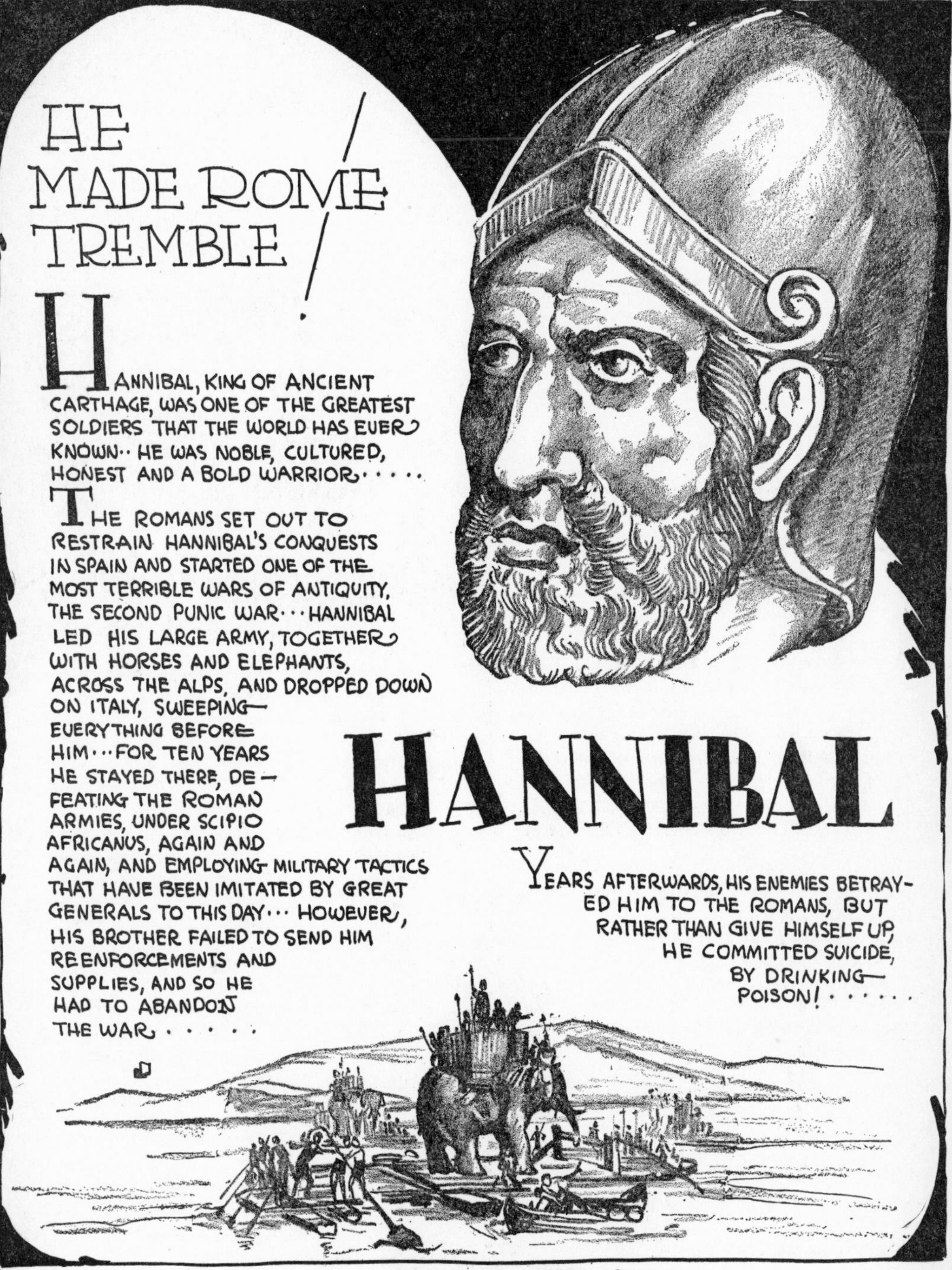
HE MADE ROME TREMBLE!
HANNIBAL, KING OF ANCIENT CARTHAGE, WAS ONE OF THE GREATEST SOLDIERS THAT THE WORLD HAS EVER KNOWN.. HE WAS NOBLE, CULTURED, HONEST AND A BOLD WARRIOR.....
THE ROMANS SET OUT TO RESTRAIN HANNIBAL'S CONQUESTS IN SPAIN AND STARTED ONE OF THE MOST TERRIBLE WARS OF ANTIQUITY, THE SECOND PUNIC WAR... HANNIBAL LED HIS LARGE ARMY, TOGETHER WITH HORSES AND ELEPHANTS, ACROSS THE ALPS, AND DROPPED DOWN ON ITALY, SWEEPING EVERYTHING BEFORE HIM... FOR TEN YEARS HE STAYED THERE, DE-FEATING THE ROMAN ARMIES, UNDER SCIPIO AFRICANUS, AGAIN AND AGAIN, AND EMPLOYING MILITARY TACTICS THAT HAVE BEEN IMITATED BY GREAT GENERALS TO THIS DAY... HOWEVER, HIS BROTHER FAILED TO SEND HIM REENFORCEMENTS AND SUPPLIES, AND SO HE HAD TO ABANDON THE WAR.....
HANNIBAL
YEARS AFTERWARDS, HIS ENEMIES BETRAY-ED HIM TO THE ROMANS, BUT RATHER THAN GIVE HIMSELF UP, HE COMMITTED SUICIDE, BY DRINKING POISON!.....

...BORN-247 B.C.-DIED-183 B.C....

THE MASTER STORY TELLER
NATHANIEL HAWTHORNE
HAWTHORNE WOVE ROMANCES AROUND THE EARLY PURITAN TIMES·· "THE SCARLET LETTER", "TWICE TOLD TALES" AND "THE HOUSE OF THE SEVEN GABLES" STAND AS MONUMENTS TO HIS GENIUS · · · ·
HAWTHORNE CAME FROM A NEW-ENGLAND FAMILY OF SEA CAPTAINS··· AS A BOY, HE LIKED GAMES, BUT WAS CRIPPLED WHILE PLAYING BALL AND SO TURNED TO READING··· AFTER GOING TO COLLEGE, HE LOCKED HIMSELF UP IN HIS HOUSE AND WROTE, DAY AFTER DAY, YEAR AFTER YEAR, TEARING UP HIS STORIES AND REWRITING THEM UNTIL THEY WERE PERFECT! · · · ·
ALTHOUGH HE WAS LATER U·S· CONSUL TO LIVERPOOL, IN HIS EARLIER YEARS, HAWTHORNE HAD TO WORK IN THE CUSTOM HOUSE TO EARN A LIVING — A JOB WHICH HE HATED · · · · ·
"THE HOUSE OF SEVEN GABLES" WHERE HAWTHORNE LIVED · · · · · ·

···BORN-1804-DIED-1864···

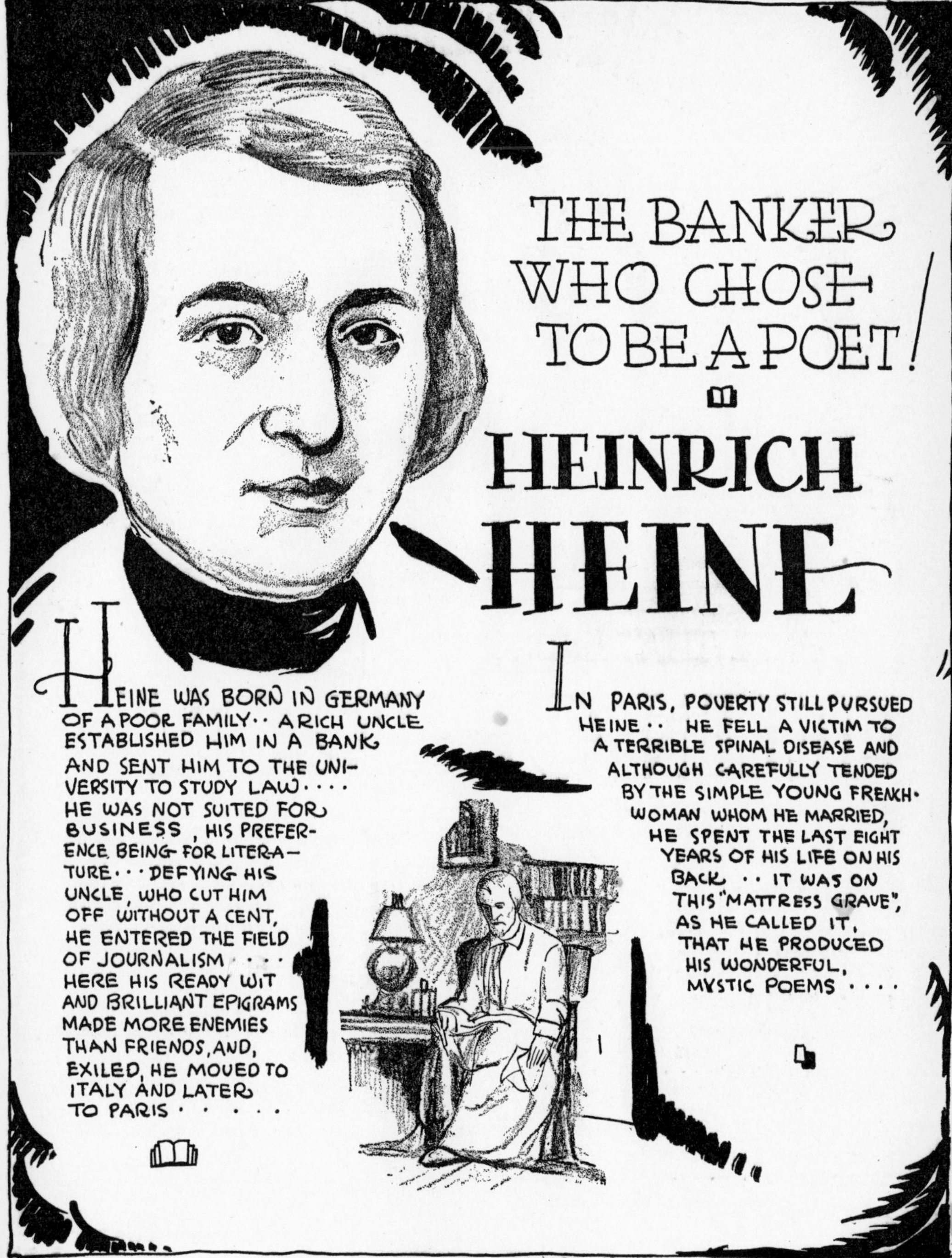
THE BANKER WHO CHOSE TO BE A POET!
HEINRICH HEINE
HEINE WAS BORN IN GERMANY OF A POOR FAMILY.. A RICH UNCLE ESTABLISHED HIM IN A BANK AND SENT HIM TO THE UNIVERSITY TO STUDY LAW.... HE WAS NOT SUITED FOR BUSINESS, HIS PREFERENCE BEING FOR LITERATURE... DEFYING HIS UNCLE, WHO CUT HIM OFF WITHOUT A CENT, HE ENTERED THE FIELD OF JOURNALISM.... HERE HIS READY WIT AND BRILLIANT EPIGRAMS MADE MORE ENEMIES THAN FRIENDS, AND, EXILED, HE MOVED TO ITALY AND LATER TO PARIS.....
IN PARIS, POVERTY STILL PURSUED HEINE.. HE FELL A VICTIM TO A TERRIBLE SPINAL DISEASE AND ALTHOUGH CAREFULLY TENDED BY THE SIMPLE YOUNG FRENCHWOMAN WHOM HE MARRIED, HE SPENT THE LAST EIGHT YEARS OF HIS LIFE ON HIS BACK.. IT WAS ON THIS "MATTRESS GRAVE", AS HE CALLED IT, THAT HE PRODUCED HIS WONDERFUL, MYSTIC POEMS....

.. BORN-1797-DIED-1856 ..

"THE FACE THAT LAUNCHED A THOUSAND SHIPS!"...

HELEN OF TROY...

HELEN WAS THE MOST BEAUTIFUL WOMAN IN ALL GREECE AND THE WIFE OF MENELAUS, AN ANCIENT SPARTAN PRINCE... WHILE HER HUSBAND WAS AWAY, PARIS, THE SON OF PRIAM, KING OF TROY, INDUCED HER TO FLEE WITH HIM TO TROY.... THE SPARTANS SET OUT TO RESCUE HELEN AND THE RESULT WAS A WAR WHICH LASTED TEN YEARS...

THE SPARTANS WERE FINALLY ENABLED TO ENTER TROY AND DESTROY IT, THROUGH THE STRATAGEM OF LEAVING A GIANT WOODEN HORSE FILLED WITH SOLDIERS ON THE BEACH, AND PRETENDING TO SAIL AWAY.. MENELAUS HAD RESOLVED TO KILL HELEN BUT HER BEAUTY STAYED HIS SWORD.. HE TOOK HER BACK TO SPARTA AND THEY "LIVED HAPPILY EVER AFTER".....

HOMER'S EPIC POEMS, "THE ILIAD" AND "THE ODYSSEY", TELL THE STORY OF THE TROJAN WAR AND OF THE TEN YEAR VOYAGE HOME AFTER THE FALL OF TROY...

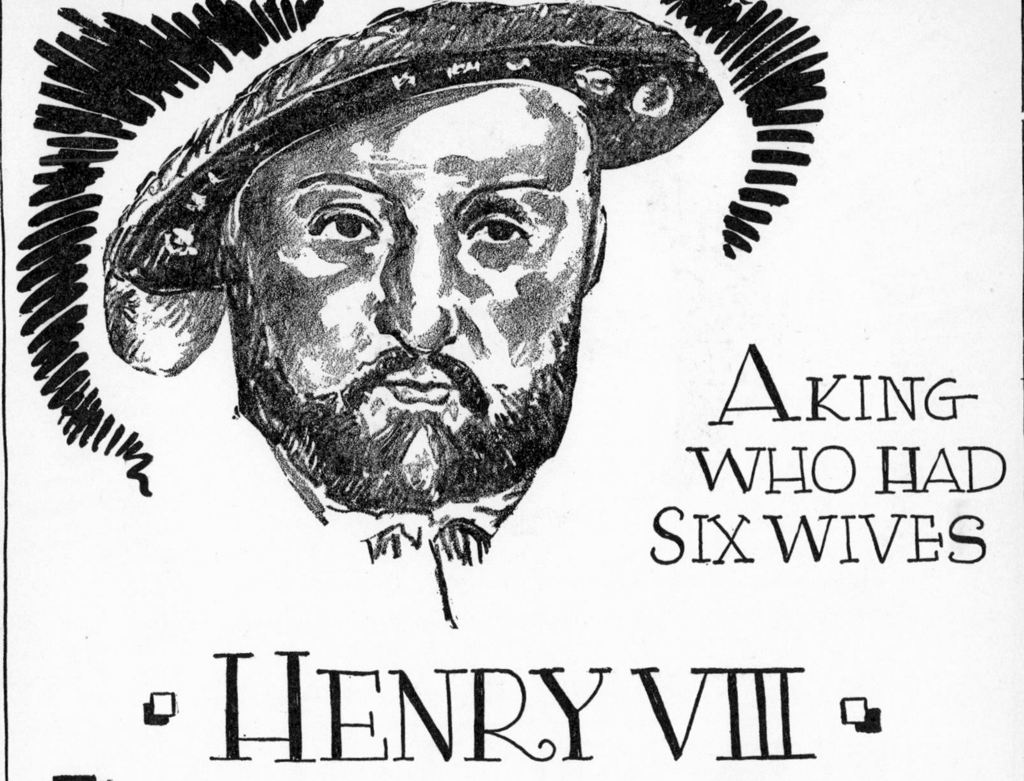

A KING WHO HAD SIX WIVES

HENRY VIII

HENRY WAS INTERESTED IN LEARNING AND ART... HE WORKED FOR THE GOOD OF ENGLAND, BUT HE REALIZED THAT IT WAS ALSO FOR HIS OWN GOOD.. HE MADE THE ENGLISH NAVY GREAT.. BUT FOR HIS WORK, DEFEAT OF THE SPANISH ARMADA BY THE ENGLISH YEARS LATER WOULD HAVE BEEN IMPOSSIBLE.. KING FRANCIS I, OF FRANCE AND HENRY ONCE MET ON A FIELD COVERED WITH 3000 TENTS MADE OF GOLD CLOTH... THIS PLACE BECAME KNOWN AS THE, "FIELD OF THE CLOTH OF GOLD" . . . .

KING HENRY HAD SIX WIVES, AMONG THEM THE FAMOUS ANN BOLEYN.. THREE OF HIS WIVES WERE EXECUTED; THE OTHERS TWO HE DIVORCED... THESE DIVORCES WERE CONTRARY TO THE POPE'S DOCTRINE.. HENRY DEFIED THE CHURCH AND MADE THE PROTESTANT FAITH THE OFFICIAL RELIGION OF ENGLAND.

BORN-1491 — DIED 1547

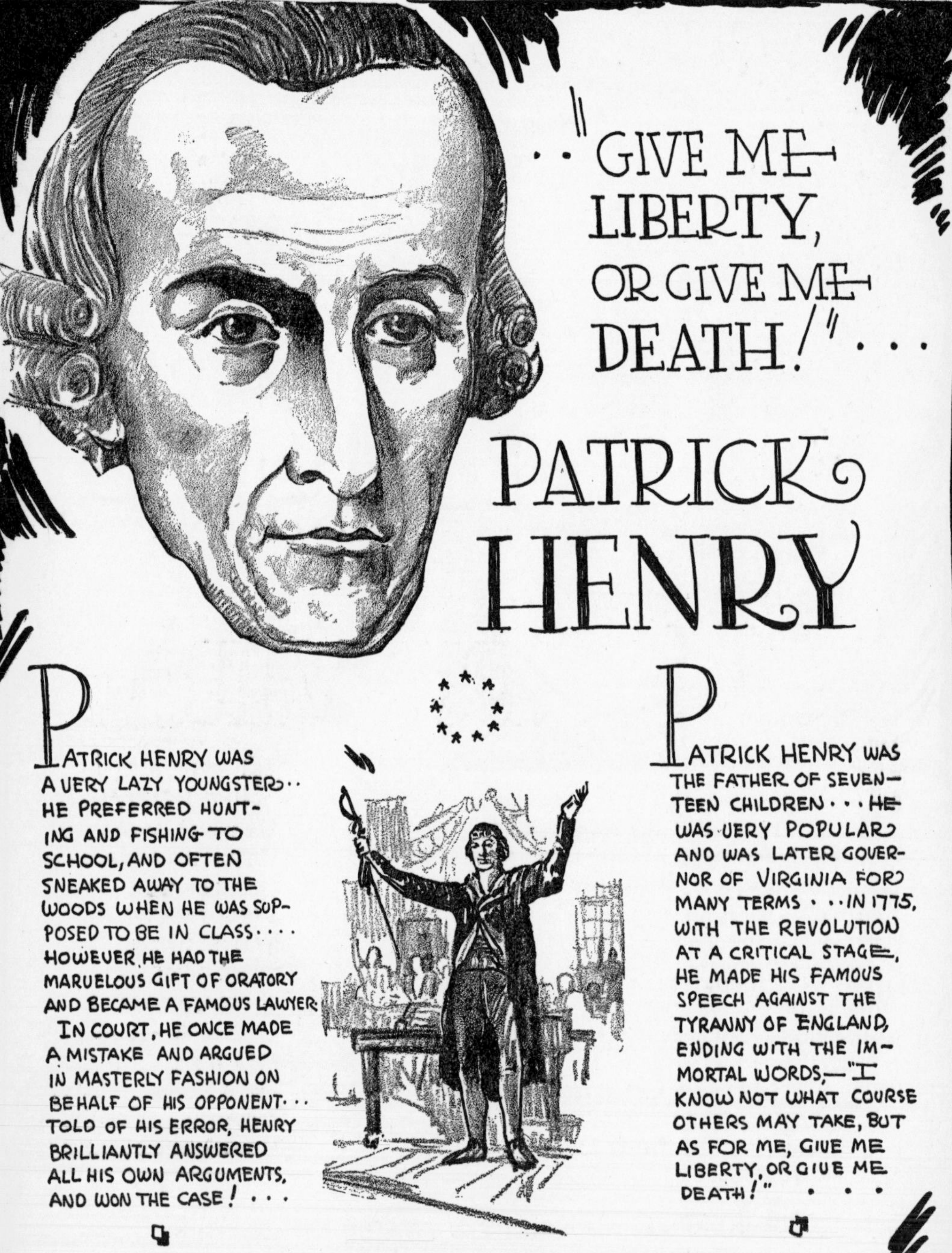

.. "GIVE ME LIBERTY, OR GIVE ME DEATH!" ...
PATRICK HENRY
PATRICK HENRY WAS A VERY LAZY YOUNGSTER.. HE PREFERRED HUNTING AND FISHING TO SCHOOL, AND OFTEN SNEAKED AWAY TO THE WOODS WHEN HE WAS SUPPOSED TO BE IN CLASS.... HOWEVER HE HAD THE MARVELOUS GIFT OF ORATORY AND BECAME A FAMOUS LAWYER.
IN COURT, HE ONCE MADE A MISTAKE AND ARGUED IN MASTERLY FASHION ON BEHALF OF HIS OPPONENT... TOLD OF HIS ERROR, HENRY BRILLIANTLY ANSWERED ALL HIS OWN ARGUMENTS, AND WON THE CASE! ...
PATRICK HENRY WAS THE FATHER OF SEVENTEEN CHILDREN... HE WAS VERY POPULAR AND WAS LATER GOVERNOR OF VIRGINIA FOR MANY TERMS ... IN 1775, WITH THE REVOLUTION AT A CRITICAL STAGE, HE MADE HIS FAMOUS SPEECH AGAINST THE TYRANNY OF ENGLAND, ENDING WITH THE IMMORTAL WORDS,—"I KNOW NOT WHAT COURSE OTHERS MAY TAKE, BUT AS FOR ME, GIVE ME LIBERTY, OR GIVE ME DEATH!" ...

..BORN-1739—DIED-1799..

KING OF MEN . . . HATER OF TYRANTS AND LOVER OF CHILDREN!

VICTOR HUGO.

EXILED! . . . THIS GREAT DEFENDER OF JUSTICE DEVOTED ALL HIS TIME TO BATTLING FOR HUMAN LIFE. **HUGO** ONCE MADE A THRILLING SPEECH AT A TRIAL DEFENDING HIS OWN SON. BECAUSE OF HIS WRITINGS AND SPEECHES AGAINST THE UNJUST GOVERNMENT **HUGO** WAS EXPELLED FROM **FRANCE**. FOR TWENTY YEARS HE LIVED IN EXILE AWAY FROM HIS BELOVED LAND . . . . .

CHILDREN LOVED **HUGO**, BECAUSE HE LOVED THEM. HE GAVE PARTIES FOR THEM AND FED THEM WHEN THEY WERE HUNGRY.

HUGO WAS THE GREATEST ORATOR AND WRITER IN FRANCE. HIS HOUSE IN PARIS IS NOW A MUSEUM FILLED WITH RELICS AND PICTURES OF HIS LIFE . . .

· · BORN · 1802 · DIED · 1885 · ·

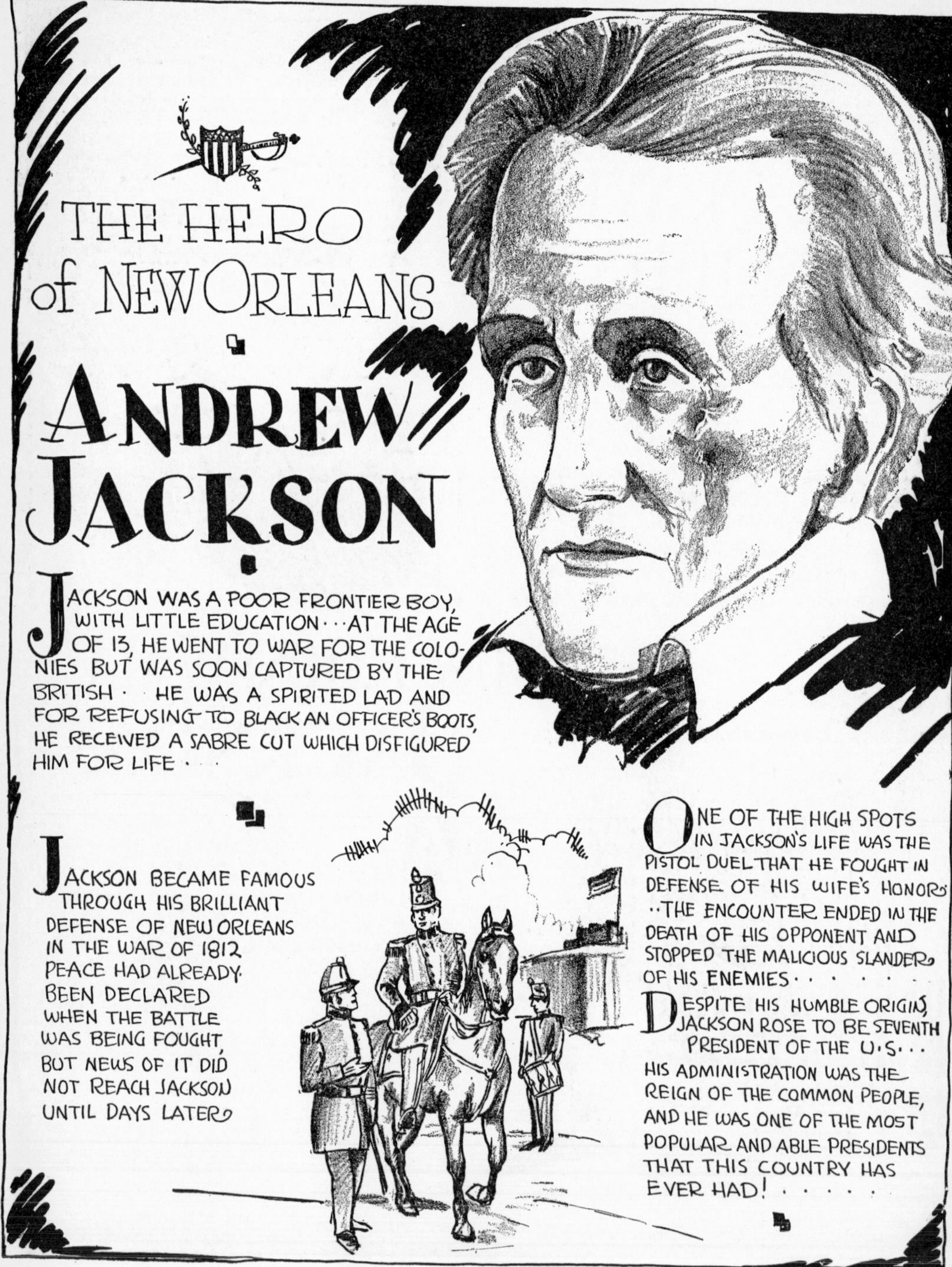
THE HERO of NEW ORLEANS
ANDREW JACKSON
JACKSON WAS A POOR FRONTIER BOY, WITH LITTLE EDUCATION... AT THE AGE OF 13, HE WENT TO WAR FOR THE COLONIES BUT WAS SOON CAPTURED BY THE BRITISH. HE WAS A SPIRITED LAD AND FOR REFUSING TO BLACK AN OFFICER'S BOOTS, HE RECEIVED A SABRE CUT WHICH DISFIGURED HIM FOR LIFE...
JACKSON BECAME FAMOUS THROUGH HIS BRILLIANT DEFENSE OF NEW ORLEANS IN THE WAR OF 1812 PEACE HAD ALREADY BEEN DECLARED WHEN THE BATTLE WAS BEING FOUGHT, BUT NEWS OF IT DID NOT REACH JACKSON UNTIL DAYS LATER
ONE OF THE HIGH SPOTS IN JACKSON'S LIFE WAS THE PISTOL DUEL THAT HE FOUGHT IN DEFENSE OF HIS WIFE'S HONOR ..THE ENCOUNTER ENDED IN THE DEATH OF HIS OPPONENT AND STOPPED THE MALICIOUS SLANDER OF HIS ENEMIES......
DESPITE HIS HUMBLE ORIGIN, JACKSON ROSE TO BE SEVENTH PRESIDENT OF THE U.S... HIS ADMINISTRATION WAS THE REIGN OF THE COMMON PEOPLE, AND HE WAS ONE OF THE MOST POPULAR AND ABLE PRESIDENTS THAT THIS COUNTRY HAS EVER HAD!.....

..BORN-1767- DIED-1845.

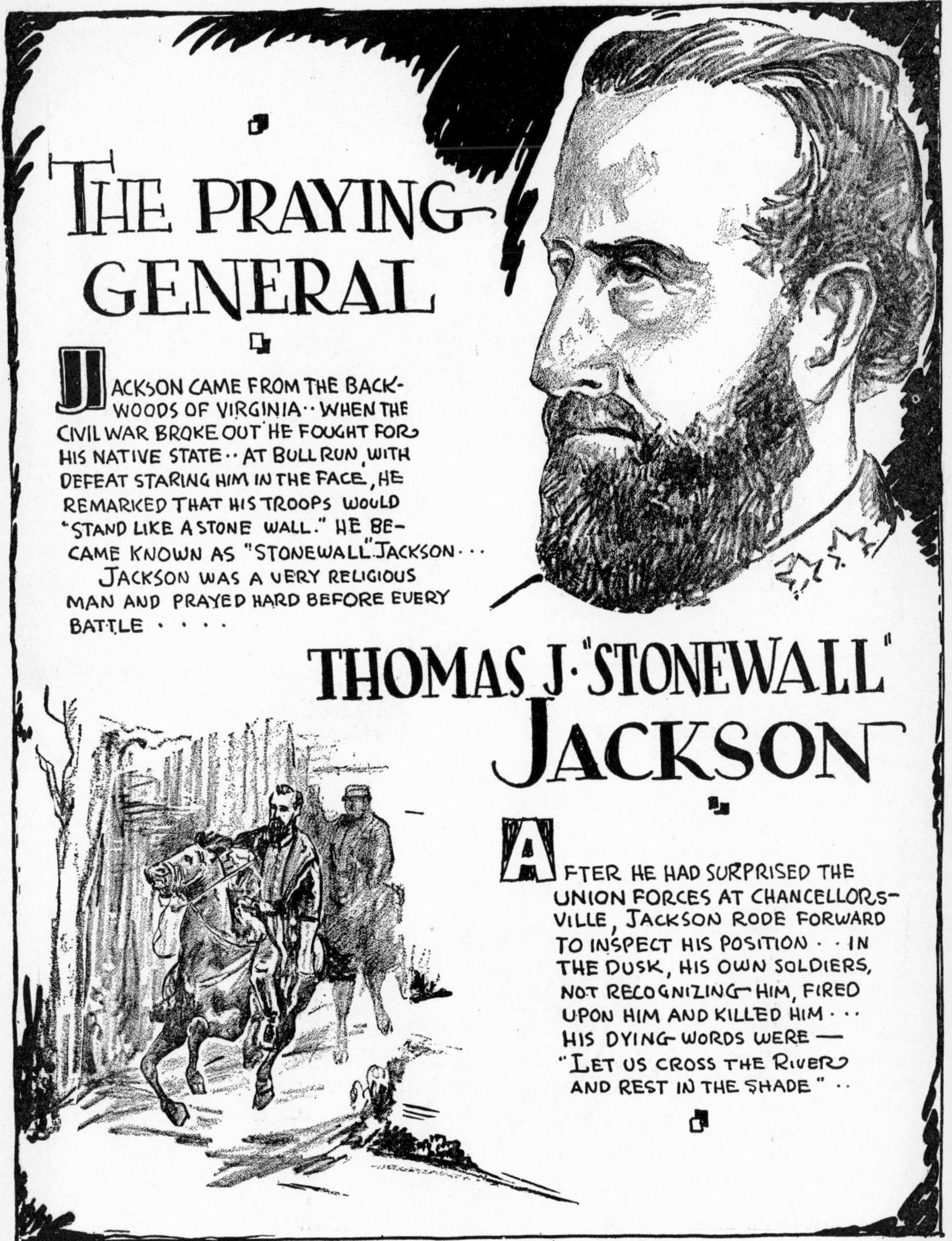
THE PRAYING GENERAL
JACKSON CAME FROM THE BACKWOODS OF VIRGINIA·· WHEN THE CIVIL WAR BROKE OUT HE FOUGHT FOR HIS NATIVE STATE·· AT BULL RUN, WITH DEFEAT STARING HIM IN THE FACE, HE REMARKED THAT HIS TROOPS WOULD "STAND LIKE A STONE WALL." HE BECAME KNOWN AS "STONEWALL" JACKSON···
JACKSON WAS A VERY RELIGIOUS MAN AND PRAYED HARD BEFORE EVERY BATTLE · · · ·
THOMAS J· "STONEWALL" JACKSON
AFTER HE HAD SURPRISED THE UNION FORCES AT CHANCELLORSVILLE, JACKSON RODE FORWARD TO INSPECT HIS POSITION · · IN THE DUSK, HIS OWN SOLDIERS, NOT RECOGNIZING HIM, FIRED UPON HIM AND KILLED HIM · · · HIS DYING WORDS WERE — "LET US CROSS THE RIVER AND REST IN THE SHADE" · ·

·· BORN-1824-DIED-1862··

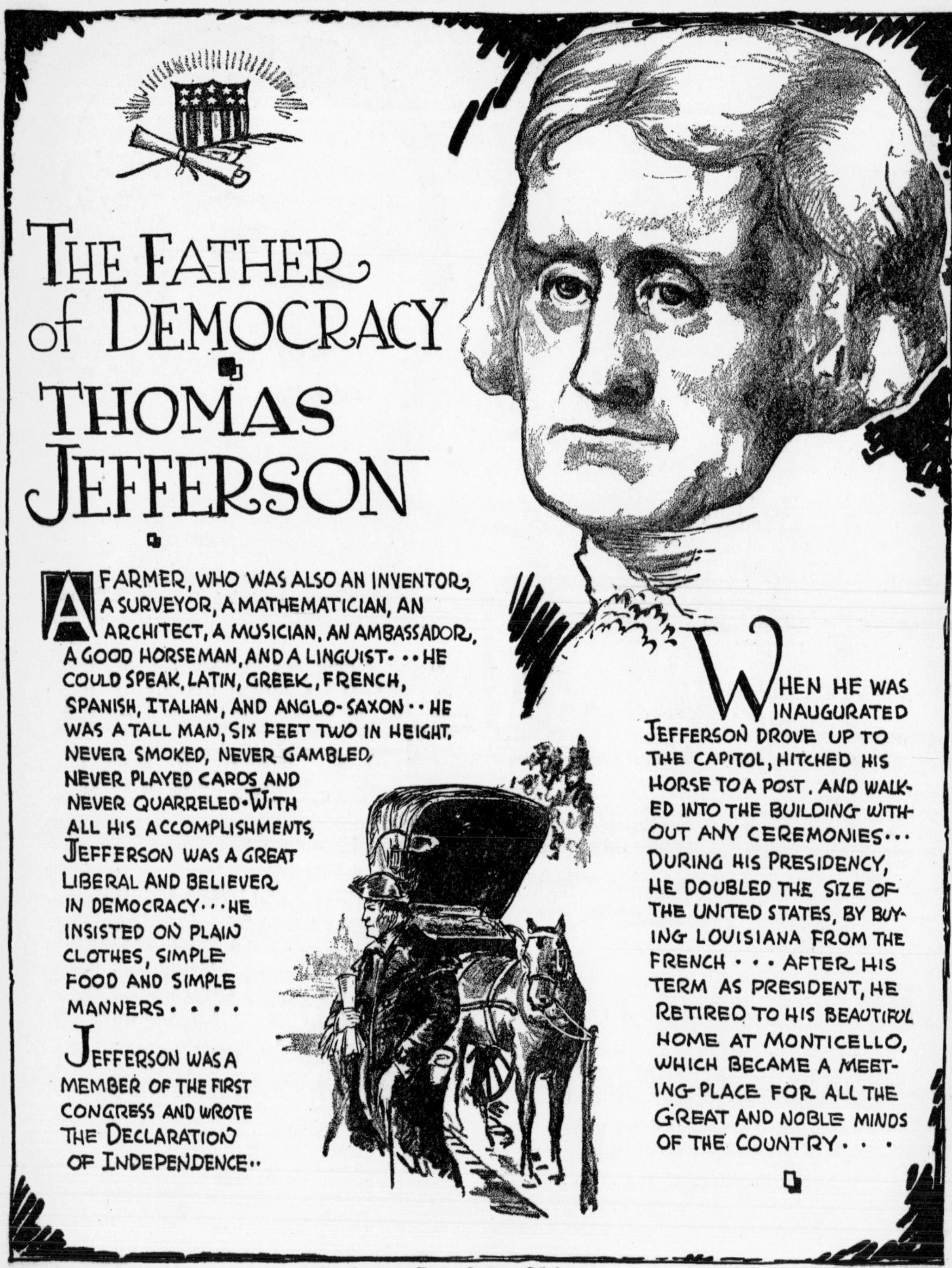
THE FATHER of DEMOCRACY
THOMAS JEFFERSON
A FARMER, WHO WAS ALSO AN INVENTOR, A SURVEYOR, A MATHEMATICIAN, AN ARCHITECT, A MUSICIAN, AN AMBASSADOR, A GOOD HORSEMAN, AND A LINGUIST . . . HE COULD SPEAK LATIN, GREEK, FRENCH, SPANISH, ITALIAN, AND ANGLO-SAXON . . HE WAS A TALL MAN, SIX FEET TWO IN HEIGHT, NEVER SMOKED, NEVER GAMBLED, NEVER PLAYED CARDS AND NEVER QUARRELED. WITH ALL HIS ACCOMPLISHMENTS, JEFFERSON WAS A GREAT LIBERAL AND BELIEVER IN DEMOCRACY . . . HE INSISTED ON PLAIN CLOTHES, SIMPLE FOOD AND SIMPLE MANNERS . . . .
JEFFERSON WAS A MEMBER OF THE FIRST CONGRESS AND WROTE THE DECLARATION OF INDEPENDENCE . .
WHEN HE WAS INAUGURATED JEFFERSON DROVE UP TO THE CAPITOL, HITCHED HIS HORSE TO A POST, AND WALKED INTO THE BUILDING WITHOUT ANY CEREMONIES . . . DURING HIS PRESIDENCY, HE DOUBLED THE SIZE OF THE UNITED STATES, BY BUYING LOUISIANA FROM THE FRENCH . . . AFTER HIS TERM AS PRESIDENT, HE RETIRED TO HIS BEAUTIFUL HOME AT MONTICELLO, WHICH BECAME A MEETING-PLACE FOR ALL THE GREAT AND NOBLE MINDS OF THE COUNTRY . . .

. . BORN 1743 . . . DIED 1826 . .

THE LITTLE SHEPHERDESS WHO BECAME A SAINT!
JOAN OF ARC
JOAN WAS A YOUNG GIRL DOING CHORES ON HER FATHER'S FARM WHEN THE ENGLISH INVADED FRANCE. SHE FELT HERSELF CALLED TO SAVE HER NATION.. JOAN PUT ON WHITE ARMOR AND RODE AT THE HEAD OF THE ARMY ON A WHITE HORSE.. SHE INSPIRED THE SOLDIERS WITH HER OWN BRAVERY AND THEY DROVE THE ENGLISH FROM THE CITY OF ORLEANS . . . .
JOAN THEN BROUGHT THE DAUPHIN (THE HEIR TO THE THRONE) TO THE CATHEDRAL AT RHEIMS WHERE HE WAS CROWNED KING CHARLES VII
THROUGH TREACHERY, SHE WAS ALLOWED TO FALL INTO THE HANDS OF THE ENGLISH.. THEY ACCUSED HER OF BEING A WITCH AND BURNT HER AT THE STAKE.. HER SIMPLE SPIRIT LIVES ON AS A GLOWING EXAMPLE OF FAITH AND COURAGE . . . . .

· · BORN · 1412 · · DIED 1431 · ·

THE FATHER of the AMERICAN NAVY
JONES WAS BORN IN SCOTLAND, HIS REAL NAME BEING JOHN PAUL. HE WAS REARED ON THE SEA, AND AT THE OUTBREAK OF THE AMERICAN REVOLUTION, HE EQUIPPED A SMALL FLEET TO HARASS ENGLISH SHIPPING. . HIS SURPRIZE ATTACKS AND DARING COUPS STRUCK TERROR IN THE HEARTS OF THE BRITISH AND EARNED THE SYMPATHY OF EUROPE FOR THE AMERICAN CAUSE
JOHN PAUL JONES
THE ENCOUNTER BETWEEN JONE'S SHIP, THE "BON HOMME RICHARD", AND THE BRITISH FRIGATE, THE "SERAPIS", WAS ONE OF THE MOST FAMOUS SEA ENGAGEMENTS OF HISTORY IN A FIERCE THREE AND A HALF HOUR BATTLE, FOUGHT BY MOON-LIGHT, JONES, HIS OWN SHIP BADLY SHATTERED, NEVERTHELESS FORCED HIS SUPERIOR OPPONENT TO STRIKE HER COLORS . . . . .
AFTER THE WAR, JONES WAS INVITED BY RUSSIA TO BUILD UP HER NAVY . . . DISCREDITED THROUGH THE JEALOUSY OF THE RUSSIAN OFFICERS, HE RETURNED TO PARIS, WHERE HE DIED IN 1913 HIS BODY WAS BELATEDLY BROUGHT TO AMERICA TO BE BURIED AT ANNAPOLIS .

. . . BORN-1747- DIED-1792 .

O RARE
BEN JONSON!
BRICKLAYER . . LATIN SCHOLAR . . .
ACTOR . . . DRUNKARD . . . PLAYWRIGHT . .
SOLDIER . . KEEN WIT . . POET AND RAKE!
THE WRITER CAMDEN DISCOVERED BEN AS A LAD OF TWELVE, CHASING A GROUP OF FELLOW SCHOOL-MATES AND CURSING AT THEM IN LATIN . . . CAMDEN TOOK HIM UNDER HIS WING AND EDUCATED HIM . . . JONSON WROTE MANY PLAYS IN WHICH HE MOCKED HIS BROTHER WRITERS OF THE DAY . . . HIS PLAYS AND PAGEANTS SOON MADE HIM THE PET OF THE ENGLISH COURT . . . .
SHAKESPEARE AND JONSON WERE GREAT FRIENDS AND SPENT MANY EVENINGS TOGETHER IN A TAVERN . . BEN TRAVELLED ALL OVER FRANCE, AS A SOLDIER AND AS A TUTOR OF SIR WALTER RALEIGH'S SON . . . HE WAS OFTEN DRUNK AND GOT INTO MANY SCRAPES . . . HE ONCE FOUGHT A DUEL WITH AN ACTOR AND KILLED HIM IN SELF-DEFENCE, BUT WAS RELEASED FROM PRISON AFTER BEING BRANDED ON THE THUMB . . . .
ON HIS GRAVE, A STONE-CUTTER WAS ORDERED TO CHISEL "ORARE BEN JONSON"— IN LATIN, "PRAY FOR BEN JONSON" . . THE MAN MADE A MISTAKE AND WROTE "O RARE BEN JONSON" ———.

. . BEN JONSON WORKING AS A BRICKLAYER . .

— BORN – 1573 – DIED – 1637 —

A GREAT SOUL IN A TORTURED BODY! ...

Samuel Johnson lived a life of physical torture... He had a strong, muscular body, but suffered from nervous spells and twitchings... His eyes were very weak and his manners were crude.... In addition to this for fifty years he struggled against hopeless poverty and went around in rags.. He married a coarse, fat woman, 21 years older than himself, but to the day of her death he loved her and thought she was pretty. . . . .

DR. SAMUEL JOHNSON

Despite these tremendous handicaps, Johnson was a keen scholar and a very learned man... His books, especially the huge English dictionary which he wrote, made him famous...He became a professor at Oxford University and a circle of prominent literary men gathered at his feet... One of them, James Boswell, wrote a long and intimate biography of him which is itself a classic . . . .

Johnson wrote his famous story "Rasselas", in a week's time to pay the expenses of his mother's funeral.....

...BORN-1709—DIED-1789...

AN EMPEROR'S PLAYTHING!
JOSEPHINE
JOSEPHINE WAS A CREOLE, BORN ON THE ISLAND OF MARTI-NIQUE OFF THE COAST OF SOUTH AMERICA · · · SHE WAS INDIFFER-ENTLY EDUCATED, NEVER READ, AND HATED MUSIC AND SPORTS · · HER ONLY INTEREST WAS RICH CLOTHES AND PLEASURES · · · HER FIRST HUSBAND WAS KILLED DURING THE FRENCH REVOLUTION AND ALTHOUGH SHE WAS IN PRISON WITH HIM, READY TO BE BEHEADED, HER FRIENDS SAVED HER · · ·
NAPOLEON FELL MADLY IN LOVE WITH HER · · · SHE MARRIED HIM BUT WHILE HE WAS AWAY ON HIS CAMPAIGNS SHE FLIRTED OUT-RAGEOUSLY · · · NAPOLEON FORGAVE HER AND PAID HER EXTRAVAGANT DEBTS · · SHE WAS CROWNED EMPRESS OF FRANCE, BUT NAPOLEON LATER DIVORCED HER · · SHE RETIRED TO THE COUNTRY OUTSIDE OF PARIS AND RAISED PLANTS AND FLOWERS · · · · · · · ·
DESPITE HER FAULTS SHE WAS A VERY POPULAR AND LOVE-ABLE WOMAN · · · · · ·

· · · BORN – 1763 · · DIED – 1814 · · ·

The
NOBLEST ROMAN
OF THEM ALL!
... JULIUS
CAESAR
.. GREAT AS A GENERAL!
.. GREAT AS A STATESMAN!
.. GREAT AS A WRITER!
JULIUS CAESAR WAS A WISE AND KIND RULER .. HE TRIED TO MAKE THE ROMAN EMPIRE THE GREATEST IN THE WORLD! ...
HOWEVER, THERE WERE SOME PEOPLE WHO WERE AFRAID HE WANTED TO BE CROWNED KING .. ALTHOUGH HE REFUSED THE CROWN THREE TIMES, THEY PLOTTED AGAINST HIM AND STABBED HIM TO DEATH .....
CAESAR WROTE A FAMOUS BOOK ABOUT HIS WARS IN GAUL, WHICH IS NOW READ BY ALL LATIN STUDENTS ... AFTER A GREAT BATTLE FROM WHICH HE EMERGED VICTORIOUS, HE WROTE BACK TO ROME — "VENI, VIDI, VICI!" .. THIS MEANS — "I CAME, I SAW I CONQUERED!"

.. BORN-B.C.100-DIED B.C.44 ..

"A THING OF BEAUTY IS A JOY FOREVER!"

KEATS WAS THE SON OF A STABLE-KEEPER.. HE STUDIED MEDICINE, BUT SOON GAVE UP HIS WORK IN THE HOSPITALS TO WRITE POETRY..

THE CRITICS ATTACKED HIS WRITINGS, BUT HE CONTINUED TO PRODUCE SUCH WONDERFUL IMAGINATIVE POEMS THAT HIS NAME HAS BECOME SYNONYMOUS WITH BEAUTY.......

JOHN KEATS

KEATS LIKED TO WANDER AROUND LONDON, MEETING PEOPLE.. THUS HE MET FANNY BRAWNE WHO INSPIRED MANY OF HIS POEMS .. LIVING IN THE OPEN CONTINUOUSLY, HE DEVELOPED THROAT TROUBLE, WHICH LATER TURNED INTO TUBERCULOSIS.. HE WENT TO ITALY FOR HIS HEALTH, BUT IT WAS TOO LATE. HE WAS DEAD AT TWENTY-SIX!.

..BORN-1795-DIED-1821..

THE FRENCH AMBASSADOR OF LIBERTY!
LAFAYETTE
THE DESCENDANT OF A VERY ANCIENT FAMILY, MARIE JOSEPH PAUL, MARQUIS DE LAFAYETTE FOUND HIMSELF AT THIRTEEN AN ORPHAN WITH A PRINCELY FORTUNE ··· WHEN THE COLONIES REVOLTED AGAINST ENGLAND, SIX YEARS LATER, LAFAYETTE, DESPITE THE STRICT ORDERS OF THE FRENCH KING, LEFT FRANCE WITH BARON DE KALB, TO AID THEM ···· HE BECAME THE LIFE-LONG FRIEND OF GEORGE WASHINGTON AND FOUGHT VALIANTLY UNDER THE AMERICAN FLAG—
LAFAYETTE RETURNED TO FRANCE IN 1787 TO THROW HIS ENERGIES INTO THE FRENCH REVOLUTION, AND INTRODUCED THE TRICOLOR COCKADE OF LIBERTY IN FRANCE ·· HOWEVER, THE TIDE TURNED IN 1792, AND HE WAS IMPRISONED FOR FIVE YEARS, FINALLY BEING RELEASED BY NAPOLEON ···
IN 1825, LAFAYETTE REVISITED AMERICA ··· HE RECEIVED A TREMENDOUS OVATION AND WAS SHOWERED WITH GIFTS OF LAND AND MONEY ···

·· BORN - 1757 - DIED - 1834 ··

A BOOKKEEPER WHO WROTE BOOKS
CHARLES LAMB
CHARLES LAMB WAS AN INCURABLE STUTTERER AND THIS BARRED HIM FROM THE CHURCH AND UNIVERSITY.... HE WENT TO WORK AS A BOOKKEEPER IN THE EAST INDIA HOUSE AND WORKED THERE FOR THIRTY-THREE YEARS, PRODUCING THE ACCOUNTING BOOKS WHICH HE CALLED HIS TRUE WORKS.
WHEN LAMB WAS 21, HIS SISTER MARY WENT INSANE AND STABBED HIS MOTHER TO DEATH.. WITH A CHARACTERISTIC LOYALTY AND SELF-RENUNCIATION WHICH WAS A PIECE OF REAL HEROISM, LAMB UNDERTOOK TO NURSE HER AND DEVOTED THE REST OF HIS LIFE TO HER CARE ......
LAMB WAS MUCH BELOVED AND HAD MANY FAMOUS LITERARY FRIENDS .... HIS BOOK "ESSAYS OF ELIA" IS FILLED WITH A GENTLE NON-SENSICAL HUMOR WHICH MAKES IT CHARMING .... TOGETHER WITH HIS SISTER MARY, HE WROTE THE FAMOUS "TALES FROM SHAKESPEARE" ...
LAMB MOVED TO THE COUNTRY BECAUSE OF HIS SISTER'S HEALTH.. WHILE WALKING ONE DAY, HE SUFFERED A FATAL FALL. HIS SUDDEN DEATH WAS A GREAT SHOCK TO THE LITERARY WORLD .....

..BORN-1775- DIED-1834..

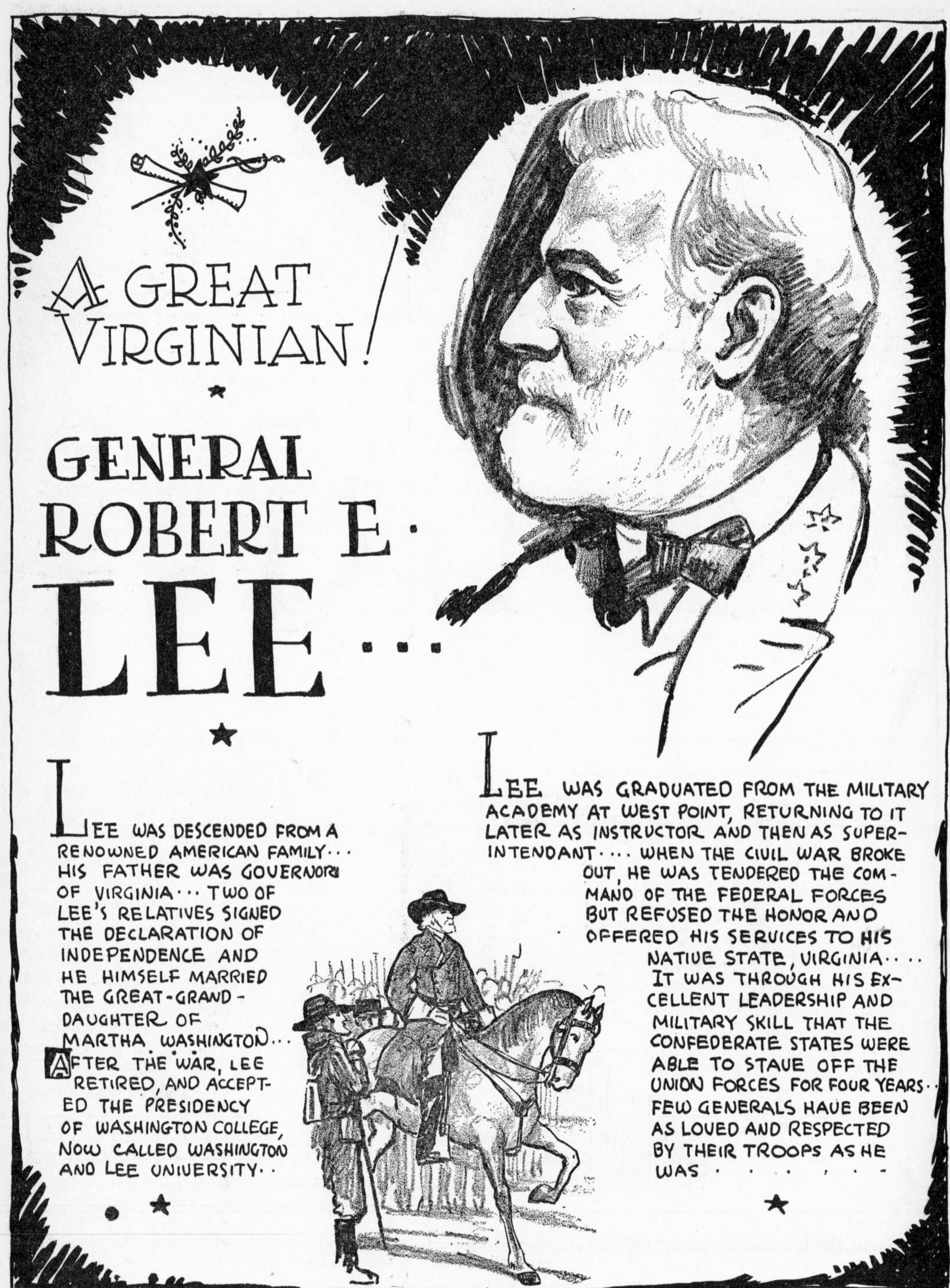
A GREAT VIRGINIAN!
GENERAL ROBERT E. LEE...
LEE WAS DESCENDED FROM A RENOWNED AMERICAN FAMILY... HIS FATHER WAS GOVERNOR OF VIRGINIA... TWO OF LEE'S RELATIVES SIGNED THE DECLARATION OF INDEPENDENCE AND HE HIMSELF MARRIED THE GREAT-GRAND-DAUGHTER OF MARTHA WASHINGTON...
AFTER THE WAR, LEE RETIRED, AND ACCEPTED THE PRESIDENCY OF WASHINGTON COLLEGE, NOW CALLED WASHINGTON AND LEE UNIVERSITY..
LEE WAS GRADUATED FROM THE MILITARY ACADEMY AT WEST POINT, RETURNING TO IT LATER AS INSTRUCTOR AND THEN AS SUPERINTENDANT.... WHEN THE CIVIL WAR BROKE OUT, HE WAS TENDERED THE COMMAND OF THE FEDERAL FORCES BUT REFUSED THE HONOR AND OFFERED HIS SERVICES TO HIS NATIVE STATE, VIRGINIA....
IT WAS THROUGH HIS EXCELLENT LEADERSHIP AND MILITARY SKILL THAT THE CONFEDERATE STATES WERE ABLE TO STAVE OFF THE UNION FORCES FOR FOUR YEARS.. FEW GENERALS HAVE BEEN AS LOVED AND RESPECTED BY THEIR TROOPS AS HE WAS

... BORN—1807—DIED—1870...

THE RUSSIAN
EMANCIPATOR
LENIN
VLADIMIR LENIN SPENT HIS EARLY YEARS STUDYING LAW AND THE WORKS OF KARL MARX, THE GREAT SOCIALIST .... HE WROTE NEWSPAPER ARTICLES AND CARRIED ON PROPAGANDA FOR THE LIBERATION OF THE WORKING CLASS ... AS A RESULT, AT 26, HE WAS EXILED TO SIBERIA FOR THREE YEARS ... AT THE SAME TIME, HIS OLDER BROTHER WAS EXECUTED FOR ATTEMPTING TO KILL TZAR ALEXANDER III
LIVING OUTSIDE OF RUSSIA FROM 1907 TO 1917, HE NEVERTHELESS, ORGANIZED THE BOLSHEVIK PARTY AFTER A STUDY OF THE EVILS OF THE PROLETARIAT SYSTEM ALL OVER THE WORLD .. WHEN THE TZAR WAS OVERTHROWN IN 1917, LENIN WENT TO RUSSIA .. DESPITE FIERCE OPPOSITION, HE LED THE PEASANTS AND WORKERS TO FREEDOM AND BECAME THE FOUNDER AND DICTATOR OF THE SOVIET REPUBLIC . HE SET OUT TO DEVELOP THE INDUSTRIES OF RUSSIA, BUT THE LONG YEARS OF HARD WORK HAD AT LAST BEGUN TO TELL .. HIS DEATH WAS MOURNED BY MILLIONS AND THE NAME OF THE CITY OF PETROGRAD WAS CHANGED TO LENINGRAD IN HIS HONOR.
... BORN - 1870 - DIED - 1924 ..

A MAN FOR THE AGES!

ABRAHAM LINCOLN

LINCOLN—WHO WAS BORN IN A LOG CABIN·· KEPT A COUNTRY STORE··· FLOATED DOWN THE MISSISSIPPI ON A FLAT BOAT···STUDIED LAW IN HIS SPARE TIME···BECAME FAMOUS AS A TRIAL LAWYER·· LOVED ANN RUTLEDGE, MOURNED HER PASSING··AND TRAVELLED OVER THE COUNTRY-SIDE, DEBATING THE SLAVERY QUESTION WITH HIS POLITICAL OPPONENT- STEPHEN DOUGLAS·

LINCOLN, THE MASTER POLITICIAN···WHO BECAME PRESIDENT···FREED THE SLAVES··· MADE THE GETTYSBURG ADDRESS· ··LED THE NATION THROUGH A GREAT CIVIL WAR AND PRESERVED THE UNION!···AND IN HIS MOMENT OF VICTORY DIED AT THE HANDS OF A CRAZED ASSASSIN···A HOMELY BACKWOODS MAN WHO WILL FOREVER BE REVERED AS ONE OF THE GRANDEST MEN OF ALL TIME!··

··BORN·1809—DIED—1865··

JENNY LIND

THE SWEDISH NIGHTINGALE

JENNY LIND WAS BORN IN SWEDEN AND BEGAN TO SING OPERA AT THE AGE OF SEVENTEEN... SHE BECAME A SENSATION ALL OVER EUROPE AND AMERICA:.. PEOPLE STARVED TO BUY TICKETS TO HEAR THE SLIM SHY GIRL WITH THE MARVELOUS VOICE... AT THE HEIGHT OF HER CAREER, SHE RETIRED FROM OPERA AND DEVOTED HER HUGE FORTUNE TO HOSPITALS AND CHARITY...

JENNY LIND WAS BROUGHT TO AMERICA BY P. T. BARNUM, UNDER A CONTRACT WHICH CALLED FOR 150 PERFORMANCES AT 1,000 DOLLARS A PERFORMANCE . . . .

HER GREATEST SONG WAS MENDELSSOHN'S "I KNOW THAT MY REDEEMER LIVETH," AND THESE WORDS ARE INSCRIBED ON HER MEMORIAL . . . .

—BORN-1820—DIED 1887—

THE
PRINCE
OF PIANISTS!
FRANZ
LISZT
AS A YOUNG STUDENT LISZT
HEARD THE GREAT VIOLINIST
PAGANINI PLAY · · THE WONDER-
FUL PERFORMANCE MADE A DEEP
IMPRESSION ON HIM AND HE RE-
SOLVED TO DO AS WELL ON THE
PIANO · · · HE BECAME SO FAMOUS
THAT HE EARNED THE TITLE "PRINCE
OF PIANISTS" · · · · · · ·
THIS VENERABLE MUSICIAN WAS
ALSO A REMARKABLE CONDUCTOR,
TEACHER AND COMPOSER OF HUNGARIAN
MUSIC · · · HE WAS THE FEARLESS CHAMP-
ION OF THE NOBLE IN ART AND EN-
COURAGED YOUNG MUSICIANS LIKE
BERLIOZ AND RICHARD WAGNER · · · ·
HIS DAUGHTER COSIMA MARRIED WAGNER
AND WAS A LEADER AMONG MUSICIANS
HERSELF · · ·
TOWARD THE END OF HIS
LIFE HE JOINED A MON-
ASTERY AND RETIRED FROM
THE WORLD TO DEVOTE HIM-
SELF TO MUSIC ·

· · BORN · 1811 — DIED · 1886 · ·

A WEAVER OF LYRICAL LEGENDS . . .
HENRY WADSWORTH LONGFELLOW
LONGFELLOW, THE SON OF A LAWYER, WAS BORN IN PORTLAND, MAINE . . . HE STUDIED IN EUROPE AND BECAME A MARVELOUS LINGUIST . . AT 22, HE WAS ALREADY A PROFESSOR OF LANGUAGES AND TRANSLATED POEMS FROM NEARLY ALL THE FOREIGN TONGUES . . . .
FOR YEARS, LONGFELLOW TAUGHT AT HARVARD . . HIS SMOOTH HAPPY EXISTENCE WAS INTERRUPTED ONLY ONCE BY A GREAT TRAGEDY, WHEN HIS WIFE DIED IN A FIRE! . .
LONGFELLOW WAS A GENTLE, DIGNIFIED MAN AND LOVED CHILDREN . . . THAT IS WHY HIS BEAUTIFUL LEGENDS OF "EVANGELINE" "HIAWATHA" AND "THE COURTSHIP OF MILES STANDISH" ARE BELOVED BY YOUNG AND OLD . . . .
LONGFELLOW WATCHING THE VILLAGE BLACKSMITH "UNDER THE SPREADING CHESTNUT TREE" . . . . . .

BORN 1807 . . . DIED 1882

THE GREAT REFORMER
MARTIN LUTHER
THE SON OF A PEASANT, LUTHER WAS SENT TO THE GERMAN UNIVERSITIES TO STUDY LATIN, PHILOSOPHY AND LAW · · WHILE STUDYING HE EARNED HIS BREAD BY SINGING IN THE STREETS · · · · CAUGHT IN A THUNDERSTORM, ONE DAY, WHEN HE WAS 24 YEARS OLD, HE WAS OVERTAKEN BY A SUDDEN FEAR OF DEATH AND BECAME A MONK · · · ·
LUTHER WROTE A PROTEST AGAINST THE CHURCH PRACTICE OF ACCEPTING MONEY TO FORGIVE SINS AND POSTED IT ON A CHURCH DOOR IN WITTENBERG · · · HE WAS ORDERED BY THE POPE TO RETRACT HIS STATEMENTS · · · · BEING PUGNACIOUS AND AFRAID OF NO ONE, NO MATTER HOW MIGHTY, LUTHER REFUSED AND WAS EXCOMMUNICATED · · · · · · ·
HOWEVER, THE PEASANTS SIDED WITH LUTHER IN HIS ATTEMPTS TO REFORM THE CHURCH AND REVOLTED · · · THEY ACCEPTED HIS VERSION OF THE BIBLE AND HIS FOLLOWERS BECAME KNOWN AS LUTHERANS · · · ·

··· BORN · 1483 – DIED · 1546 ···

THE SPIDER OF FLORENCE
NICCOLO MACHIAVELLI
MACHIAVELLI WAS A CULTURED AND ARISTOCRATIC FLORENTINE THINKER, AND A SHREWD STATESMAN . . . HE BECAME A CLERK AND AMBASSADOR FOR THE MEDICI AND BORGIA FAMILIES, WHO RULED FLORENCE . . . A UNITED ITALY, FREE FROM THE FETTERS OF THE INVADER WAS HIS DREAM AND HE LIT THE TORCH OF THE 350 YEAR STRUGGLE WHICH FINALLY BROKE ITALY'S SHACKLES . .
MACHIAVELLI WAS A WITTY AND SARCASTIC WRITER . . HIS BITING SATIRE AND GRIM JESTS MAKE HIS FARCE "MANDRAGOLA" ONE OF THE BOLDEST AND MOST ENJOYABLE IN ITALIAN LITERATURE . . HIS GREATEST WORK WAS "THE PRINCE", IN WHICH HE OUTLINES A SYSTEM OF UNSCRUPULOUS, POLITICAL TRICKERY WHEREBY A SINGLE MAN MAY DOMINATE A NATION . . BECAUSE OF THIS BOOK HIS NAME HAS BECOME AN ADJECTIVE MEANING CRAFTY OR TREACHEROUS . . . . . .

. . . BORN-1469-DIED-1527 . . .

THE GREAT NAVIGATOR!
FERDINAND
MAGELLAN
MAGELLAN WAS BORN IN PORTUGAL·· HE THOUGHT THAT THE EARTH WAS ROUND BUT THE PORTUGUESE KING WOULD NOT LISTEN TO HIM··· THE KING OF SPAIN FINALLY GAVE HIM FIVE SHIPS AND TOGETHER WITH 250 MEN, HE SET SAIL WESTWARD!
HE FOUND THE STRAIT OF MAGELLAN AT THE SOUTHERN TIP OF SOUTH AMERICA AND AFTER VERY SEVERE STORMS, HE CAME TO THE GREAT OCEAN WHICH HE NAMED THE PACIFIC·· BUT THE HARDSHIPS AND PRIVATIONS GREW WORSE·· THE MEN MUTINIED, THEY FELL SICK, THEY STARVED AND HAD TO EAT LEATHER AND RATS!
FINALLY, THEY SIGHTED THE SOUTH SEA ISLANDS··· IN A BATTLE WITH HOSTILE NATIVES, FOUGHT IN THE WATER, MAGELLAN WAS KILLED··· AFTER THREE LONG YEARS ONE SHIP WITH 18 MEN STAGGERED HOME AT LAST, WITHOUT ITS LEADER···
BUT, MAGELLAN HAD PROVEN THAT THE EARTH IS ROUND!

··BORN-1480?—DIED·1521··

The SPENDTHRIFT QUEEN!
MARIE ANTOINETTE
MARIE ANTOINETTE WAS THE DAUGHTER OF MARIA THERESA, QUEEN OF AUSTRIA. AT 15, SHE CAME TO THE FRENCH COURT AS THE WIFE OF LOUIS XVI ... SHE WAS EXTRAVAGANT IN HER DRESS AND AMUSEMENTS AND HAD A TASTE FOR GAIETY AND PLEASURE .. SHE WAS HATED BY THE FRENCH PEOPLE, WHO BLAMED HER FOR THE BANKRUPT CONDITION OF THE COUNTRY
WHEN TOLD THAT THE PEOPLE HAD NO BREAD TO EAT, SHE REPLIED, "LET THEM EAT CAKE!"
LOUIS XVI, HER HUSBAND, WAS A WEAK CHARACTER, AND WHEN THE REVOLUTION BROKE OUT, IT WAS MARIE ANTOINETTE WHO DIRECTED THE POLICIES OF THE NATION ... IN HER ATTEMPTS TO SAFEGUARD THE THRONE AND PROTECT HER HUSBAND AND SON, SHE REVEALED THE PLANS OF THE FRENCH GENERALS TO AUSTRIA .. SHE WAS CONVICTED OF BETRAYING FRANCE AND FOLLOWED LOUIS TO THE GUILLOTINE!

.. BORN-1755 - DIED-1793 ...

A MARTYR QUEEN!
MARY
QUEEN OF SCOTS
MARY WAS A VERY ABLE AND INTELLIGENT WOMAN.. SHE WAS A KIND, LOYAL FRIEND BUT A DEADLY DANGEROUS ENEMY.. A VERY COURAGEOUS YOUNG GIRL, SHE ESCAPED FROM AN ISLAND PRISON AND LED AN ARMY TO REGAIN SCOTLAND'S THRONE. AFTER BEING DEFEATED, SHE FLED SIXTY MILES IN THREE DAYS, SLEEPING ON HARD GROUND, LIVING ON OATMEAL AND SOUR MILK, AND TRAVELLING AT NIGHT IN THE COLD.
MARY BECAME QUEEN OF SCOTLAND WHEN HER FATHER DIED, A FEW DAYS AFTER SHE WAS BORN... SHE MARRIED THE FRENCH KING'S ELDEST SON AND WAS AFTERWARDS QUEEN OF FRANCE AS WELL AS SCOTLAND... IN EXILE MOST OF HER LIFE MARY REMAINED FAITHFUL TO SCOTLAND, BECAUSE OF A SECRET PLOT SHE WAS CONDEMNED TO DEATH BY QUEEN ELIZABETH AND BEHEADED.......

..BORN·1542—DIED 1587..

MICHELANGELO
A PAINTER OF THE HEAVENS
WHO CHISELED STONE
INTO LIFE! . . . .
IN THE VATICAN, IN ROME, STANDS A MOST GLORIOUS MONUMENT TO MICHEL-ANGELO, THE SISTINE CHAPEL · · COVERING THE WALLS AND CEILING OF THIS CHAPEL IS THE STORY OF THE WHOLE ADVENTURE OF MAN ON EARTH, BEGINNING WITH THE CREATION AND ENDING WITH THE LAST JUDGE-MENT · · FOR FOUR YEARS MICHELANGELO LABOURED ALONE TO COMPLETE THIS VAST UNDERTAKING, AND IN IT, IS REFLECTED THE SUBLIME IMAGINATION AND TERRIBLE FORCE OF HIS GENIUS ·
MICHELANGELO WAS THE FRIEND OF POPES AND KINGS THROUGH-OUT HIS NINETY YEARS · · ALTHOUGH HE WROTE SONNETS ABOUT WOMEN AND CARVED STATUES OF THEM, HE NEVER MARRIED · · HE PREFERRED SOLITUDE, AND DEVOTION TO HIS ART · · · · · · ·

· · BORN 1475 · DIED 1564 · ·

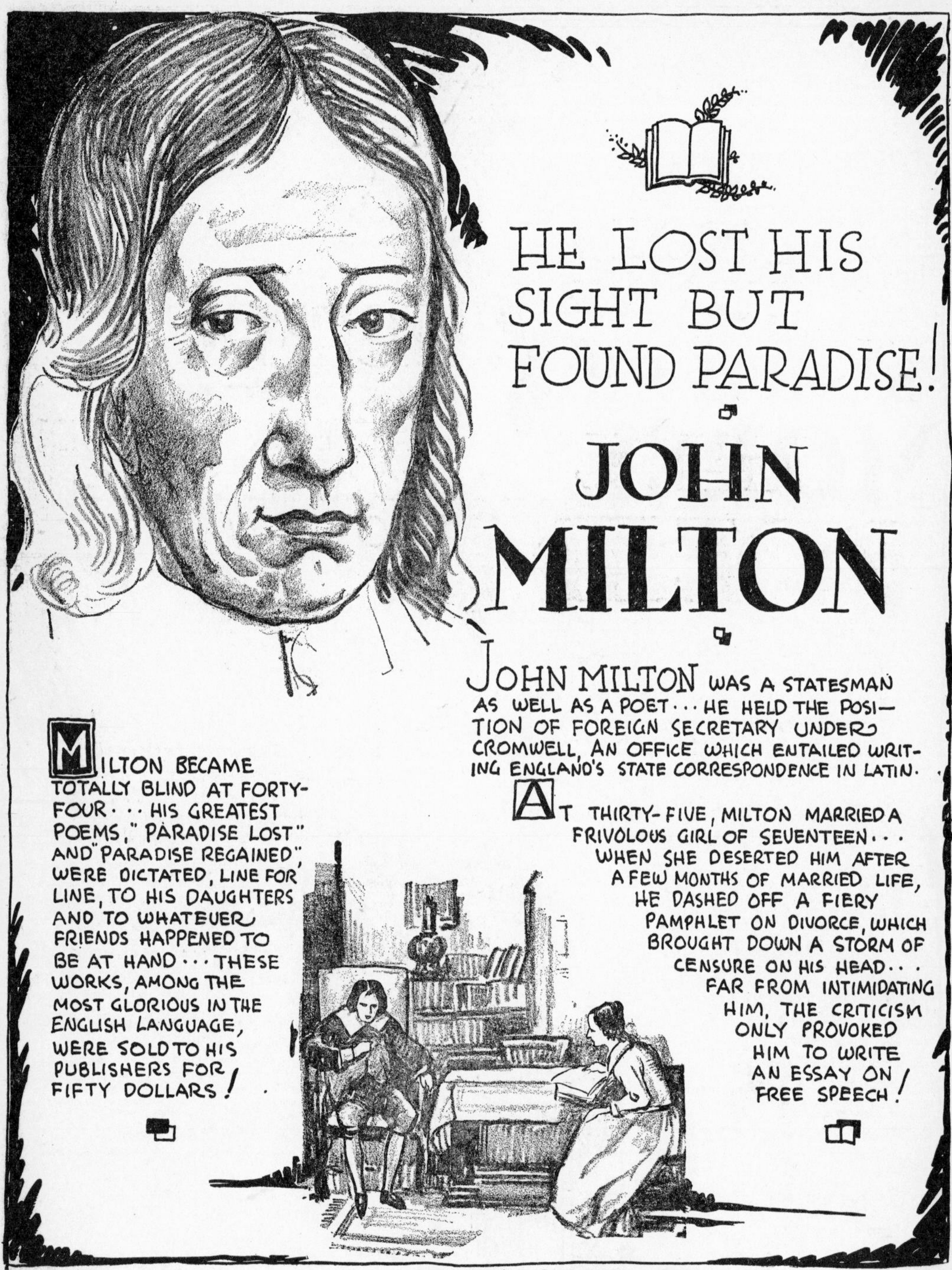
HE LOST HIS SIGHT BUT FOUND PARADISE!
JOHN MILTON
JOHN MILTON WAS A STATESMAN AS WELL AS A POET... HE HELD THE POSITION OF FOREIGN SECRETARY UNDER CROMWELL, AN OFFICE WHICH ENTAILED WRITING ENGLAND'S STATE CORRESPONDENCE IN LATIN.
MILTON BECAME TOTALLY BLIND AT FORTY-FOUR... HIS GREATEST POEMS, "PARADISE LOST" AND "PARADISE REGAINED", WERE DICTATED, LINE FOR LINE, TO HIS DAUGHTERS AND TO WHATEVER FRIENDS HAPPENED TO BE AT HAND... THESE WORKS, AMONG THE MOST GLORIOUS IN THE ENGLISH LANGUAGE, WERE SOLD TO HIS PUBLISHERS FOR FIFTY DOLLARS!
AT THIRTY-FIVE, MILTON MARRIED A FRIVOLOUS GIRL OF SEVENTEEN... WHEN SHE DESERTED HIM AFTER A FEW MONTHS OF MARRIED LIFE, HE DASHED OFF A FIERY PAMPHLET ON DIVORCE, WHICH BROUGHT DOWN A STORM OF CENSURE ON HIS HEAD... FAR FROM INTIMIDATING HIM, THE CRITICISM ONLY PROVOKED HIM TO WRITE AN ESSAY ON FREE SPEECH!

... BORN-1608 - DIED - 1674 ...

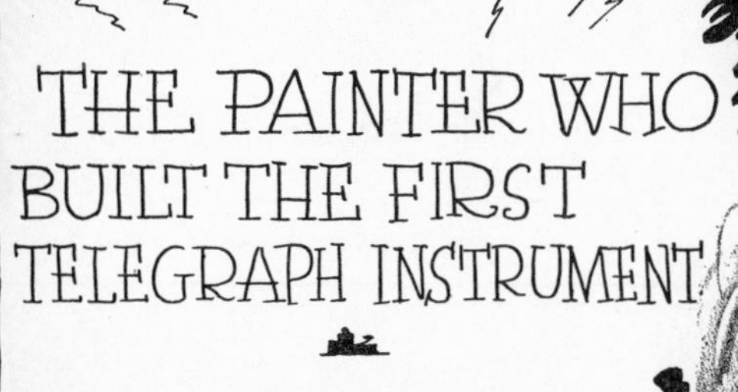

THE PAINTER WHO BUILT THE FIRST TELEGRAPH INSTRUMENT

·SAMUEL·F·B· MORSE

SAMUEL FINLEY BREESE MORSE WAS THE SON OF A PROFESSOR AND AUTHOR OF TEXT-BOOKS· HE WAS SENT TO YALE UNIVERSITY AND AFTER BEING GRADUATED, WENT TO EUROPE TO STUDY ART· · HE BECAME A SUCCESSFUL NEW YORK PORTRAIT PAINTER AND FOUNDED THE NATIONAL ACADEMY OF DESIGN

AT 42 MORSE'S INTERESTS SUDDENLY SHIFTED FROM THE ARTISTIC TO THE SCIENTIFIC· · HIS STUDIES IN ELECTRICITY SUGGESTED THE IDEA OF TELEGRAPHY TO HIM· · HE BUILT THE FIRST INSTRUMENT AND DEVISED THE MORSE ALPHABET, WHICH IS USED EVERYWHERE TELEGRAPH WIRES ARE STRUNG— ·

MORSE'S INVENTION WAS LAUGHED AT· FOR FIVE YEARS HE TRIED TO INTEREST THE U·S· AND FOREIGN POWERS IN HIS PROJECT, BUT IN VAIN· · · FINALLY CONGRESS AGREED TO STEP A LINE BETWEEN WASHINGTON AND BALTIMORE, AND OVER THIS WIRE, MORSE SENT THE FIRST TELEGRAPHIC MESSAGE IN THIS COUNTRY, THE FAMOUS WORDS,— "WHAT HATH GOD WROUGHT!"

· · · BORN-1791- DIED-1872·

A MUSICAL WONDER!
MOZART
A PRODIGY AT FIVE
THE GRAVE AT THIRTY-FIVE! ...
MOZART COMPOSED MUSIC WHEN HE WAS FIVE YEARS OLD.. AT FOURTEEN HE HAD ALREADY WRITTEN AND PRODUCED AN OPERA.... IN ITALY HE HEARD SOME FAMOUS SECRET CHURCH MUSIC, HE ASTOUNDED EVERYONE BY WRITING IT OUT FROM MEMORY, NOTE FOR NOTE, AFTER HEARING IT ONLY ONCE.
THE OVERTURE TO ONE OF HIS OPERAS WAS WRITTEN THE NIGHT BEFORE THE FIRST PERFORMANCE ... HIS WIFE KEPT HIM AWAKE WITH COFFEE AND AMUSING STORIES WHILE HE WROTE PAGE AFTER PAGE OF MUSIC.. MOZART'S LAST AND GREATEST WORK WAS THE "REQUIEM". HE WAS VERY ILL WHEN HE WROTE IT AND NEVER LIVED TO FINISH IT. HIS DYING WISH WAS TO HEAR IT SUNG BY A GROUP OF FRIENDS.

..BORN 1756 — DIED 1792..

"Il Duce!"
BENITO MUSSOLINI
"Live Dangerously" - IS HIS MOTTO!
HE LIKES TO SPEED IN AUTOS AND AEROPLANES.. HE THINKS HIS LIFE IS CHARMED. THERE HAVE BEEN FIVE ATTEMPTS TO KILL HIM, WITH GUNS AND BOMBS.. FOR RELAXATION HE PLAYS THE VIOLIN...
A BLACKSMITH'S SON, MUSSOLINI WORKED AS A HOD-CARRIER. HE HAD TO SLEEP UNDER BRIDGES IN POURING RAINS, OFTEN NEARLY STARVED. HE WAS ONCE ARRESTED FOR VAGRANCY.
MUSSOLINI ORGANIZED THE FASCISTI TO RECONSTRUCT AND PURIFY ITALY... IN 1922, HE MARCHED ON ROME WITH AN ARMY OF 100,000 — MEN.. THE KING — ASKED HIM TO TAKE OVER THE GOVERNMENT, AND HE HAS BEEN ITALY'S POWERFUL LEADER SINCE...
— BORN 1886 —

ENGLAND'S
GREATEST
NAVAL HERO!
LORD
NELSON
HORATIO NELSON ENTERED THE NAVY AS A YOUNGSTER... A BRAVE SEAMAN AND A CONFIDENT LEADER, HE ROSE RAPIDLY FROM THE RANKS.. THOUGH HE WAS THE SOUL OF HONOR AND LOYALTY IN HIS PUBLIC CAREER, HE WAS LESS CONSCIENTIOUS IN HIS PRIVATE LIFE... HE BECAME INVOLVED IN A LOVE AFFAIR WITH LADY HAMILTON, WHICH LED TO A SEPARATION FROM HIS WIFE AND CREATED ONE OF THE GREAT SCANDALS OF THE DAY....
NELSON COMMANDED THE BRITISH NAVY AT THE BATTLE OF TRAFALGAR.. HIS FLAGSHIP, "THE VICTORY", BROKE THE FRENCH LINE AND HE HIMSELF WAS WOUNDED AND DIED DURING THE BATTLE ... HIS STIRRING PHRASE, "ENGLAND EXPECTS THAT EVERY MAN WILL DO HIS DUTY!" HAS BECOME A WATCH WORD FOR MILITARY MEN,.. IN TRAFALGAR SQUARE, IN LONDON, A TALL STONE COLUMN RISES AS A MONUMENT TO THE ADMIRAL WHO DIED DOING HIS DUTY!...

...BORN-1758- DIED-1805...

THE SINGING EMPEROR NERO

AS A YOUTH, NERO WAS VERY FRIVOLOUS. HE LIKED TO SING AND ACT, OFTEN APPEARING ON THE STAGE. AT NIGHT HE WOULD DISGUISE HIMSELF AND SEEK ADVENTURE.. ONE NIGHT HE PROVOKED A SENATOR WHO, NOT RECOGNIZING THE EMPEROR, GAVE HIM A PAIR OF BLACK EYES....

AT FIRST NERO WAS A WISE RULER, BUT LATER HE BECAME CRUEL AND BLOODTHIRSTY.. HE BURNT AND PERSECUTED A GREAT MANY PEOPLE.. A TREMENDOUS FIRE BROKE OUT IN ROME AND LASTED FOR NINE DAYS.. IT IS SAID THAT HE PLAYED HIS HARP AND SANG WHILE THE CITY BURNED........

FINALLY THE PEOPLE REVOLTED AGAINST HIM.. IN TERROR HE FLED FROM ROME AND SLEW HIMSELF....

..BORN 37 A.D. — DIED 68 A.D.

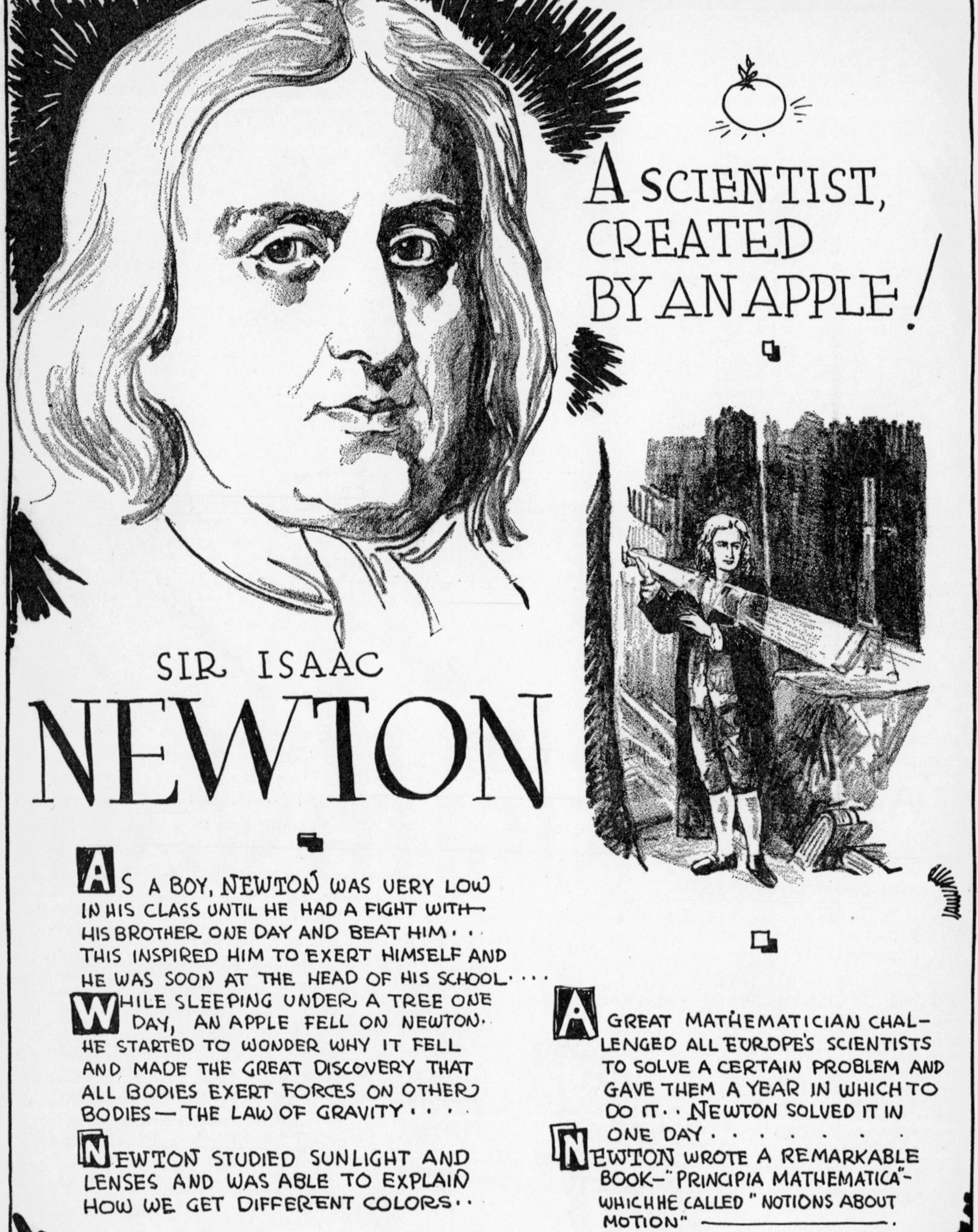
A SCIENTIST, CREATED BY AN APPLE!
SIR ISAAC
NEWTON

AS A BOY, NEWTON WAS VERY LOW IN HIS CLASS UNTIL HE HAD A FIGHT WITH HIS BROTHER ONE DAY AND BEAT HIM . . THIS INSPIRED HIM TO EXERT HIMSELF AND HE WAS SOON AT THE HEAD OF HIS SCHOOL . . .

WHILE SLEEPING UNDER A TREE ONE DAY, AN APPLE FELL ON NEWTON. HE STARTED TO WONDER WHY IT FELL AND MADE THE GREAT DISCOVERY THAT ALL BODIES EXERT FORCES ON OTHER BODIES — THE LAW OF GRAVITY . . . .

NEWTON STUDIED SUNLIGHT AND LENSES AND WAS ABLE TO EXPLAIN HOW WE GET DIFFERENT COLORS . .

A GREAT MATHEMATICIAN CHALLENGED ALL EUROPE'S SCIENTISTS TO SOLVE A CERTAIN PROBLEM AND GAVE THEM A YEAR IN WHICH TO DO IT . . NEWTON SOLVED IT IN ONE DAY . . . .

NEWTON WROTE A REMARKABLE BOOK—"PRINCIPIA MATHEMATICA"—WHICH HE CALLED "NOTIONS ABOUT MOTION" ——————.

. . . BORN-1642—DIED . . 1727 . . .

THE LADY WITH THE LAMP!
FLORENCE NIGHTINGALE WAS A WEALTHY, ENGLISH SOCIETY GIRL... SHE WANTED TO BE A NURSE, BUT IN THOSE DAYS NURSING WAS A DISREPUTABLE AND IMMORAL PROFESSION.. DESPITE THE STRENUOUS OBJECTIONS OF HER FAMILY, SHE SECRETLY TRAINED HERSELF, AND THE CARE OF THE SICK BECAME HER LIFE WORK....
FLORENCE NIGHTINGALE
WHEN THE CRIMEAN WAR BETWEEN ENGLAND, RUSSIA AND TURKEY BROKE OUT, SHE WENT TO SCUTARI, A SUBURB OF CONSTANTINOPLE... FIGHTING AGAINST THE BASEST SORT OF INEFFICIENCY, LACK OF MONEY AND SUPPLIES, AND THE DERISION OF THE ENGLISH OFFICERS, SHE REVOLUTIONIZED THE HORRIBLE CONDITIONS IN THE BARRACKS OF THE WOUNDED, AND SAVED THE LIVES OF HUNDREDS OF SOLDIERS....
FOR HALF A CENTURY, UNTIL HER DEATH AT THE AGE OF NINETY, MISS NIGHTINGALE QUIETLY CARRIED ON HER WORK OF HOSPITAL REFORM, AND EARNED THE ADORATION AND HOMAGE OF THE ENTIRE WORLD....
...BORN-1820-DIED..1910

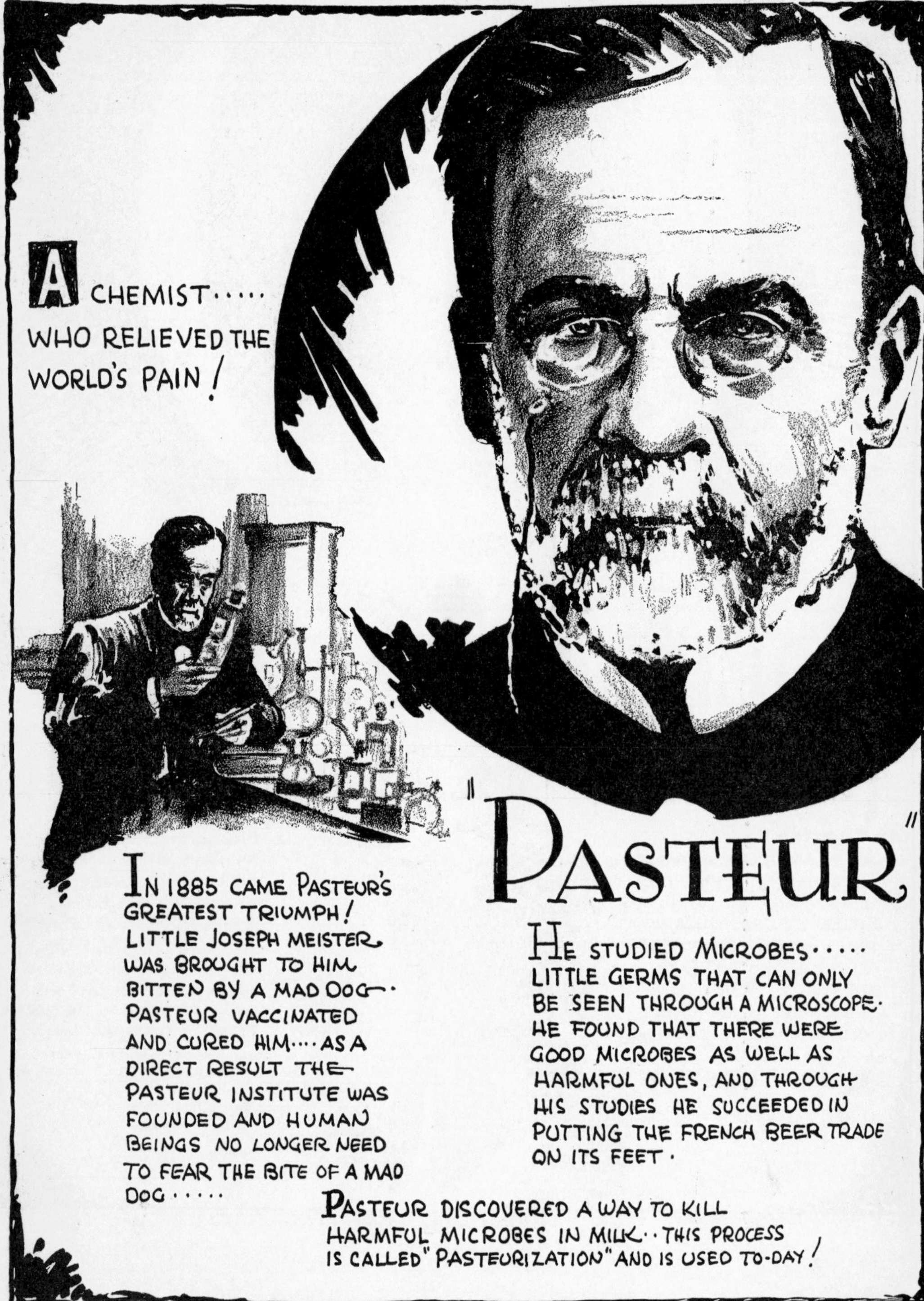
A CHEMIST.....
WHO RELIEVED THE
WORLD'S PAIN!
"PASTEUR"
IN 1885 CAME PASTEUR'S
GREATEST TRIUMPH!
LITTLE JOSEPH MEISTER
WAS BROUGHT TO HIM
BITTEN BY A MAD DOG.
PASTEUR VACCINATED
AND CURED HIM.... AS A
DIRECT RESULT THE
PASTEUR INSTITUTE WAS
FOUNDED AND HUMAN
BEINGS NO LONGER NEED
TO FEAR THE BITE OF A MAD
DOG.....
HE STUDIED MICROBES.....
LITTLE GERMS THAT CAN ONLY
BE SEEN THROUGH A MICROSCOPE.
HE FOUND THAT THERE WERE
GOOD MICROBES AS WELL AS
HARMFUL ONES, AND THROUGH
HIS STUDIES HE SUCCEEDED IN
PUTTING THE FRENCH BEER TRADE
ON ITS FEET.
PASTEUR DISCOVERED A WAY TO KILL
HARMFUL MICROBES IN MILK.. THIS PROCESS
IS CALLED "PASTEURIZATION" AND IS USED TO-DAY!

..BORN.1822. DIED.1895

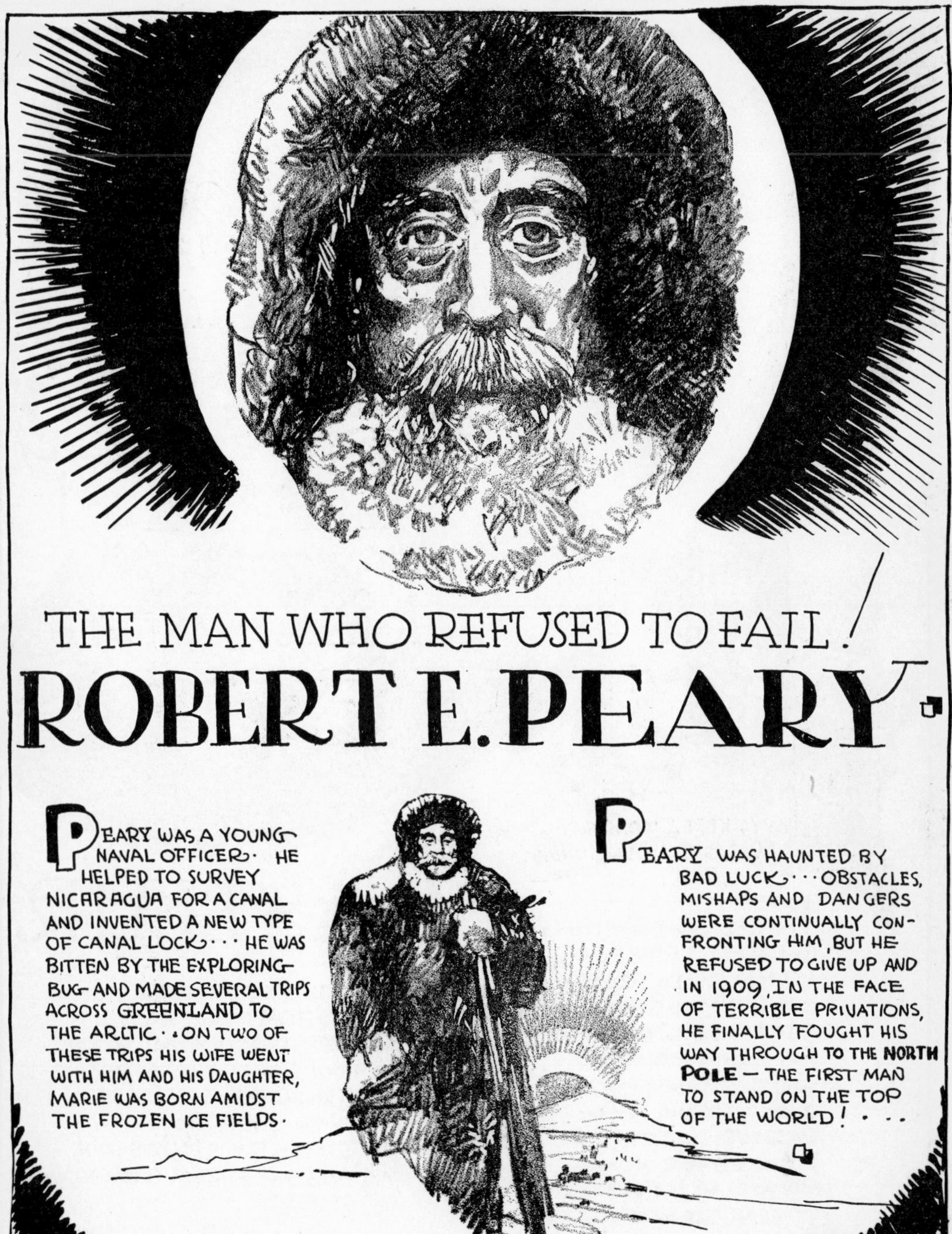
THE MAN WHO REFUSED TO FAIL!
ROBERT E. PEARY
PEARY WAS A YOUNG NAVAL OFFICER. HE HELPED TO SURVEY NICARAGUA FOR A CANAL AND INVENTED A NEW TYPE OF CANAL LOCK... HE WAS BITTEN BY THE EXPLORING BUG AND MADE SEVERAL TRIPS ACROSS GREENLAND TO THE ARCTIC. ON TWO OF THESE TRIPS HIS WIFE WENT WITH HIM AND HIS DAUGHTER, MARIE WAS BORN AMIDST THE FROZEN ICE FIELDS.
PEARY WAS HAUNTED BY BAD LUCK... OBSTACLES, MISHAPS AND DANGERS WERE CONTINUALLY CONFRONTING HIM, BUT HE REFUSED TO GIVE UP AND IN 1909, IN THE FACE OF TERRIBLE PRIVATIONS, HE FINALLY FOUGHT HIS WAY THROUGH TO THE NORTH POLE — THE FIRST MAN TO STAND ON THE TOP OF THE WORLD!...

··BORN—1856—DIED·1920··

A TAILOR'S SON WHO MADE HISTORY LIVE!

SAMUEL PEPYS

PEPYS KEPT A WONDERFUL DIARY, IN A SECRET CODE, IN WHICH HE WROTE DOWN EVERYTHING HE THOUGHT AND DID FROM DAY TO DAY, FOR A PERIOD OF TEN YEARS.. THIS DIARY CONTAINS MARVELOUS DESCRIPTIONS OF ENGLAND OF THAT TIME.. IT TELLS US ABOUT THE GREAT PLAGUE OF LONDON IN WHICH 70,000 PEOPLE DIED.. IT ALSO TELLS US ABOUT PEPYS' PERSONAL LIFE, HIS FRIENDS, HIS QUARRELS WITH HIS WIFE, AND HIS FLIRTATIONS

PEPYS WAS KNOWN AS THE "FATHER OF THE ROYAL NAVY".. HE WAS PRESIDENT OF THE ROYAL SOCIETY, A GROUP OF SCIENTISTS AND WRITERS AND WAS A SHREWD BUSINESS MAN.. NOTHING WAS KNOWN ABOUT HIM TILL ONE HUNDRED YEARS AGO, WHEN A COLLEGE STUDENT DECIPHERED THE DIARY AND PUBLISHED IT . . . . .

... BORN·1633— DIED·1703...

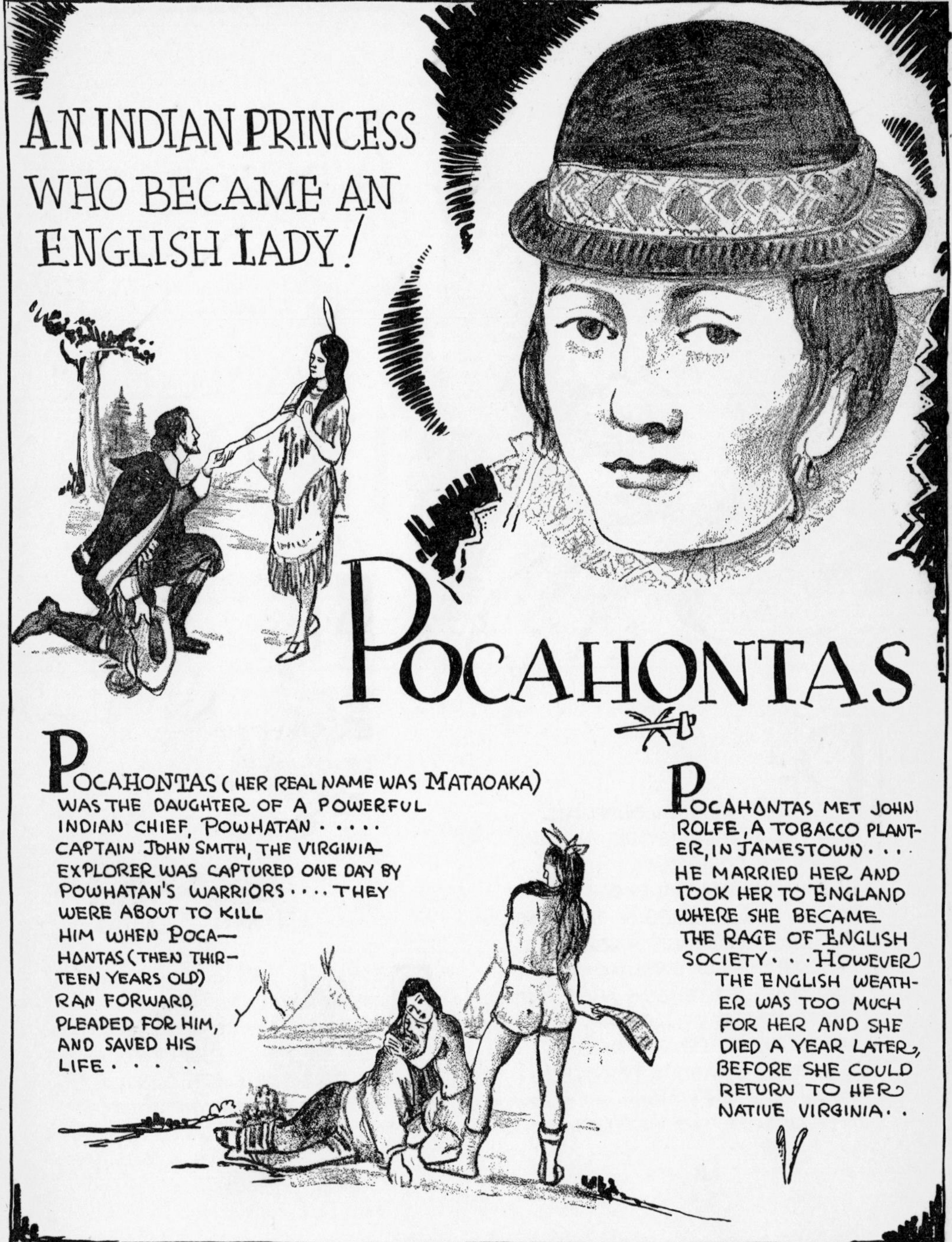
AN INDIAN PRINCESS
WHO BECAME AN
ENGLISH LADY!
POCAHONTAS
POCAHONTAS (HER REAL NAME WAS MATAOAKA) WAS THE DAUGHTER OF A POWERFUL INDIAN CHIEF, POWHATAN . . . . . CAPTAIN JOHN SMITH, THE VIRGINIA EXPLORER WAS CAPTURED ONE DAY BY POWHATAN'S WARRIORS . . . . THEY WERE ABOUT TO KILL HIM WHEN POCAHONTAS (THEN THIRTEEN YEARS OLD) RAN FORWARD, PLEADED FOR HIM, AND SAVED HIS LIFE . . . ..
POCAHONTAS MET JOHN ROLFE, A TOBACCO PLANTER, IN JAMESTOWN . . . . HE MARRIED HER AND TOOK HER TO ENGLAND WHERE SHE BECAME THE RAGE OF ENGLISH SOCIETY . . . HOWEVER THE ENGLISH WEATHER WAS TOO MUCH FOR HER AND SHE DIED A YEAR LATER, BEFORE SHE COULD RETURN TO HER NATIVE VIRGINIA . .

. . . BORN-1594 — DIED-1617 . . .

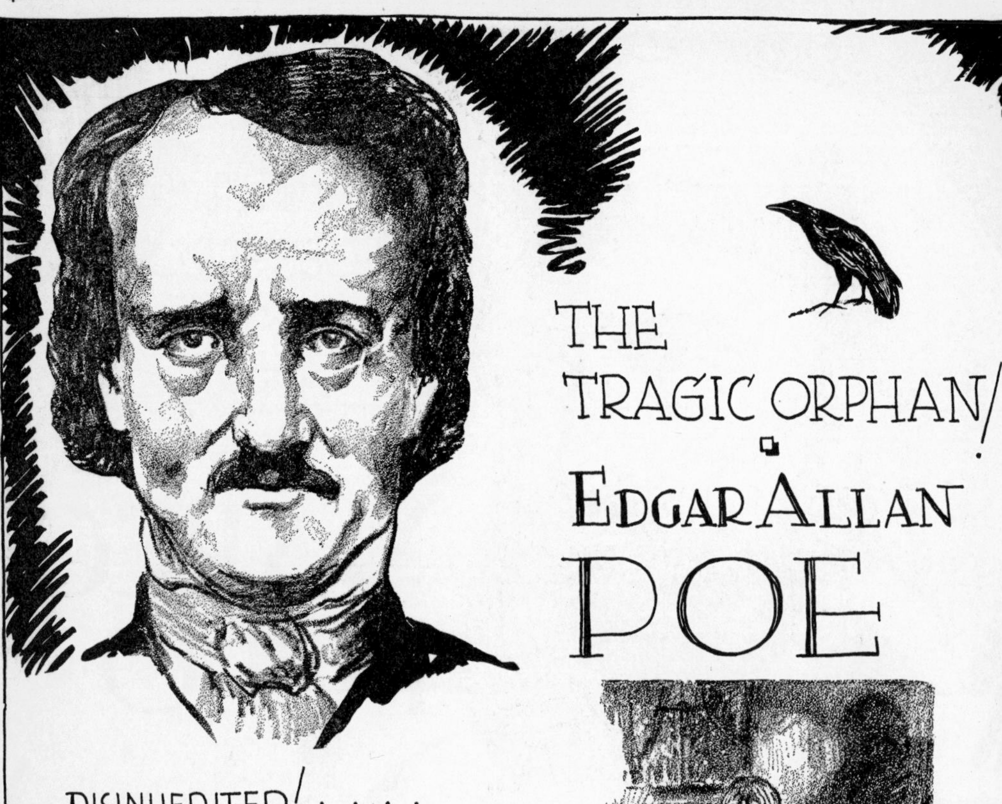

THE TRAGIC ORPHAN! EDGAR ALLAN POE

DISINHERITED! . . . .

BOTH OF POE'S PARENTS DIED WHEN HE WAS TWO YEARS OLD.. A TOBACCO PLANTER BROUGHT HIM UP AND SENT HIM TO COLLEGE. POE WAS A BRILLIANT STUDENT, BUT FELL AN EASY VICTIM TO DRINK AND GAMBLING— LATER HE RAN AWAY AND JOINED THE ARMY.. FOR THIS, HIS GUARDIAN DISINHERITED HIM

POE WROTE SOME OF HIS GREATEST WORKS WHILE HE WAS UNDER THE INFLUENCE OF LIQUOR . . . TWO OF HIS POEMS, "THE BELLS" AND "THE RAVEN" ARE POPULAR THE WORLD OVER . . . .

POE LIVED A LIFE FULL OF MISERY AND SORROW . . . HIS BEAUTIFUL POEMS ARE FILLED WITH SAD HAUNTING MUSIC . . .

POE'S HOBBY WAS SECRET CODES AND HIS THRILLING MYSTERY STORIES ARE UNSURPASSED TO THIS DAY . . . . .

. . BORN . 1809 — DIED . 1849

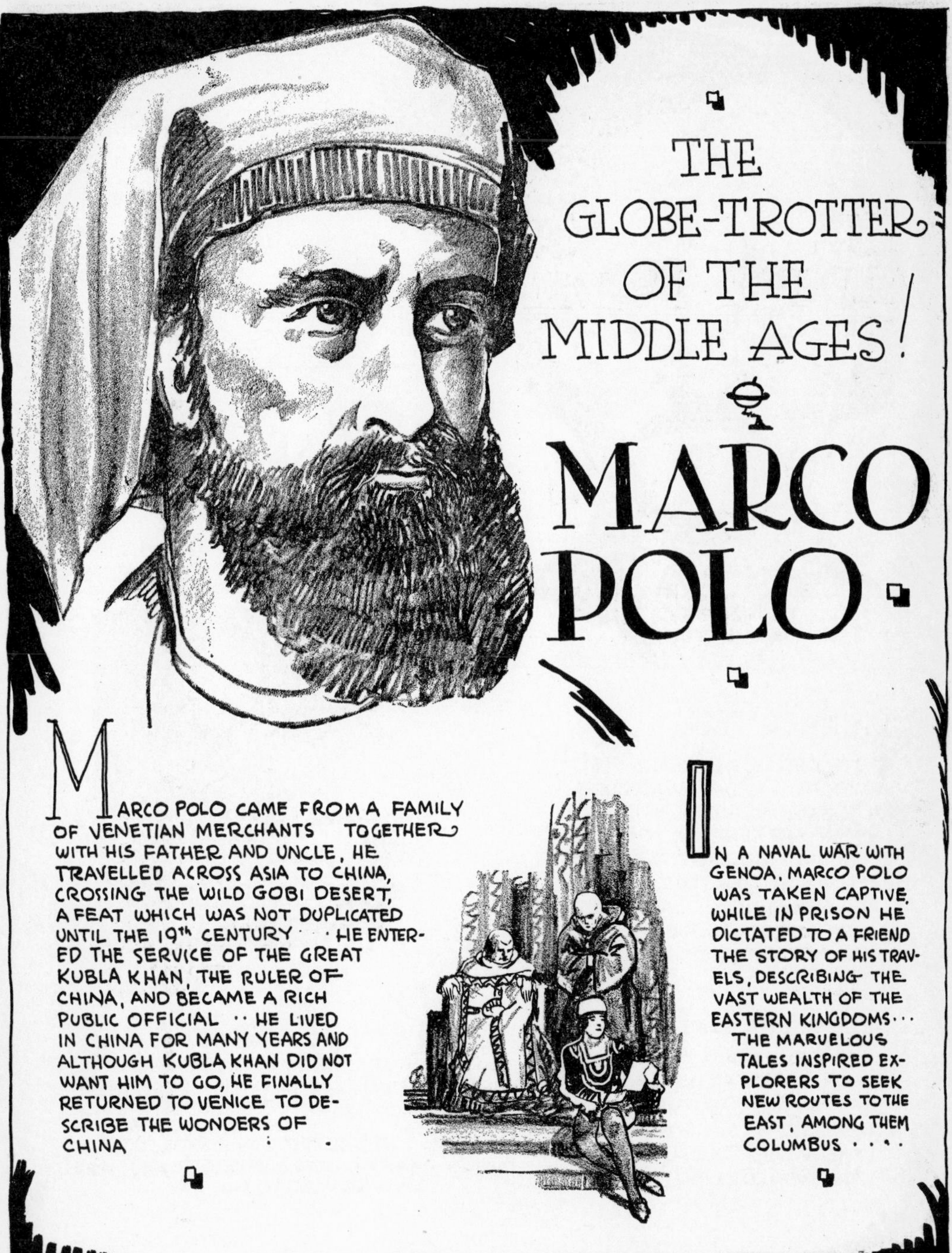
THE GLOBE-TROTTER OF THE MIDDLE AGES!
MARCO POLO
MARCO POLO CAME FROM A FAMILY OF VENETIAN MERCHANTS TOGETHER WITH HIS FATHER AND UNCLE, HE TRAVELLED ACROSS ASIA TO CHINA, CROSSING THE WILD GOBI DESERT, A FEAT WHICH WAS NOT DUPLICATED UNTIL THE 19th CENTURY ··· HE ENTERED THE SERVICE OF THE GREAT KUBLA KHAN, THE RULER OF CHINA, AND BECAME A RICH PUBLIC OFFICIAL ·· HE LIVED IN CHINA FOR MANY YEARS AND ALTHOUGH KUBLA KHAN DID NOT WANT HIM TO GO, HE FINALLY RETURNED TO VENICE TO DESCRIBE THE WONDERS OF CHINA
IN A NAVAL WAR WITH GENOA, MARCO POLO WAS TAKEN CAPTIVE. WHILE IN PRISON HE DICTATED TO A FRIEND THE STORY OF HIS TRAVELS, DESCRIBING THE VAST WEALTH OF THE EASTERN KINGDOMS··· THE MARVELOUS TALES INSPIRED EXPLORERS TO SEEK NEW ROUTES TO THE EAST, AMONG THEM COLUMBUS ····
···BORN-1254?-DIED-1324··

THE QUEEN IN ALL BUT NAME!
MADAME POMPADOUR
JEANNE ANTOINETTE POISSON, MARQUISE de POMPADOUR, WAS OF LOW BIRTH: · HER EDUCATION WAS TAKEN IN HAND BY A WEALTHY FINANCIER, WHO DESTINED HER TO BE THE MISTRESS OF THE FRENCH KING, LOUIS XV. SHE MARRIED THE FINANCIER'S NEPHEW, BUT LEFT HIM AFTER SHE MET LOUIS AT A BALL · · · FALLING COMPLETELY UNDER THE SWAY OF HER BEAUTY, LOUIS ESTABLISHED HER AT VERSAILLES, AND GAVE HER TITLES AND LANDS
MME POMPADOUR IMMEDIATELY TOOK A DECISIVE HOLD ON THE POLITICAL SITUATION IN FRANCE LOUIS WAS LIKE PUTTY IN HER HANDS, AND SHE DIRECTED THE ARMIES, CHANGED RICHELIEU'S POLICY OF WEAKENING AUSTRIA AND ENTERED INTO AN ALLIANCE WHICH LED TO THE DISASTROUS SEVEN YEARS WAR · · · SHE BECAME INDISPENS-ABLE BOTH IN LOUIS' PRIVATE LIFE AND IN AFFAIRS OF STATE, AND FRANCE AS WELL AS LOUIS MOURNED HER DEATH AT THE EARLY AGE OF 42 ·

· · · BORN – 1721 – DIED – 1764 · · ·

THE MASTER OF MOCKERY!

·FRANÇOIS·RABELAIS·

RABELAIS WAS BROUGHT UP, EDUCATED, AND SPENT HALF HIS LIFE IN A MONASTERY··· HE GREW DISGUSTED WITH THE LIFE OF A MONK AND RESOLVED TO BECOME A DOCTOR··· HE WROTE MEDICAL BOOKS, WORKED IN HOSPITALS AT LYONS, AND BECAME FAMOUS AS A LECTURER ON MEDICAL SUBJECTS · · · · ·

RABELAIS WROTE "GARGANTUA AND PANTAGRUEL"-- FIVE HUMOROUS VOLUMES IN WHICH HE RIDICULED AND BURLESQUED THE EXCESSIVE EATING AND DRINKING, THE SCHOOLS, THE POLITICS AND THE RELIGION OF HIS DAY. HE WAS ATTACKED BY THE CLERGY AND SOCIETY ALIKE, BUT HIS POWERFUL FRIENDS PROTECTED HIM FROM HARM. HIS NAME HAS BECOME AN ADJECTIVE FOR BROAD, SATIRICAL WIT · · · · · ·

···BORN-1495?—DIED·1553···

HE GAINED A NEW WORLD, BUT LOST HIS HEAD!
SIR WALTER RALEIGH
AS A LAD, RALEIGH FREQUENTLY WENT DOWN TO THE SEASHORE AND HEARD THE STORIES OF THE OLD SEAMEN ABOUT THE RICHES OF THE NEW WORLD·· THESE STORIES LATER INSPIRED HIM TO MAKE TRIPS TO VIRGINIA AND SOUTH AMERICA AND CREATE BRITISH COLONIES··· BECAUSE ONE OF THESE TRIPS WAS UNSUCCESSFUL, HIS ENEMIES BROUGHT HIM TO TRIAL AND HAD HIM BEHEADED! . . . . .
WHILE WALKING ONE DAY, QUEEN ELIZABETH CAME TO A PUDDLE OF MUD··· RALEIGH WHIPPED OFF HIS RICH PLUSH JACKET AND SPREAD IT FOR THE QUEEN TO STEP ON··· FROM THEN ON HE WAS ONE OF THE QUEEN'S GREATEST FAVORITES··
IT WAS SIR WALTER WHO INTRODUCED TOBACCO TO THE CIVILIZED WORLD··
BESIDES BEING A GREAT ADMIRAL, RALEIGH WAS A POET AND WRITER· WHILE IMPRISONED IN THE TOWER OF LONDON, HE WROTE A "HISTORY OF THE WORLD".

— BORN-1552?—DIED·1618 —

HE GAVE A SOUL TO PAINTING!
RAPHAEL
RAPHAEL WAS A VERY POPULAR AND PROFICIENT ARTIST.. HE IS FAMOUS FOR HIS BEAUTIFUL MADONNAS AND FOR HIS SCENES FROM THE SCRIPTURES, PAINTED ON THE WALLS OF THE VATICAN, IN ROME.. HE CHANGED HIS STYLE OFTEN AND LEARNED MORE ABOUT PAINTING IN A YEAR THAN MOST PAINTERS COULD IN A CENTURY.. "I AM STILL LEARNING", HE USED TO SAY, RIGHT UP TO HIS DEATH, ALTHOUGH ALREADY FAMOUS....
RAPHAEL WAS A HANDSOME AND CHARMING YOUTH.. LEFT AN ORPHAN AT AN EARLY AGE, HE WAS ALWAYS IN THE COMPANY OF DISTINGUISHED SCHOLARS AND ARTISTS. HE REMAINED SINCERELY MODEST AND WAS LIKED BY EVERYONE....

...BORN 1483 — DIED 1520...

A PAINTER WHO PLAYED WITH SHADOWS!
REMBRANDT
THIS GREAT ARTIST WAS A TIRELESS WORKER.. HE MADE MORE THAN 900 MASTERPIECES.. AT 24, HE HAD ALREADY LEFT HIMSELF NO ROOM FOR IMPROVEMENT, AS AN ETCHER
THE MILLER'S SON... WHO MADE PICTURES LIVE! .....
REMBRANDT WAS NOT SATISFIED TO IMITATE OTHER ARTISTS.. HE LIKED TO EXPERIMENT AND MAKE HIS CHARACTERS LOOK LIKE REAL LIVE PEOPLE INSTEAD OF JUST PICTURES.. THE PUBLIC COULD NOT UNDERSTAND HIS GREAT DISCOVERIES AND REFUSED TO BUY HIS PICTURES. HE BECAME VERY POOR, BUT LIKE A TRUE ARTIST, HE CONTINUED TO PAINT IN HIS OWN WAY.
REMBRANDT WAS A SIMPLE MAN AND A VERY ABSENT MINDED ONE. A FRIEND ONCE FOUND HIM CALMLY DRAWING IN THE OPEN, DURING A HEAVY BOMBARDMENT. HE WAS UNAWARE THAT HIS CITY WAS AT WAR .....

.. BORN. 1606—DIED 1669 ..

THE
MIDNIGHT RIDER
WHO ROUSED
A NATION!
PAUL
REVERE
PAUL REVERE WAS A GOLD-AND SILVER-SMITH, A TRADE WHICH HE LEARNED IN HIS FATHER'S SHOP. A FINE COPPER ENGRAVER, HE WAS THE PIONEER OF COPPER MANUFACTURING IN AMERICA.....
AN OFFICER OF THE MILITIA, REVERE WAS A BRAVE PATRIOT AND TOOK PART IN THE BOSTON TEA PARTY... HE INDUCED THE COLONISTS TO SEIZE ENGLISH STORES AND TO CAPTURE FORT WILLIAM AND MARY— ONE OF THE FIRST BATTLES OF THE REVOLUTIONARY WAR!
REVERE WAS A MEMBER OF THE BAND OF 30 PATRIOTS WHO FORMED A PATROL TO WATCH THE MOVEMENTS OF THE BRITISH FORCES.... LONGFELLOW, IN HIS WELL-KNOWN POEM, HAS COMMEMORATED THE FAMOUS RIDE OF PAUL REVERE AT MIDNIGHT ON APRIL 18th 1775, TO ROUSE THE FARMERS AND WARN THEM OF THE APPROACH OF THE BRITISH FORCES

...BORN-1735-DIED-1818...

THE LION HEARTED!
KING RICHARD I
RICHARD WAS A COURAGEOUS SOLDIER AND A FAMOUS CRUSADER... HE SPENT HIS YOUTH WARRING AGAINST HIS FATHER AND HIS OLDER BROTHER, HENRY.. HENRY WAS KILLED IN A BATTLE AND RICHARD BECAME KING OF ENGLAND WHEN HIS FATHER, HENRY II, DIED.......
RICHARD LED HIS KNIGHTS ON A CRUSADE TO THE HOLY LAND... WHILE HE WAS AWAY, HIS BROTHER JOHN CARRIED ON INTRIGUES WITH NORMANDY AND TRIED TO USURP HIS THRONE... READERS OF SCOTT'S "IVANHOE" WILL REMEMBER HOW RICHARD WAS DELAYED BY STORMS AND WARS AND HELD CAPTIVE IN AUSTRIA FOR TWO YEARS... HE FINALLY RETURNED TO ENGLAND AS THE "BLACK PRINCE" AND REGAINED HIS THRONE....

..BORN-1157-DIED-1199..

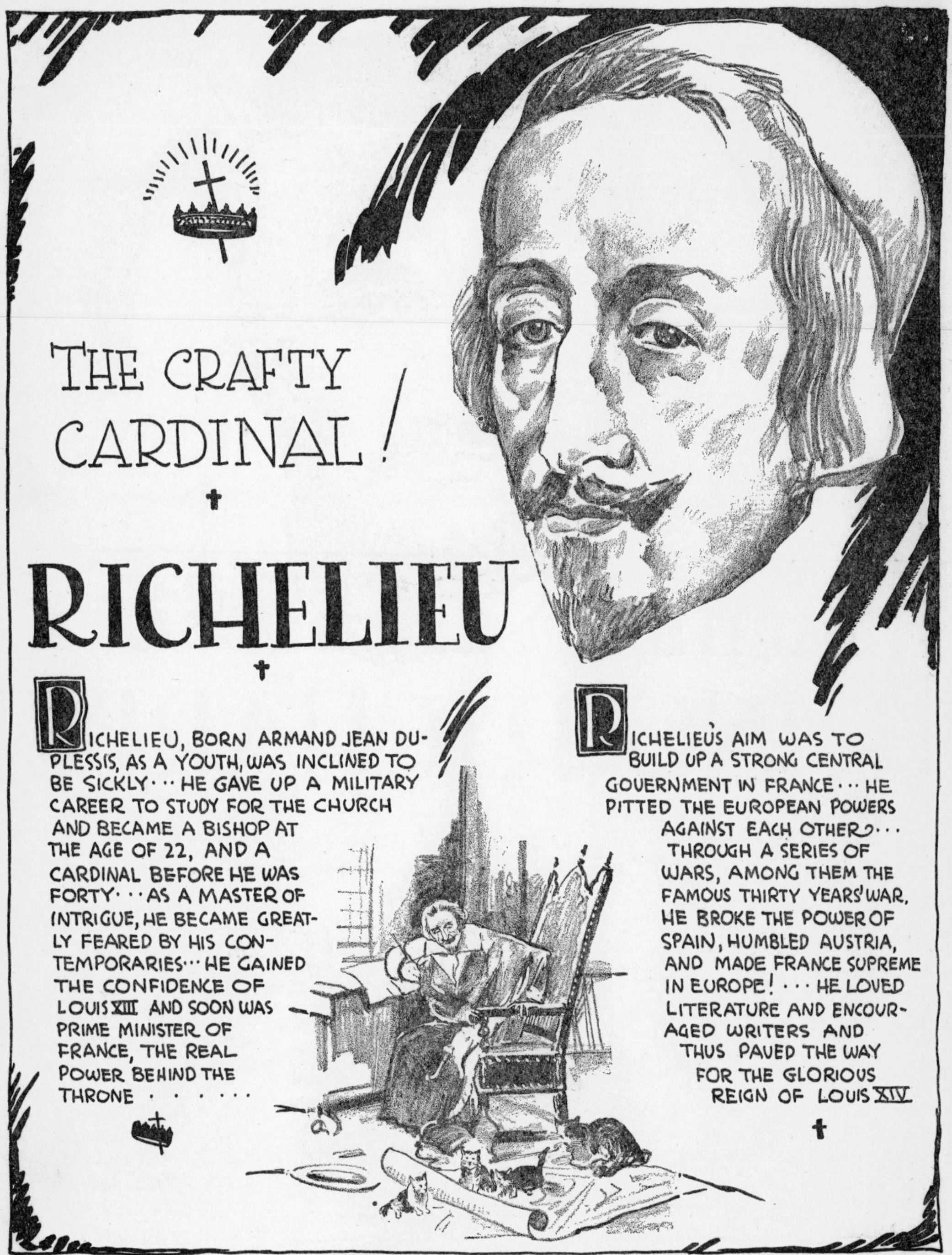
THE CRAFTY CARDINAL!
RICHELIEU
RICHELIEU, BORN ARMAND JEAN DU-PLESSIS, AS A YOUTH, WAS INCLINED TO BE SICKLY ··· HE GAVE UP A MILITARY CAREER TO STUDY FOR THE CHURCH AND BECAME A BISHOP AT THE AGE OF 22, AND A CARDINAL BEFORE HE WAS FORTY ··· AS A MASTER OF INTRIGUE, HE BECAME GREATLY FEARED BY HIS CONTEMPORARIES ··· HE GAINED THE CONFIDENCE OF LOUIS XIII AND SOON WAS PRIME MINISTER OF FRANCE, THE REAL POWER BEHIND THE THRONE · · · · · ·
RICHELIEU'S AIM WAS TO BUILD UP A STRONG CENTRAL GOVERNMENT IN FRANCE ··· HE PITTED THE EUROPEAN POWERS AGAINST EACH OTHER ··· THROUGH A SERIES OF WARS, AMONG THEM THE FAMOUS THIRTY YEARS' WAR, HE BROKE THE POWER OF SPAIN, HUMBLED AUSTRIA, AND MADE FRANCE SUPREME IN EUROPE! ··· HE LOVED LITERATURE AND ENCOURAGED WRITERS AND THUS PAVED THE WAY FOR THE GLORIOUS REIGN OF LOUIS XIV

·· BORN ·· 1585 – DIED ·· 1642 ···

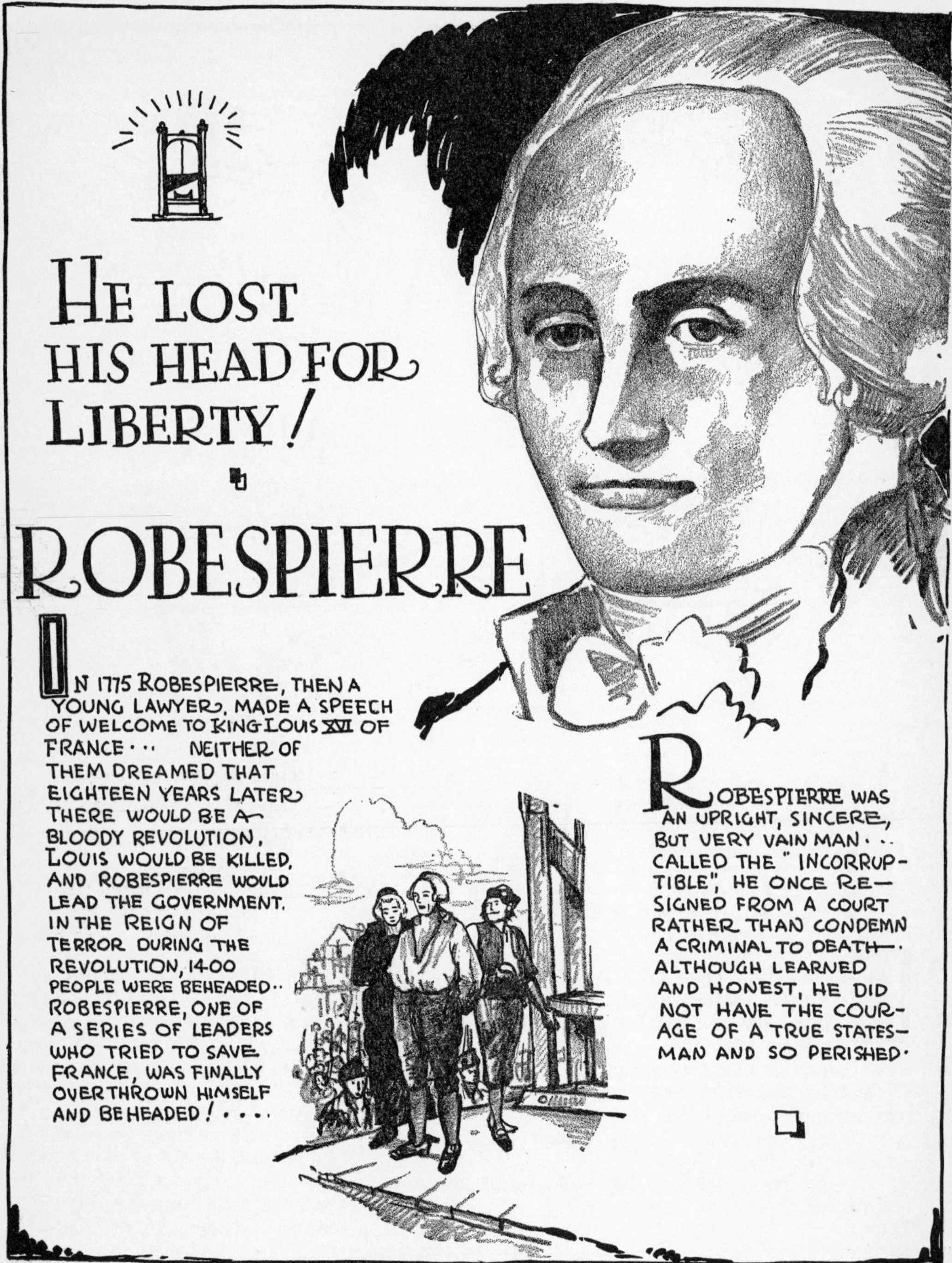
He lost his head for Liberty!
ROBESPIERRE
In 1775 Robespierre, then a young lawyer, made a speech of welcome to King Louis XVI of France... Neither of them dreamed that eighteen years later there would be a bloody revolution, Louis would be killed, and Robespierre would lead the government. In the Reign of Terror during the Revolution, 1400 people were beheaded.. Robespierre, one of a series of leaders who tried to save France, was finally overthrown himself and beheaded!....
Robespierre was an upright, sincere, but very vain man... Called the "Incorruptible", he once resigned from a court rather than condemn a criminal to death. Although learned and honest, he did not have the courage of a true statesman and so perished.

··BORN·1758—DIED·1794·

A MAN AMONG MEN!
THEODORE ROOSEVELT
ROOSEVELT CAME FROM A DUTCH FAMILY THAT HAS LIVED IN AMERICA ALMOST 300 YEARS·· A VERY WEAK BOY HE COULD NOT GO TO SCHOOL, BUT WAS EDUCATED BY TUTORS·· LIVING ON A WESTERN RANCH, WORKING HARD, HE GRADUALLY GREW STRONG·· HE BECAME ASSISTANT SECRETARY OF THE NAVY, BUT WITH THE OUT BREAK OF THE SPANISH-AMERICAN WAR, HE RESIGNED AND WENT TO CUBA TO FIGHT AT THE HEAD OF THE "ROUGH RIDERS" · ·
AT ONE TIME ROOSEVELT WAS POLICE COMMISSIONER OF NEW YORK CITY·
HE EARNED A REPUTATION AS A FEARLESS FIGHTER AGAINST CRIME AND CORRUPTION·· IN ORDER TO SHIFT HIM OUT OF THE WAY, HE WAS ELECTED VICE-PRESIDENT OF THE UNITED STATES·· WITH THE DEATH OF PRESIDENT MCKINLEY, HE CAME TO THE WHITE HOUSE, THE YOUNGEST PRESIDENT IN THE HISTORY OF THE COUNTRY··· ROOSEVELT WAS BLIND IN ONE EYE, THE RESULT OF A BOXING MATCH WITH A YOUNG OFFICER··

·BORN- 1858— DIED 1919··

BETSY ROSS
THE MAKER OF THE STARS AND STRIPES!
BETSY ROSS WAS BORN IN PHILADELPHIA AND KEPT A LITTLE UPHOLSTERY SHOP . . . . SHE WAS THE SISTER-IN-LAW OF GEN. GEORGE ROSS, ONE OF THE SIGNERS OF THE DECLARATION OF INDEPENDENCE . . . .
WASHINGTON, TOGETHER WITH ROBERT MORRIS AND GENERAL ROSS, CALLED AT HER SHOP AND, SHOWING HER A SKETCH, ASKED IF SHE WOULD MAKE THE FLAG . . . THEY HAD SELECTED A SIX POINTED STAR BECAUSE IT WAS EASIER TO MAKE, BUT SHE SHOWED THEM HOW TO MAKE A FIVE-POINTED STAR WITH ONE CLIP OF THE SCISSORS . . . . .
WASHINGTON, THEN AND THERE, CHANGED THE SKETCH AND BETSY ROSS SET TO WORK TO MAKE THIS COUNTRY'S FIRST FLAG . . . .

. . . BORN · 1752 – DIED · 1836 ·

THE MASTER OF SONG!

FRANZ SCHUBERT

ONE OF EIGHTEEN CHILDREN, SCHUBERT EARLY FELT THE PINCH OF POVERTY · · ONLY THROUGH HIS DEVOTED FRIENDS WAS HE KEPT FROM STARVING AND SUPPLIED WITH THE SO NECESSARY MUSIC PAPER · · · IN RETURN, HE PRESENTED TO THE WORLD A TREASURE OF 600 SONGS · · · IN ONE YEAR ALONE, HIS EIGHTEENTH, HE COMPOSED FIVE OPERAS, TWO SYMPHONIES, TWO MASSES, AND 146 SONGS! — FIFTEEN OF THEM WRITTEN IN THE SPACE OF TWO DAYS! · · · THE LOVELY "HARK, HARK, THE LARK," WAS JOTTED ON THE BACK OF A MENU IN A TAVERN, AND THE EQUALLY FAMOUS, "WHO IS SYLVIA"? WAS COMPOSED LATER ON IN THE SAME DAY · · ·

AT 25, SCHUBERT BEGAN THE EXQUISITE "UNFINISHED SYMPHONY", BUT JUST AS HE WAS ENTERING THE MOST PROMISING AND ABUNDANT PERIOD OF HIS LIFE, HE DIED AT THE TRAGIC AGE OF 31 · · · HIS EPITAPH READS "MUSIC BURIED HERE A RICH POSSESSION AND YET FAIRER HOPES".

· · · BORN-1797-DIED-1828 · · ·

SCOTLAND'S MINSTREL!
SIR WALTER SCOTT
A WRITER ON HORSEBACK! . . . .
SCOTT WAS A SHERIFF AND TRAVELLED
OVER THE COUNTRY-SIDE ON A HORSE . . .
HE LEARNED TO KNOW SCOTLAND AND ITS
PEOPLE AND WROTE ABOUT THEM IN THE
FAMOUS WAVERLY NOVELS . . . .
THIS GREAT WRITER LOVED LIFE
AND FREEDOM . . . AS A YOUNGSTER HE
ONCE REFUSED TO LIVE IN A HOUSE BE-
CAUSE IT WAS "HEMMED IN BY DITCHES AND
HEDGES, NOT TO MENTION DUKES AND
DOWAGERS" . . . TO BE INTELLIGENT OR
TO BE POOR WAS TO BE HIS FRIEND . . . .
SCOTT WAS A VERY GENEROUS MAN.
HE LENT ALL HIS MONEY TO A FIRM
OF PUBLISHERS WHO LATER BECAME
BANKRUPT . . HE SHOULDERED HIS
DEBTS AND WORKED HIMSELF TO DEATH
TO PAY HIS CREDITORS . . . HE DID NOT
THINK LIFE AND HEALTH TOO GREAT
A PRICE TO PAY FOR SELF-RESPECT . . .

· · BORN 1771 — DIED 1832 · ·

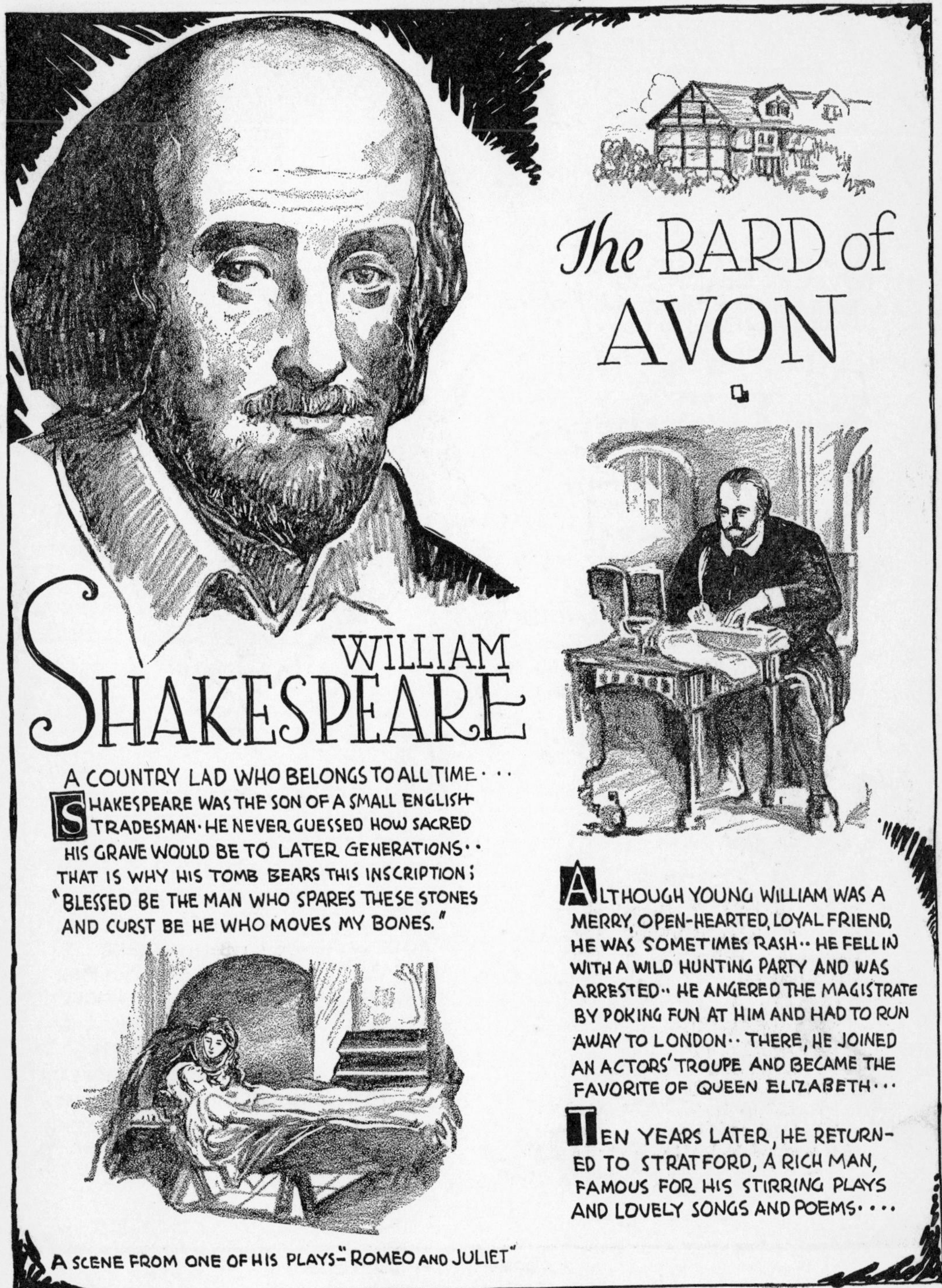
The BARD of AVON
WILLIAM SHAKESPEARE
A COUNTRY LAD WHO BELONGS TO ALL TIME · · ·
SHAKESPEARE WAS THE SON OF A SMALL ENGLISH TRADESMAN· HE NEVER GUESSED HOW SACRED HIS GRAVE WOULD BE TO LATER GENERATIONS · · THAT IS WHY HIS TOMB BEARS THIS INSCRIPTION;
"BLESSED BE THE MAN WHO SPARES THESE STONES AND CURST BE HE WHO MOVES MY BONES."
ALTHOUGH YOUNG WILLIAM WAS A MERRY, OPEN-HEARTED, LOYAL FRIEND, HE WAS SOMETIMES RASH·· HE FELL IN WITH A WILD HUNTING PARTY AND WAS ARRESTED·· HE ANGERED THE MAGISTRATE BY POKING FUN AT HIM AND HAD TO RUN AWAY TO LONDON·· THERE, HE JOINED AN ACTORS' TROUPE AND BECAME THE FAVORITE OF QUEEN ELIZABETH · · ·
TEN YEARS LATER, HE RETURNED TO STRATFORD, A RICH MAN, FAMOUS FOR HIS STIRRING PLAYS AND LOVELY SONGS AND POEMS · · · ·
A SCENE FROM ONE OF HIS PLAYS-"ROMEO AND JULIET"

· · BORN 1564 — DIED 1616 · ·

"THE REBELLIOUS ANGEL!"
PERCY BYSSHE SHELLEY
SHELLEY CAME FROM A WEALTHY, OLD FAMILY.. ALTHOUGH HE WAS A SHY, SENSITIVE, GENEROUS AND VERY HANDSOME YOUNG MAN, HE WAS HEADSTRONG AND HAD A VIOLENT TEMPER... HE HAD HIS OWN NOTIONS OF JUSTICE AND FREEDOM, AND PRACTISED THEM... HE WAS EXPELLED FROM OXFORD FOR WRITING A BOOK ON ATHEISM.....
CUT OFF BY HIS FATHER, SHELLEY RAN AWAY TO SCOTLAND AND MARRIED A YOUNG FRIEND OF HIS SISTER'S.. THEY LIVED HAPPILY UNTIL HE FELL IN LOVE WITH MARY GODWIN AND ELOPED WITH HER...TWO YEARS LATER, HIS FIRST WIFE COMMITTED SUICIDE!....
SHELLEY AND MARY WENT TO LIVE IN ITALY AND IT WAS THERE THAT HE WROTE HIS MOST BEAUTIFUL POEMS, FILLING THEM WITH AN IDEALISM AND MUSIC THAT MAKES HIM ONE OF THE GREATEST POETS WHO EVER LIVED....
SHELLEY LOVED BOATING—.... WHILE HE WAS SAILING ONE DAY IN LEGHORN HARBOR, (ITALY) WITH TWO OF HIS FRIENDS, A STORM CAME UP AND THE THREE WERE DROWNED— SHELLEY BEING ONLY 30 YEARS OLD... HIS BODY WAS RECOVERED, SEVERAL DAYS LATER, AND WAS BURNT ON THE BEACH, AS WAS THE CUSTOM WITH THE ANCIENT GREEKS........
..BORN-1792—DIED-1822.

"LITTLE PHIL"
SHERIDAN WAS BORN IN ALBANY, N.Y. OF AN IRISH FAMILY, BUT WAS BROUGHT UP IN OHIO ... WHEN HE WAS TEN YEARS OLD, "LITTLE PHIL" COULD LICK EVERY BOY HIS SIZE AND WEIGHT IN THE VILLAGE WHERE HE LIVED ... WITH THE HELP OF HIS DOG HE ONCE CORNERED HIS SCHOOLMASTER AND DROVE HIM UP A TREE ....
SHERIDAN ENTERED WEST POINT, AND AFTER BEING GRADUATED BECAME ENGAGED IN THE INDIAN WARFARE ALONG THE TEXAS BORDER ... AT THE OUTBREAK OF THE CIVIL WAR HE WAS A LIEUTENANT BUT ROSE RAPIDLY TO THE CHIEF COMMAND OF THE UNITED STATES CAVALRY ....
GEN. PHILIP SHERIDAN
DURING THE CIVIL WAR, SHERIDAN WAS CALLED AWAY TO WASHINGTON.. COMING BACK, HE WAS TWENTY MILES AWAY FROM HIS ARMY, WHEN A TERRIBLE ATTACK FELL ON IT .... SHERIDAN HEARD THE GUNS AND GALLOPED TOWARD WINCHESTER ... ARRIVING ON HIS FOAM-FLECKED HORSE, HE RALLIED HIS SOLDIERS, CHARGED THE ENEMY AND DEFEATED THEM ......

·· BORN - 1831 — DIED ·· 1888 ··

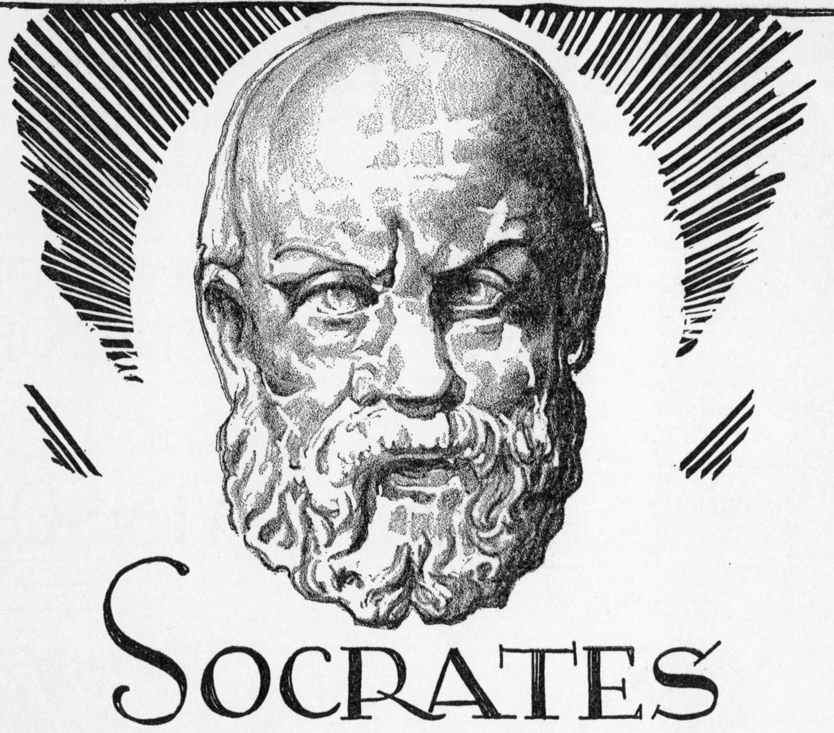

SOCRATES

...THE STONE-MASON WHO DIED FOR HIS IDEALS.

SOCRATES WAS A LABOURER AND A SOLDIER.. HE WAS A VERY UGLY OLD MAN BUT SINCERE AND WITTY, AND HE WON MANY FRIENDS AND FOLLOWERS.. HE LIKED TO WANDER THROUGH THE STREETS OF ATHENS QUESTIONING PEOPLE AND STIMULATING THEIR THOUGHTS....

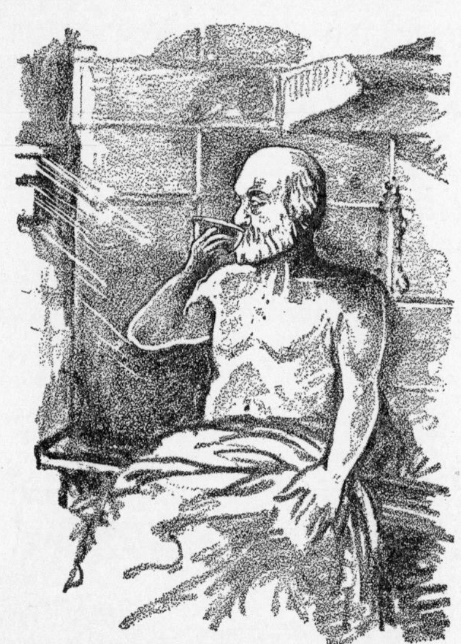

SOCRATES TAUGHT THAT THE MOST IMPORTANT KIND OF KNOWLEDGE WAS FOR A MAN TO KNOW HIMSELF.. THE ATHENIANS DID NOT LIKE HIS INFLUENCE ON THE YOUNG MEN AND THEY CONDEMNED HIM TO POISON HIMSELF BY DRINKING HEMLOCK.. WHILE HE WAS DYING, HE TALKED CHEERFULLY TO HIS FRIENDS, HAVING NO FEAR OF DEATH.

..BORN.B.C.470 — DIED.B.C.400?..

THE POET OF CHILDHOOD!
ROBERT LOUIS STEVENSON
BURIED ON A SOUTH SEA ISLAND!
STEVENSON WAS A SICKLY MAN AND LIVED FOR A TIME IN A CABIN IN THE ADIRONDACK MOUNTAINS IN NEW YORK STATE...
LATER, HE BUILT HIMSELF A HUT ON AN ISLAND IN THE PACIFIC OCEAN....
DESPITE HIS BAD HEALTH HE WAS A GENTLE AND KIND MAN AND THE NATIVES OF THE ISLAND LOVED AND RESPECTED HIM.. THEY MADE HIM A CHIEF AND WHEN HE DIED THEY BURIED HIM ON TOP OF A MOUNTAIN OVERLOOKING THE PACIFIC......
STEVENSON WROTE MANY ESSAYS AND ROMANTIC STORIES, AMONG THEM "TREASURE ISLAND".. EVERY SCHOOL BOY AND SCHOOL GIRL KNOWS HIS BEAUTIFUL CHILDRENS' POEMS.....

..BORN.1850.—DIED 1894..

1664
"OLD PEG LEG"
PETER STUYVESANT
AS GOVERNOR OF NEW AMSTERDAM (THE DUTCH NAME FOR NEW YORK), HE SUPPRESSED THE INDIAN UPRISINGS AND BROUGHT ORDER TO THE CITY . . . HIS STERN METHODS AROUSED OP-POSITION AND SO, WHEN THE ENGLISH SAILED INTO THE HARBOR IN 1664, HE WAS UNABLE TO RESIST THEM . . . THE ENGLISH CHANGED THE NAME OF THE CITY TO NEW YORK . . . . .
DISGRACED IN HOLLAND AS A RESULT OF HIS DEFEAT, STUYVESANT RETURNED TO NEW YORK AND LIVED ON HIS FARM, BOUWERIE, (FROM WHICH THE BOWERY OF TO-DAY TAKES ITS NAME) . . . . HE LIES BURIED IN ST. MARK'S CHURCH IN NEW YORK . . .
STUYVESANT WAS BORN IN HOLLAND AND BECAME A SOLDIER IN THE WEST INDIA COMPANY . . . HAVING LOST HIS LEG WHILE FIGHTING FOR THE DUTCH COLONIES, HE WORE A WOODEN PEG, BOUND WITH SILVER BANDS . . . .

. . . . BORN - 1592 - DIED - 1672 . . . .

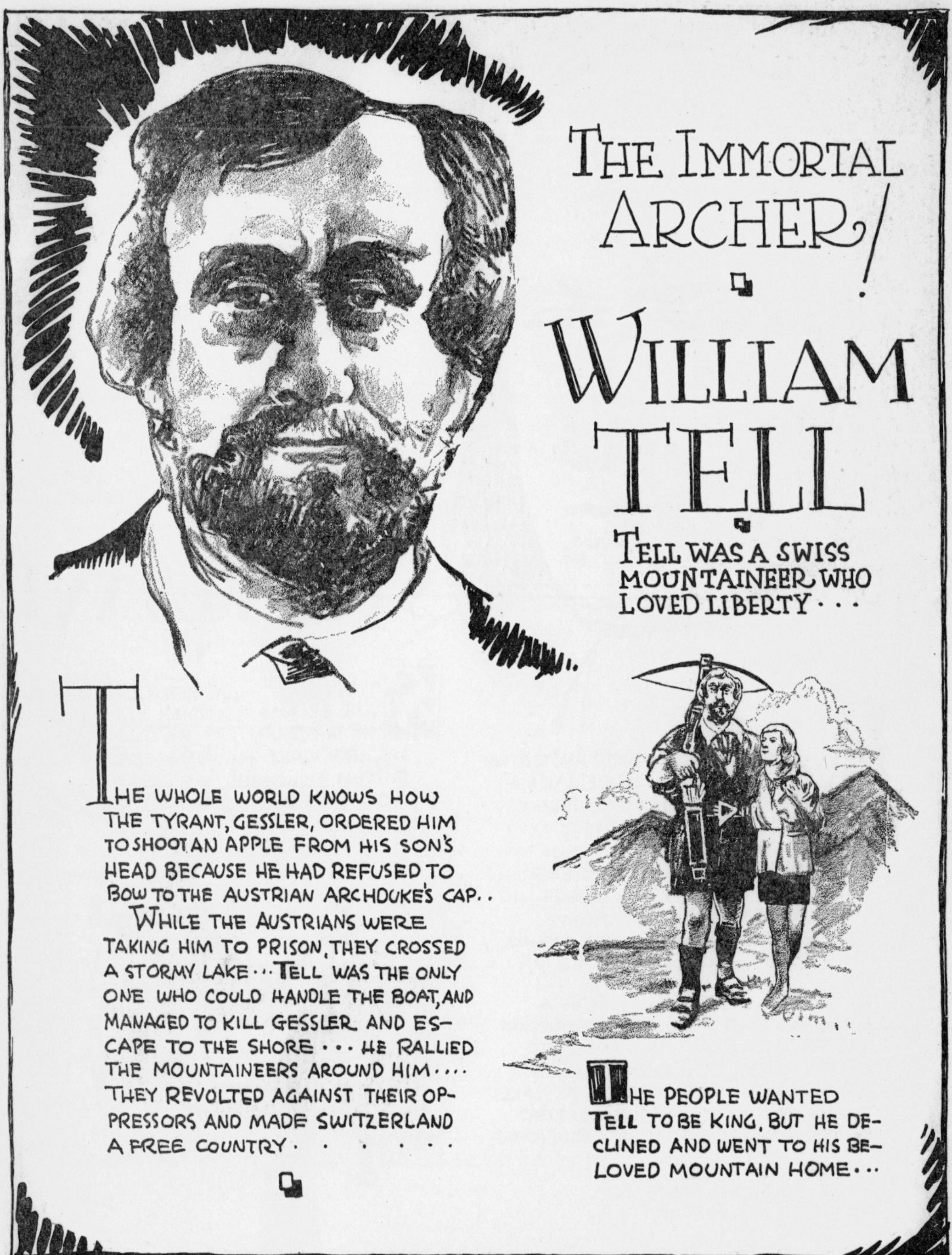
THE IMMORTAL ARCHER!
WILLIAM TELL
TELL WAS A SWISS MOUNTAINEER WHO LOVED LIBERTY . . .
THE WHOLE WORLD KNOWS HOW THE TYRANT, GESSLER, ORDERED HIM TO SHOOT AN APPLE FROM HIS SON'S HEAD BECAUSE HE HAD REFUSED TO BOW TO THE AUSTRIAN ARCHDUKE'S CAP. .
WHILE THE AUSTRIANS WERE TAKING HIM TO PRISON, THEY CROSSED A STORMY LAKE . . . TELL WAS THE ONLY ONE WHO COULD HANDLE THE BOAT, AND MANAGED TO KILL GESSLER AND ESCAPE TO THE SHORE . . . HE RALLIED THE MOUNTAINEERS AROUND HIM . . . . THEY REVOLTED AGAINST THEIR OPPRESSORS AND MADE SWITZERLAND A FREE COUNTRY . . . . . .
THE PEOPLE WANTED TELL TO BE KING, BUT HE DECLINED AND WENT TO HIS BELOVED MOUNTAIN HOME . . .

· BORN ABOUT 1270 · · DIED ABOUT 1340

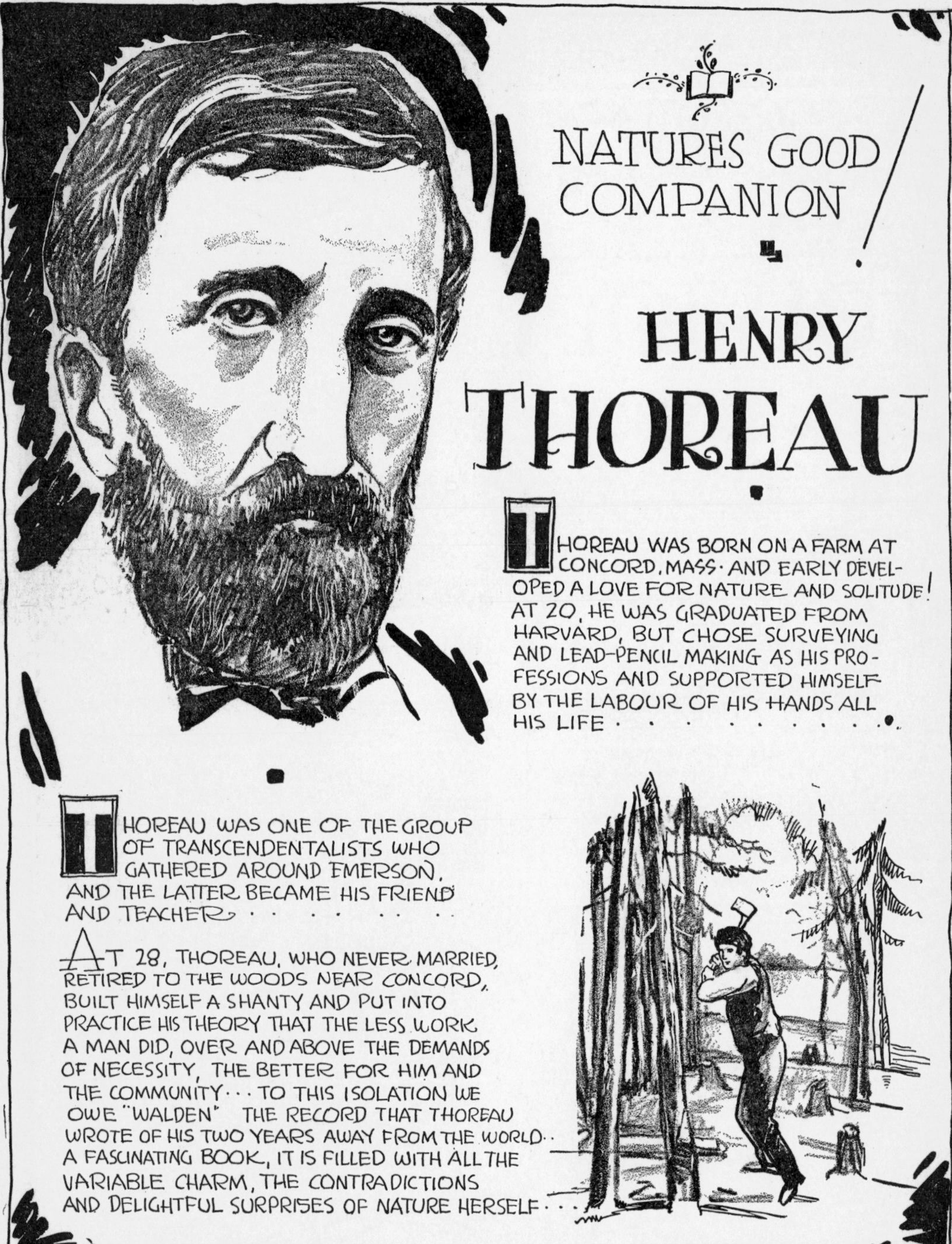
NATURES GOOD COMPANION!
HENRY
THOREAU
THOREAU WAS BORN ON A FARM AT CONCORD, MASS. AND EARLY DEVELOPED A LOVE FOR NATURE AND SOLITUDE! AT 20, HE WAS GRADUATED FROM HARVARD, BUT CHOSE SURVEYING AND LEAD-PENCIL MAKING AS HIS PROFESSIONS AND SUPPORTED HIMSELF BY THE LABOUR OF HIS HANDS ALL HIS LIFE . . . .
THOREAU WAS ONE OF THE GROUP OF TRANSCENDENTALISTS WHO GATHERED AROUND EMERSON, AND THE LATTER BECAME HIS FRIEND AND TEACHER . . . .
AT 28, THOREAU, WHO NEVER MARRIED, RETIRED TO THE WOODS NEAR CONCORD, BUILT HIMSELF A SHANTY AND PUT INTO PRACTICE HIS THEORY THAT THE LESS WORK A MAN DID, OVER AND ABOVE THE DEMANDS OF NECESSITY, THE BETTER FOR HIM AND THE COMMUNITY . . . TO THIS ISOLATION WE OWE "WALDEN" THE RECORD THAT THOREAU WROTE OF HIS TWO YEARS AWAY FROM THE WORLD . . A FASCINATING BOOK, IT IS FILLED WITH ALL THE VARIABLE CHARM, THE CONTRADICTIONS AND DELIGHTFUL SURPRISES OF NATURE HERSELF . . .

. . . BORN - 1817 - DIED - 1862 . . :

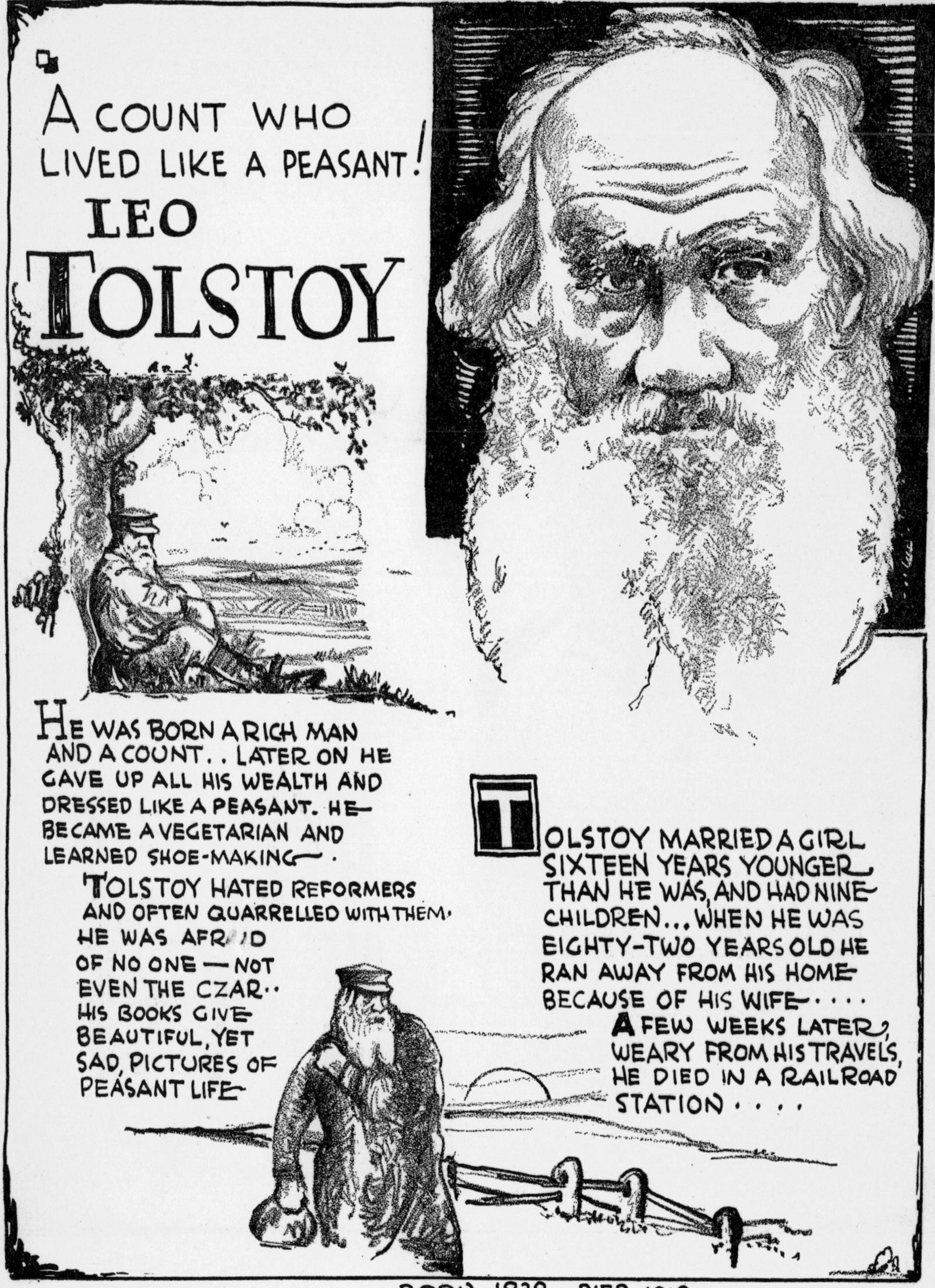
A COUNT WHO
LIVED LIKE A PEASANT!
LEO
TOLSTOY
HE WAS BORN A RICH MAN AND A COUNT . . LATER ON HE GAVE UP ALL HIS WEALTH AND DRESSED LIKE A PEASANT. HE BECAME A VEGETARIAN AND LEARNED SHOE-MAKING—.
TOLSTOY HATED REFORMERS AND OFTEN QUARRELLED WITH THEM. HE WAS AFRAID OF NO ONE — NOT EVEN THE CZAR.. HIS BOOKS GIVE BEAUTIFUL, YET SAD, PICTURES OF PEASANT LIFE
TOLSTOY MARRIED A GIRL SIXTEEN YEARS YOUNGER THAN HE WAS, AND HAD NINE CHILDREN... WHEN HE WAS EIGHTY-TWO YEARS OLD HE RAN AWAY FROM HIS HOME BECAUSE OF HIS WIFE....
A FEW WEEKS LATER, WEARY FROM HIS TRAVELS, HE DIED IN A RAILROAD STATION....

··BORN· 1828 — DIED· 1910··

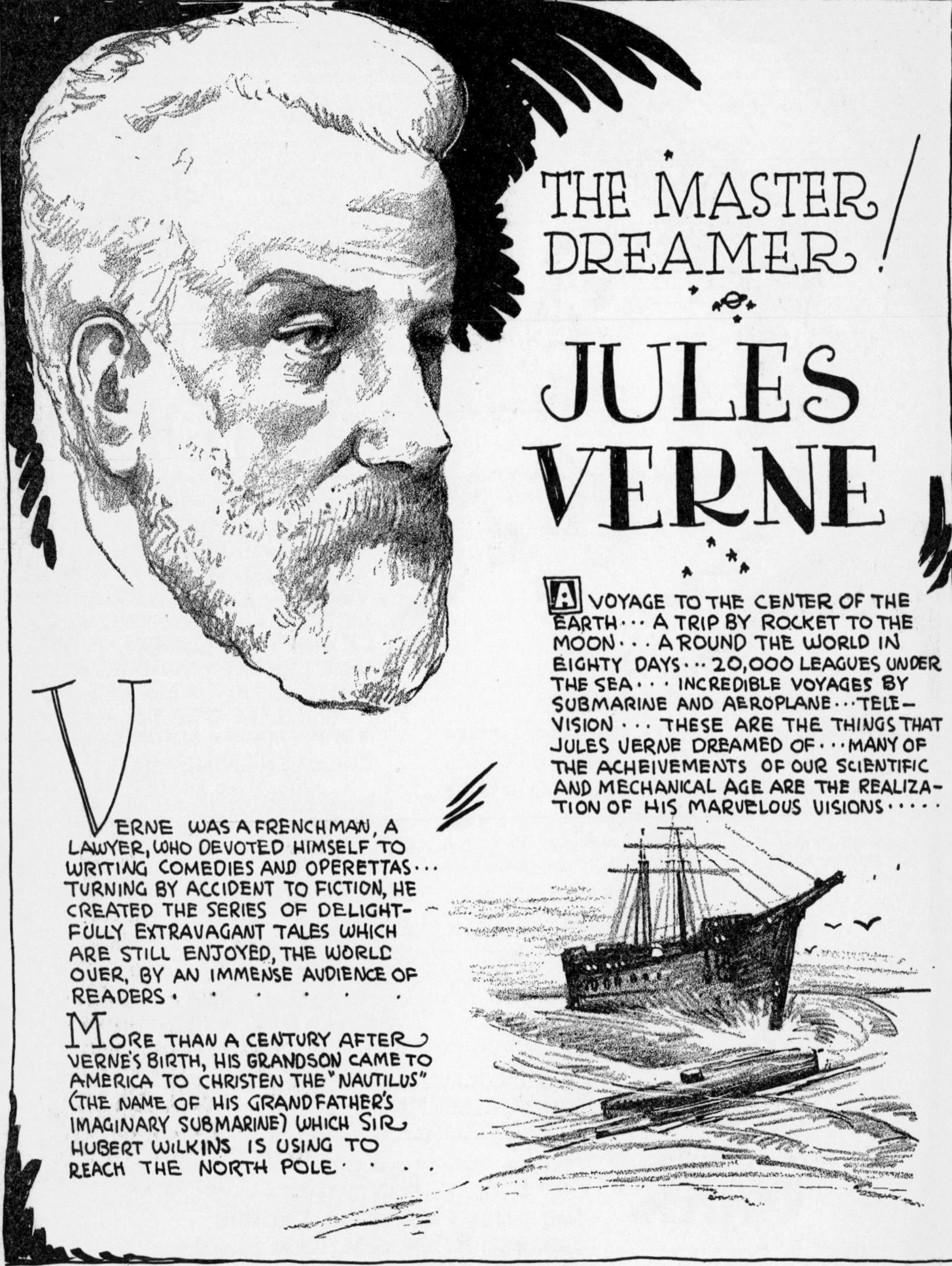
THE MASTER DREAMER!
JULES VERNE
A VOYAGE TO THE CENTER OF THE EARTH... A TRIP BY ROCKET TO THE MOON... AROUND THE WORLD IN EIGHTY DAYS... 20,000 LEAGUES UNDER THE SEA... INCREDIBLE VOYAGES BY SUBMARINE AND AEROPLANE... TELE-VISION... THESE ARE THE THINGS THAT JULES VERNE DREAMED OF... MANY OF THE ACHEIVEMENTS OF OUR SCIENTIFIC AND MECHANICAL AGE ARE THE REALIZATION OF HIS MARVELOUS VISIONS.....
VERNE WAS A FRENCHMAN, A LAWYER, WHO DEVOTED HIMSELF TO WRITING COMEDIES AND OPERETTAS... TURNING BY ACCIDENT TO FICTION, HE CREATED THE SERIES OF DELIGHTFULLY EXTRAVAGANT TALES WHICH ARE STILL ENJOYED, THE WORLD OVER, BY AN IMMENSE AUDIENCE OF READERS.......
MORE THAN A CENTURY AFTER VERNE'S BIRTH, HIS GRANDSON CAME TO AMERICA TO CHRISTEN THE "NAUTILUS" (THE NAME OF HIS GRANDFATHER'S IMAGINARY SUBMARINE) WHICH SIR HUBERT WILKINS IS USING TO REACH THE NORTH POLE...

....BORN-1828—DIED-1905....

The QUEEN of a CENTURY!
VICTORIA
SHE ASCENDED THE THRONE WHEN SHE WAS SEVENTEEN, AND RULED FOR SIXTY-FOUR YEARS.... SHE WAS TRULY THE MOTHER AND GRANDMOTHER OF KINGS AND QUEENS ... HER NINE CHILDREN MARRIED ALL THE LEADING RULERS OF EUROPE.
WHEN SHE DIED SHE HAD THIRTY-SEVEN GREAT-GRAND-CHILDREN LIVING—
VICTORIA LOVED TO SAVE LITTLE MEMENTOS OF HER LIFE -- DRESSES, FURS, DOLLS SILVER, CHINA, CURTAINS, CARPETS, PICTURES ETC.....
SHE HAD EVERYTHING CAREFULLY PHOTOGRAPHED AND PUT AWAY...
IT FORMED A TREMENDOUS COLLECTION, WORTH MILLIONS
VICTORIA MARRIED PRINCE ALBERT OF SAXE-COBURG—
IT WAS THROUGH HIS UNTIRING EFFORTS THAT THE GREAT CRYSTAL PALACE EXHIBITION OF 1851, TOOK PLACE—.

··BORN·1819—DIED 1901··

THE VAGABOND POET!
FRANÇOIS VILLON
VILLON, BORN FRANÇOIS DE MONTCORBIER, CAME OF POVERTY STRICKEN PARIS PEOPLE .. LIVING IN LAWLESS TIMES, HE WAS HIMSELF A BULLY AND OUTLAW.. HE MIXED INTO STREET SCUFFLES AND WAS ONE OF A BAND OF THIEVES THAT ROBBED A CHAPEL .. AS OFTEN AS NOT HE WAS BADLY BEATEN UP .. SOMETIMES, AS WAS THE CASE IN A SCRAP WITH A PRIEST OVER A GIRL, HIS DAGGER SAVED HIM .... THIS LONG SERIES OF RASCALLY ESCAPADES LED TO HIS BANISHMENT FROM PARIS AND HE FLED TO THE COUNTRY ....
FOR FOUR YEARS, VILLON WANDERED OVER FRANCE, HIS EXISTENCE REGULARLY PUNCTUATED BY PERIODS IN PRISON.. FINALLY, TORTURED AND CONDEMNED TO HANG LIKE SO MANY OF HIS FRIENDS, HE DISAPPEARED, PROBABLY DYING A VIOLENT DEATH ...
YET, VILLON'S KEEN INTELLECT, HIS POLISHED AND REALISTIC VERSES, MADE HIM THE IDOL OF THE PARIS OF HIS DAY AND MEDIEVAL PARIS HAS BEEN PERPETUATED IN HIS POETRY

·· BORN–1431–DIED–1463? ·

The PAINTER·· WHO WANTED TO FLY!
LEONARDO da VINCI ··
A PAINTER ······ WHO WAS ALSO AN ENGINEER··· A MUSICIAN····AN ARCHITECT·· A WRITER ·····A SCULPTOR! ·······
HIS MOST FAMOUS PAINTING IS THE "MONA LISA"· IT IS NOW HANGING IN THE LOUVRE, A MUSEUM IN PARIS, AND IS THE MOST VALUABLE SINGLE PAINTING IN THE WORLD ····
HE SPENT MORE TIME PLANNING BRIDGES AND CANALS THAN HE DID PAINTING. HE WAS EVEN INTERESTED IN AVIATION.... FOUR HUNDRED YEARS AGO HE TRIED TO BUILD A MACHINE THAT WOULD FLY·····
LEONARDO'S FAVORITE HABIT WAS TO WRITE THINGS DOWN BACKWARDS SO THAT THEY COULD ONLY BE READ BY HOLDING THEM UP TO A MIRROR.

·· BORN·1452 - DIED·1519 ··

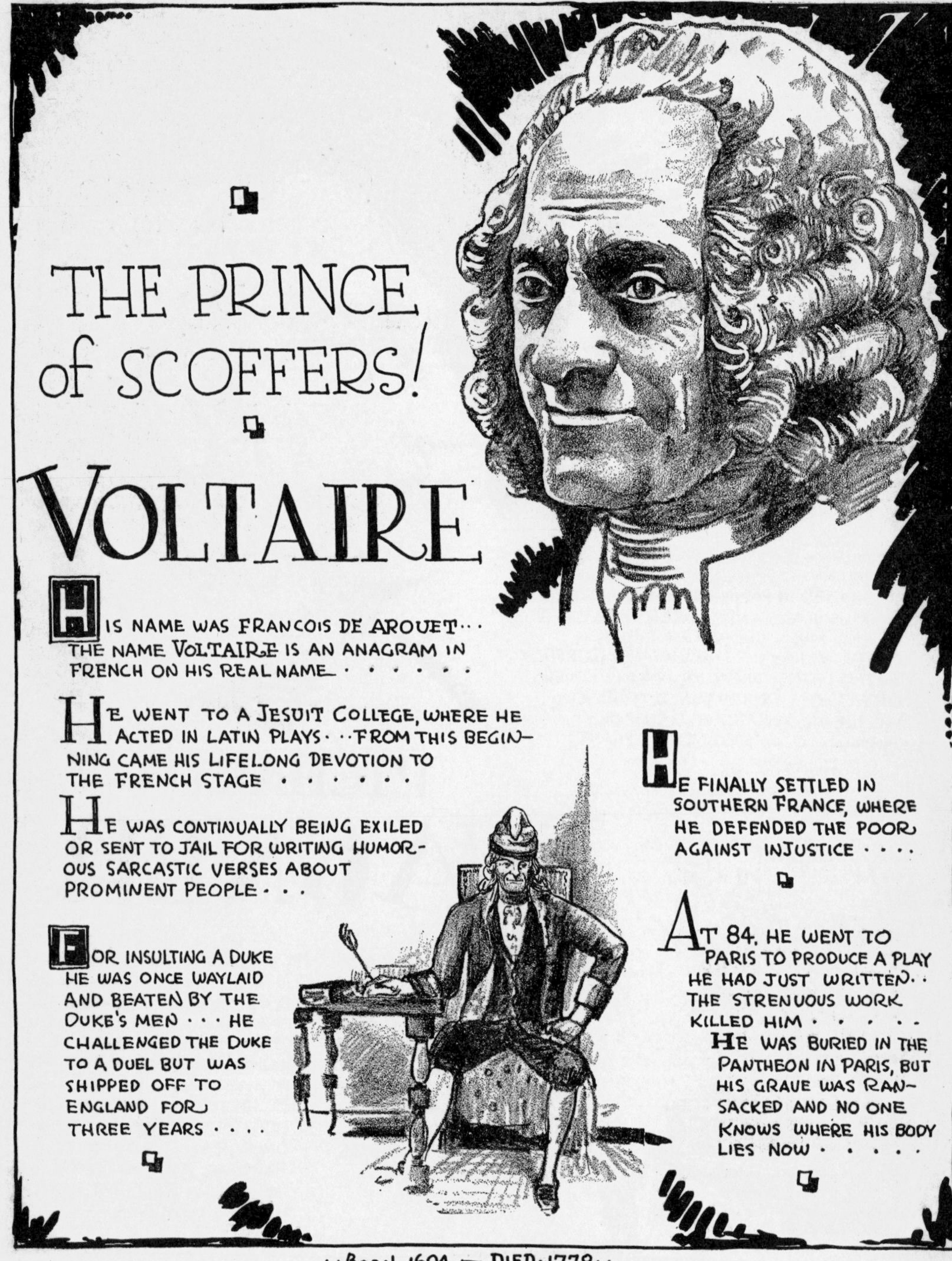
THE PRINCE of SCOFFERS!
VOLTAIRE
HIS NAME WAS FRANCOIS DE AROUET... THE NAME VOLTAIRE IS AN ANAGRAM IN FRENCH ON HIS REAL NAME......
HE WENT TO A JESUIT COLLEGE, WHERE HE ACTED IN LATIN PLAYS...FROM THIS BEGINNING CAME HIS LIFELONG DEVOTION TO THE FRENCH STAGE......
HE WAS CONTINUALLY BEING EXILED OR SENT TO JAIL FOR WRITING HUMOROUS SARCASTIC VERSES ABOUT PROMINENT PEOPLE...
FOR INSULTING A DUKE HE WAS ONCE WAYLAID AND BEATEN BY THE DUKE'S MEN... HE CHALLENGED THE DUKE TO A DUEL BUT WAS SHIPPED OFF TO ENGLAND FOR THREE YEARS....
HE FINALLY SETTLED IN SOUTHERN FRANCE, WHERE HE DEFENDED THE POOR AGAINST INJUSTICE....
AT 84, HE WENT TO PARIS TO PRODUCE A PLAY HE HAD JUST WRITTEN.. THE STRENUOUS WORK KILLED HIM.....
HE WAS BURIED IN THE PANTHEON IN PARIS, BUT HIS GRAVE WAS RANSACKED AND NO ONE KNOWS WHERE HIS BODY LIES NOW.....

··BORN 1694 — DIED·1778··

"DER MEISTERSINGER!"
WAGNER'S LIFE WAS FILLED WITH BITTER EXPERIENCES .. HIS FATHER DIED IN AN EPIDEMIC, HE WAS CONSTANTLY IN DEBT, HE WAS EXILED FROM GERMANY, HIS GREAT OPERA, "TANNHAUSER", WAS HISSED IN PARIS, HE WAS ATTACKED BY MUSICIANS AND WRITERS ALIKE AND HIS MUSIC CREATED A FIERCE CONTROVERSY .. "THE WAGNER QUESTION" TO THIS DAY IS DEBATED AMONG LOVERS OF MUSIC ... HE REMAINED TRUE TO HIS IDEALS AND FORGED STEADILY AHEAD, TO EMERGE TRIUMPHANT!
RICHARD WAGNER
WAGNER AND LISZT WERE VERY CLOSE FRIENDS ... LISZT'S DAUGHTER, COSIMA, BECAME RICHARD'S SECOND WIFE ... SHE WAS A SYMPATHETIC HELPMATE AND CARRIED ON HIS TRADITIONS .. SHE DIED IN 1930, THE LEADING SPIRIT IN BAYREUTH MUSIC CIRCLES, SINCE WAGNER'S DAY . .
WAGNER HATED THE PIANO AND NEVER COULD PLAY IT WELL .. FROM AN EARLY AGE HE WANTED TO WRITE OPERAS, INSISTING THAT THE WORDS WERE AS IMPORTANT AS THE MUSIC . HE WAS AHEAD OF HIS DAY AND PEOPLE MISUNDERSTOOD HIM, BUT SUCH OPERAS AS "LOHENGRIN" "PARSIFAL" AND THE FAMOUS NIBELUNGEN RING HAVE WON HIM LASTING FAME . . . . .

.. BORN - 1813 - DIED - 1883 ...

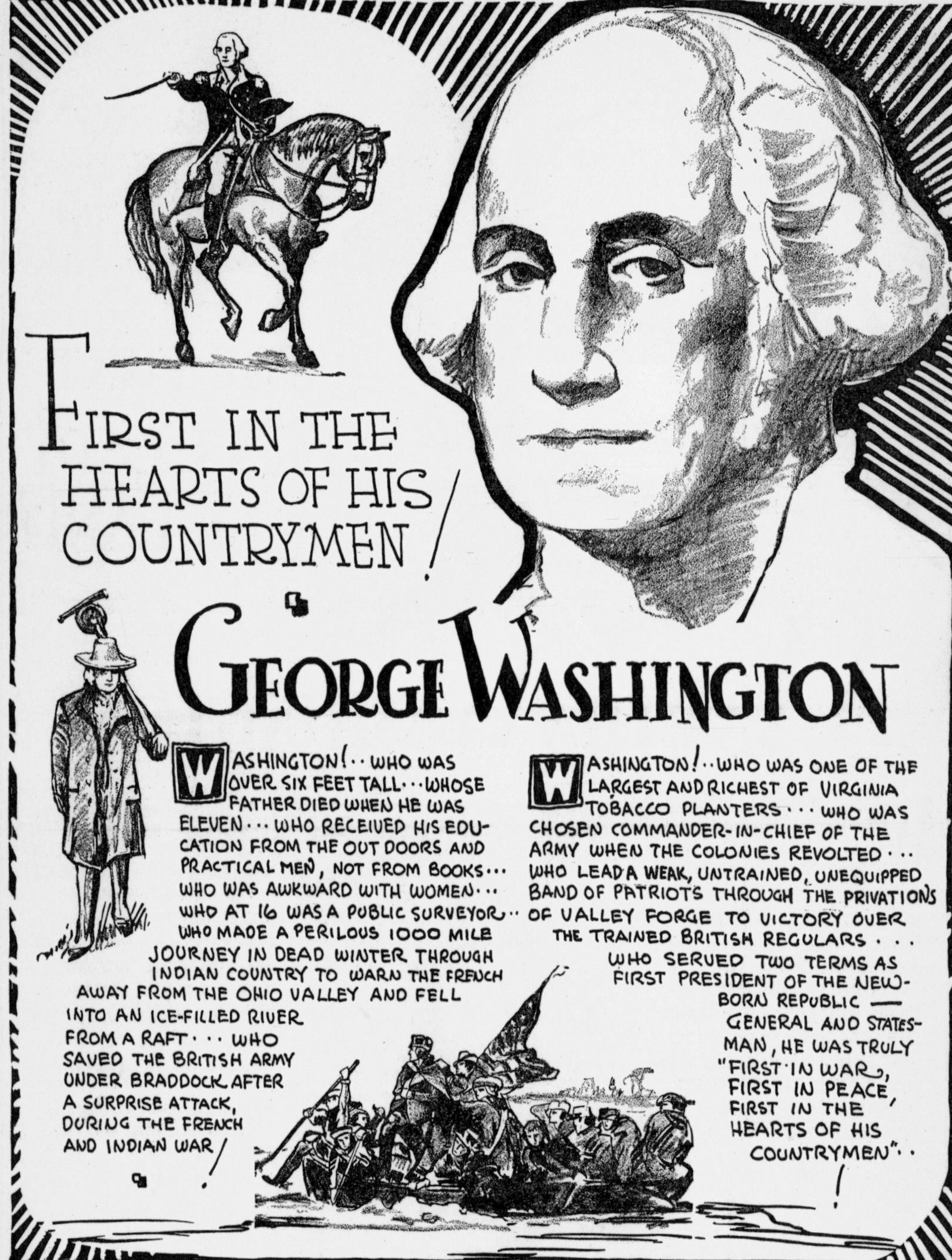
FIRST IN THE HEARTS OF HIS COUNTRYMEN!
GEORGE WASHINGTON
WASHINGTON! .. WHO WAS OVER SIX FEET TALL ... WHOSE FATHER DIED WHEN HE WAS ELEVEN ... WHO RECEIVED HIS EDUCATION FROM THE OUT DOORS AND PRACTICAL MEN, NOT FROM BOOKS ... WHO WAS AWKWARD WITH WOMEN .. WHO AT 16 WAS A PUBLIC SURVEYOR .. WHO MADE A PERILOUS 1000 MILE JOURNEY IN DEAD WINTER THROUGH INDIAN COUNTRY TO WARN THE FRENCH AWAY FROM THE OHIO VALLEY AND FELL INTO AN ICE-FILLED RIVER FROM A RAFT ... WHO SAVED THE BRITISH ARMY UNDER BRADDOCK AFTER A SURPRISE ATTACK, DURING THE FRENCH AND INDIAN WAR!
WASHINGTON! .. WHO WAS ONE OF THE LARGEST AND RICHEST OF VIRGINIA TOBACCO PLANTERS ... WHO WAS CHOSEN COMMANDER-IN-CHIEF OF THE ARMY WHEN THE COLONIES REVOLTED .. WHO LEAD A WEAK, UNTRAINED, UNEQUIPPED BAND OF PATRIOTS THROUGH THE PRIVATIONS OF VALLEY FORGE TO VICTORY OVER THE TRAINED BRITISH REGULARS ... WHO SERVED TWO TERMS AS FIRST PRESIDENT OF THE NEW-BORN REPUBLIC — GENERAL AND STATESMAN, HE WAS TRULY "FIRST IN WAR, FIRST IN PEACE, FIRST IN THE HEARTS OF HIS COUNTRYMEN" .. !

... BORN—1732 .. DIED—1799 ...

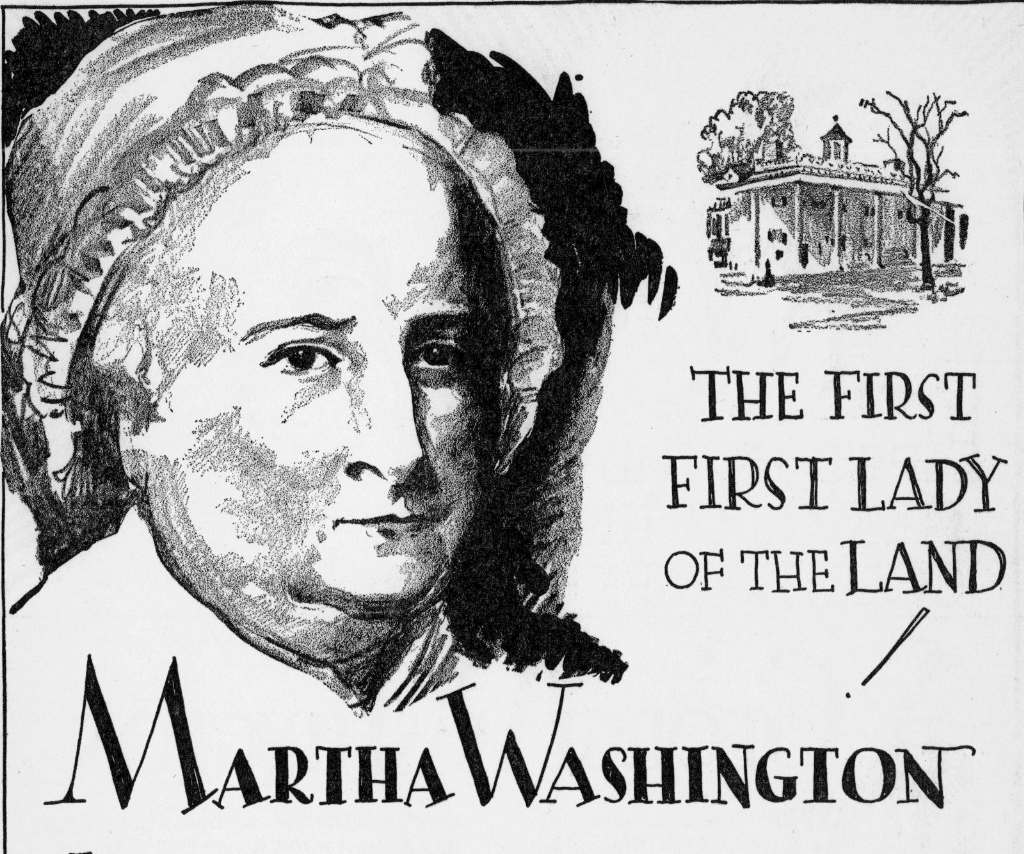
THE FIRST
FIRST LADY
OF THE LAND

MARTHA WASHINGTON

WHEN YOUNG COLONEL GEORGE WASHINGTON FIRST MET MARTHA AT THE HOME OF A FRIEND, SHE WAS YOUNG, VERY WEALTHY, AND A WIDOW WITH TWO CHILDREN... GEORGE BECAME HER SECOND HUSBAND.. SHE WAS VERY DEVOTED TO HIM, AND STAYED CLOSE TO HIM DURING THE SEVERE WINTER CAMPAIGNS OF THE REVOLUTIONARY WAR.

MARTHA (HER NICKNAME WAS PATSY) WAS A HOME WOMAN AND AN EXCELLENT COOK AND HOUSEWIFE.. WHEN WASHINGTON WAS ELECTED THE FIRST PRESIDENT, MARTHA BECAME THE GRACIOUS HOSTESS OF THE YOUNG REPUBLIC.. SHE LENT DIGNITY TO THE PRESIDENTIAL RECEPTIONS, AND WAS GREATLY BELOVED AND RESPECTED BOTH IN NEW YORK AND PHILADELPHIA . . . . . .

·· BORN 1731 — DIED 1802 ··

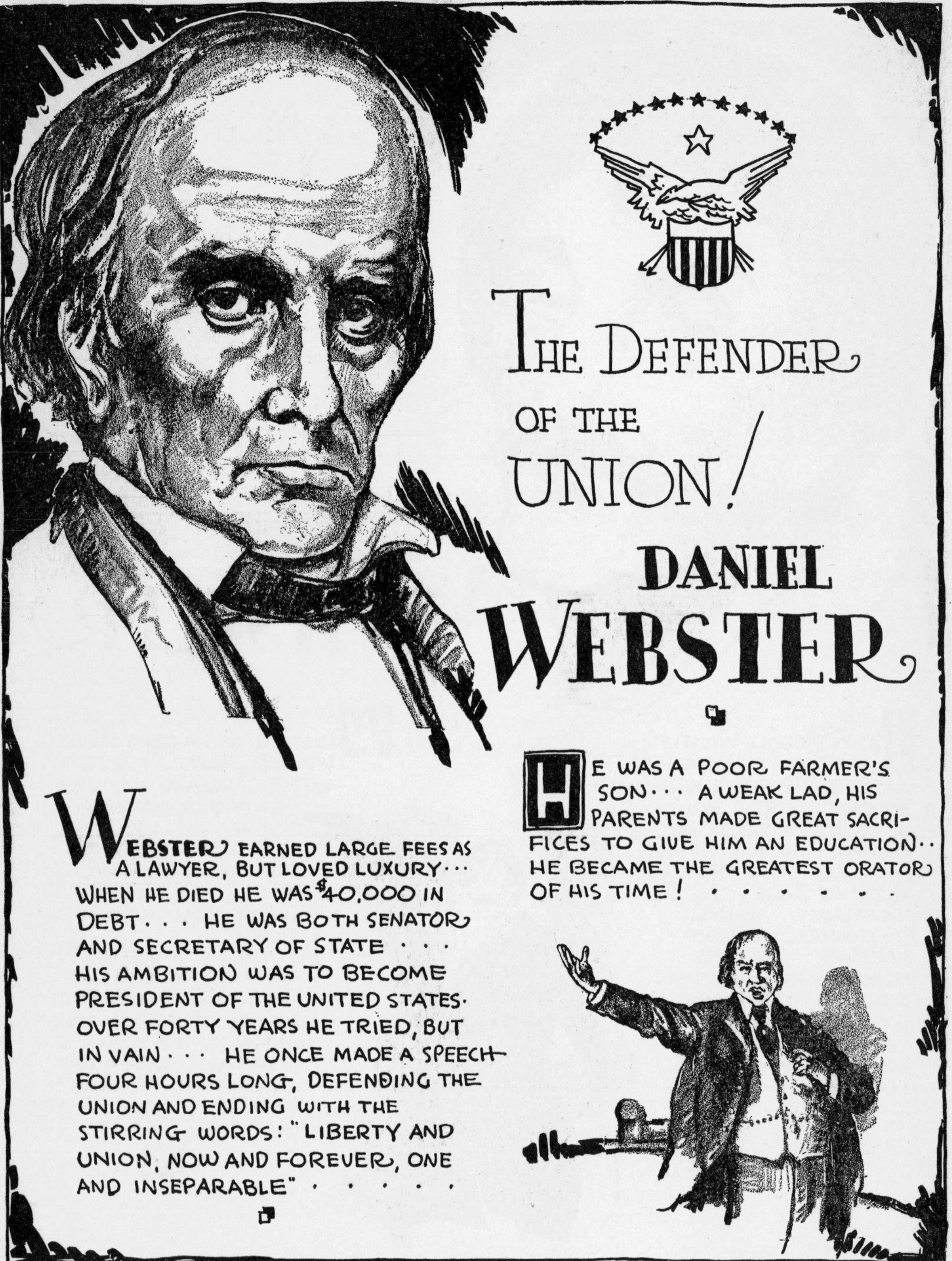
THE DEFENDER OF THE UNION!
DANIEL WEBSTER
WEBSTER EARNED LARGE FEES AS A LAWYER, BUT LOVED LUXURY... WHEN HE DIED HE WAS $40,000 IN DEBT... HE WAS BOTH SENATOR AND SECRETARY OF STATE... HIS AMBITION WAS TO BECOME PRESIDENT OF THE UNITED STATES. OVER FORTY YEARS HE TRIED, BUT IN VAIN... HE ONCE MADE A SPEECH FOUR HOURS LONG, DEFENDING THE UNION AND ENDING WITH THE STIRRING WORDS: "LIBERTY AND UNION, NOW AND FOREVER, ONE AND INSEPARABLE".....
HE WAS A POOR FARMER'S SON... A WEAK LAD, HIS PARENTS MADE GREAT SACRIFICES TO GIVE HIM AN EDUCATION.. HE BECAME THE GREATEST ORATOR OF HIS TIME! ......

...BORN-1782-DIED-1852...

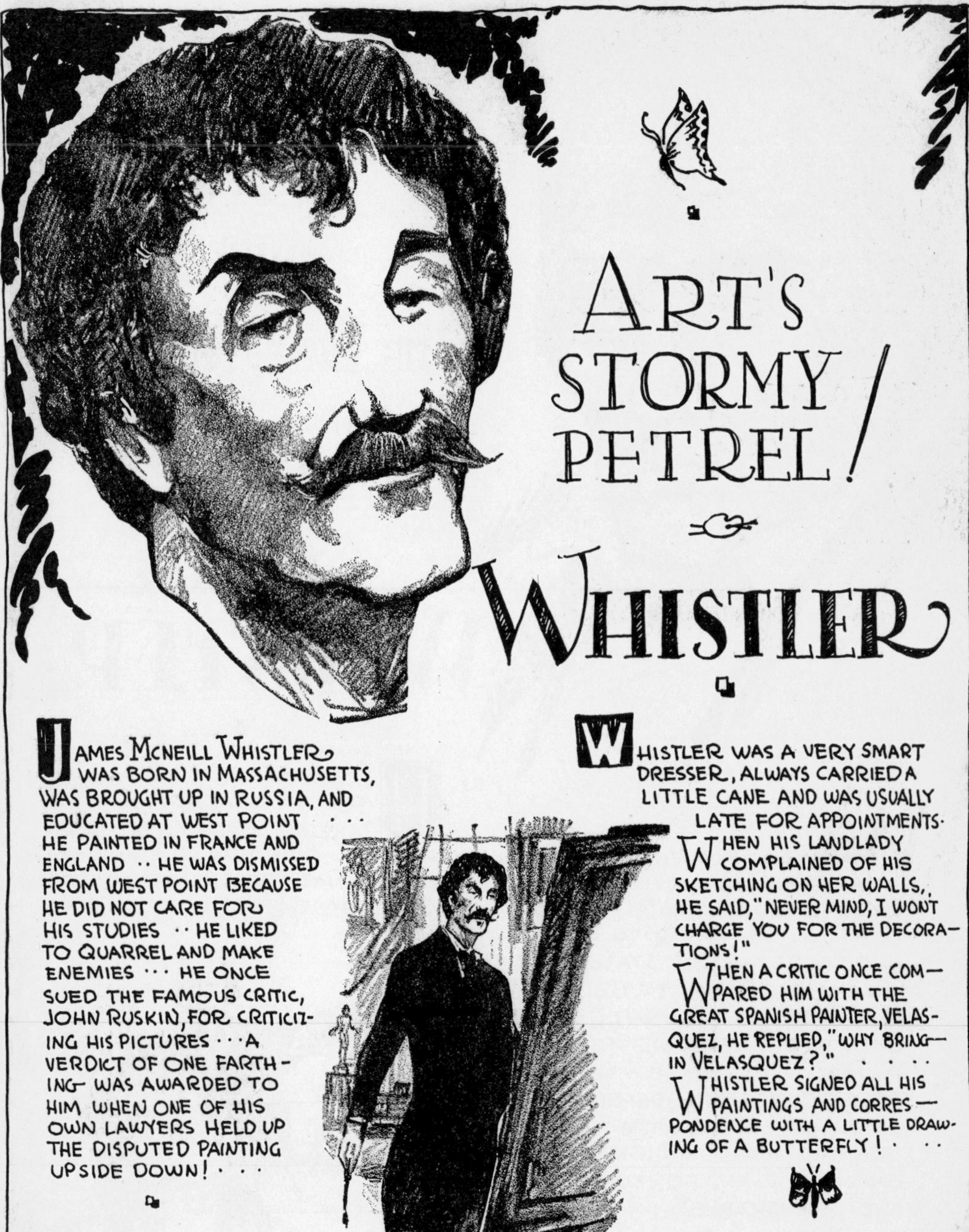
ART'S STORMY PETREL!
WHISTLER

JAMES MCNEILL WHISTLER WAS BORN IN MASSACHUSETTS, WAS BROUGHT UP IN RUSSIA, AND EDUCATED AT WEST POINT . . . HE PAINTED IN FRANCE AND ENGLAND . . HE WAS DISMISSED FROM WEST POINT BECAUSE HE DID NOT CARE FOR HIS STUDIES . . HE LIKED TO QUARREL AND MAKE ENEMIES . . . HE ONCE SUED THE FAMOUS CRITIC, JOHN RUSKIN, FOR CRITICIZING HIS PICTURES . . . A VERDICT OF ONE FARTHING WAS AWARDED TO HIM WHEN ONE OF HIS OWN LAWYERS HELD UP THE DISPUTED PAINTING UPSIDE DOWN! . . .

WHISTLER WAS A VERY SMART DRESSER, ALWAYS CARRIED A LITTLE CANE AND WAS USUALLY LATE FOR APPOINTMENTS.

WHEN HIS LANDLADY COMPLAINED OF HIS SKETCHING ON HER WALLS, HE SAID, "NEVER MIND, I WON'T CHARGE YOU FOR THE DECORATIONS!"

WHEN A CRITIC ONCE COMPARED HIM WITH THE GREAT SPANISH PAINTER, VELASQUEZ, HE REPLIED, "WHY BRING IN VELASQUEZ?" . . . .

WHISTLER SIGNED ALL HIS PAINTINGS AND CORRESPONDENCE WITH A LITTLE DRAWING OF A BUTTERFLY! . . .

. . BORN - 1834 - DIED - 1903 . .

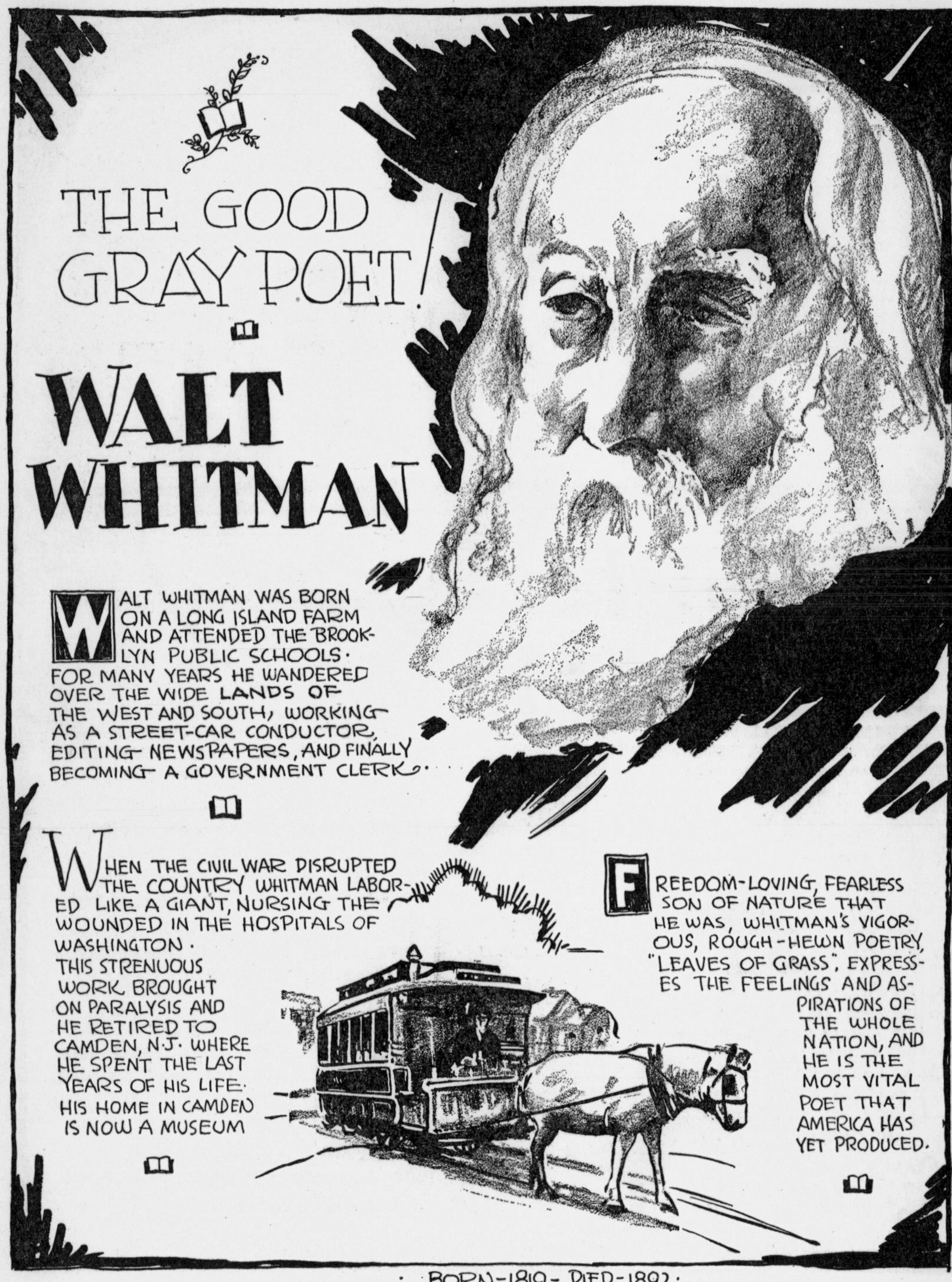
THE GOOD GRAY POET!
WALT WHITMAN
WALT WHITMAN WAS BORN ON A LONG ISLAND FARM AND ATTENDED THE BROOKLYN PUBLIC SCHOOLS. FOR MANY YEARS HE WANDERED OVER THE WIDE LANDS OF THE WEST AND SOUTH, WORKING AS A STREET-CAR CONDUCTOR, EDITING NEWSPAPERS, AND FINALLY BECOMING A GOVERNMENT CLERK...
WHEN THE CIVIL WAR DISRUPTED THE COUNTRY WHITMAN LABORED LIKE A GIANT, NURSING THE WOUNDED IN THE HOSPITALS OF WASHINGTON. THIS STRENUOUS WORK BROUGHT ON PARALYSIS AND HE RETIRED TO CAMDEN, N.J. WHERE HE SPENT THE LAST YEARS OF HIS LIFE. HIS HOME IN CAMDEN IS NOW A MUSEUM
FREEDOM-LOVING, FEARLESS SON OF NATURE THAT HE WAS, WHITMAN'S VIGOROUS, ROUGH-HEWN POETRY, "LEAVES OF GRASS", EXPRESSES THE FEELINGS AND ASPIRATIONS OF THE WHOLE NATION, AND HE IS THE MOST VITAL POET THAT AMERICA HAS YET PRODUCED.

· BORN-1819- DIED-1892 ·

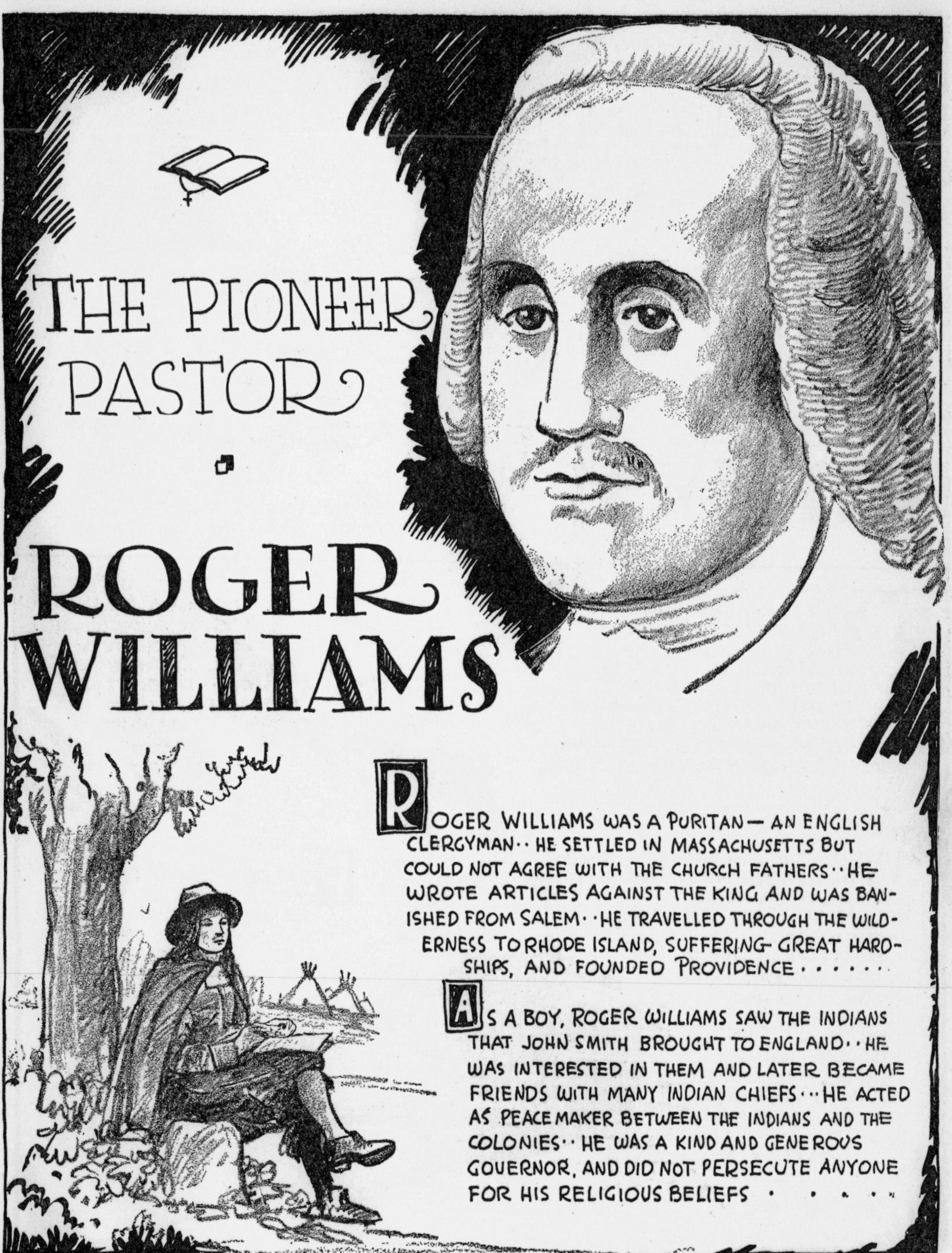
THE PIONEER PASTOR
ROGER WILLIAMS
ROGER WILLIAMS WAS A PURITAN— AN ENGLISH CLERGYMAN·· HE SETTLED IN MASSACHUSETTS BUT COULD NOT AGREE WITH THE CHURCH FATHERS·· HE WROTE ARTICLES AGAINST THE KING AND WAS BANISHED FROM SALEM·· HE TRAVELLED THROUGH THE WILDERNESS TO RHODE ISLAND, SUFFERING GREAT HARDSHIPS, AND FOUNDED PROVIDENCE······
AS A BOY, ROGER WILLIAMS SAW THE INDIANS THAT JOHN SMITH BROUGHT TO ENGLAND·· HE WAS INTERESTED IN THEM AND LATER BECAME FRIENDS WITH MANY INDIAN CHIEFS··· HE ACTED AS PEACEMAKER BETWEEN THE INDIANS AND THE COLONIES·· HE WAS A KIND AND GENEROUS GOVERNOR, AND DID NOT PERSECUTE ANYONE FOR HIS RELIGIOUS BELIEFS · · · · ·

BORN-1600?— DIED-1683 ··

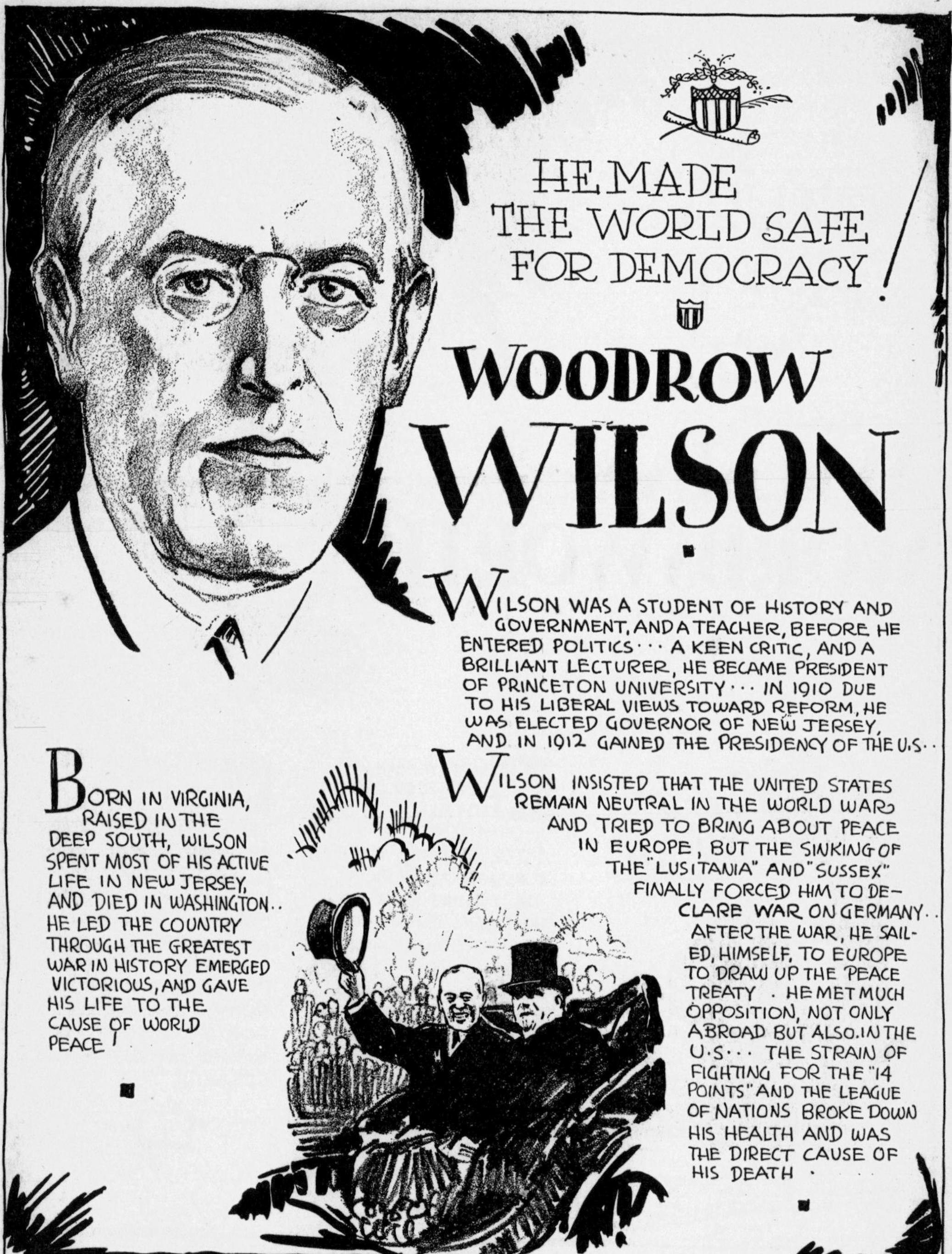
HE MADE THE WORLD SAFE FOR DEMOCRACY!
WOODROW WILSON
WILSON WAS A STUDENT OF HISTORY AND GOVERNMENT, AND A TEACHER, BEFORE HE ENTERED POLITICS . . . A KEEN CRITIC, AND A BRILLIANT LECTURER, HE BECAME PRESIDENT OF PRINCETON UNIVERSITY . . . IN 1910 DUE TO HIS LIBERAL VIEWS TOWARD REFORM, HE WAS ELECTED GOVERNOR OF NEW JERSEY, AND IN 1912 GAINED THE PRESIDENCY OF THE U.S. .
BORN IN VIRGINIA, RAISED IN THE DEEP SOUTH, WILSON SPENT MOST OF HIS ACTIVE LIFE IN NEW JERSEY, AND DIED IN WASHINGTON . . HE LED THE COUNTRY THROUGH THE GREATEST WAR IN HISTORY EMERGED VICTORIOUS, AND GAVE HIS LIFE TO THE CAUSE OF WORLD PEACE!
WILSON INSISTED THAT THE UNITED STATES REMAIN NEUTRAL IN THE WORLD WAR AND TRIED TO BRING ABOUT PEACE IN EUROPE, BUT THE SINKING OF THE "LUSITANIA" AND "SUSSEX" FINALLY FORCED HIM TO DECLARE WAR ON GERMANY . . AFTER THE WAR, HE SAILED, HIMSELF, TO EUROPE TO DRAW UP THE PEACE TREATY . HE MET MUCH OPPOSITION, NOT ONLY ABROAD BUT ALSO IN THE U.S. . . THE STRAIN OF FIGHTING FOR THE "14 POINTS" AND THE LEAGUE OF NATIONS BROKE DOWN HIS HEALTH AND WAS THE DIRECT CAUSE OF HIS DEATH .

BORN - 1856 - DIED - 1924

NATURE'S POET
WILLIAM WORDSWORTH
WORDSWORTH WAS BORN POOR AND HAD TO EXIST ON THE BARE NECESSITIES OF LIFE · · HIS SISTER, DOROTHY, WAS HIS CONSTANT COMPANION AND THE INSPIRATION FOR HIS POEMS, EVEN AFTER HE MARRIED HIS CHILDHOOD SWEETHEART · · · HE TRAVELLED OVER EUROPE AND SCOTLAND AND GREW TO LOVE NATURE · · · FAME CAME TO HIM SLOWLY BUT FINALLY HE WAS POET LAUREATE OF ENGLAND, THE GREATEST HONOR A POET CAN WIN · · · ·
WORDSWORTH'S LIFE WAS A TRANQUIL ONE, PASSED IN THE COMPANY OF LITERARY MEN · · · · THE GREAT OUTDOORS WAS HIS WORKSHOP · · · HE WROTE POEMS IN SIMPLE UNAFFECTED LANGUAGE AND DREW SUCH TRUTHFUL PICTURES OF NATURE THAT ON READING HIS POETRY, IT SEEMS THAT NATURE HERSELF IS SPEAKING—— · · · ·

·· BORN-1770 - DIED-1850 ··

THE PROPHET OF MORMONISM

Brigham Young was born in Vermont, but becoming converted to Mormonism, he moved to Nauvoo, Illinois, the Mormon centre after the death of Joseph Smith, the founder of the creed... There, the agitation against his faith and the resultant bloodshed, forced him to leave, and he led his followers westward across the plains to the "Promised Land", Utah... He laid out Salt Lake City, built tabernacles and theatres, introduced alfalfa in America, and imported the best grades of fruit and live-stock.. For 33 years, he was the dictator of the Mormon church and the supreme power in Salt Lake City........

BRIGHAM YOUNG

The Mormon Tabernacle at Salt Lake City....

Following the Mormon practice of bigamy, Young had 21 wives, and 48 children are mentioned in his will

Although Young came from poor folk and was ignorant, since he disliked books, his great enterprise and shrewd business sense, not only caused his colony to prosper, but enabled him to accumulate a personal fortune of $1,500,000.....

... Born-1801-Died-1877...